W9-BFY-736

"This book will amuse and amaze you!"

— *Michele Howe*, Newark Star-Ledger

"These guys know their onions."

— *Leonard Maltin*, Entertainment Tonight

"*O' NEW JERSEY* brings our great state to life. New Jersey has a remarkably rich and vibrant history and is filled with hidden treasures. This book tells the story of the best of the Garden State and makes me proud to call New Jersey home."

— *Christine Todd Whitman*

"Heide and Gilman have told the story of New Jersey—an exciting, vibrant, friendly place I am proud to call home. I hope their work will entice travelers to come to New Jersey and enjoy, from Sussex County to Cape May, all we have to offer—especially our people."

— *Bill Bradley*

"An eclectic travelogue taking the weekend adventurer to a pop-culture odyssey from High Point to Sandy Hook to Cape May. From Sandra Dee to submarine sandwiches, from saltwater taffy to Bruce Springsteen, the state's famous and firsts are all remembered."

— *Gail Pendleton*, New Jersey Herald

"There's a lot to like about *O' NEW JERSEY*, a pocket-size guidebook to the Garden State. Much of it comes in the form of photos—Joe's Diamond diner in Kearny, with its king-size coffee cup on the roof; the Black Cat Tavern in Absecon, where a giant neon cat stands guard; Kurt Laemmel's Pork Store in Hoboken, with architecture right out of 'Plasticville,' and, almost worth the price of the book alone, a wonderful old MGM still of Connie Francis, fetching behind her flaring eyebrows, fur wrap, and rocket beehive. If you're looking to explore New Jersey, get in your car and get going with your copy of *O' NEW JERSEY*."

— *Asbury Park Press*

"Go buy this book!"

— *Mark Simone*, NY1 News

"A gem . . . its pages are chocked with wit, humor, and solid research."

— *Library Journal*

O' New Jersey

Daytripping, Backroads, Eateries, Funky Adventures

3rd Edition

O' New Jersey

Daytripping, Backroads, Eateries, Funky Adventures

3rd Edition

NEW JERSEY TURNPIKE UNDERPASSES THE PULASKI SKYWAY

Robert Heide and John Gilman

St. Martin's Griffin ❦ New York

www.stmartins.com

Library of Congress Cataloging-in-Publication Data

Heide, Robert, 1939–
    O'New Jersey : daytripping, backroads, eateries, funky adventures / Robert Heide and John Gilman—3rd ed.
      p. cm.
    Includes index
    ISBN 0-312-34156-3
    EAN 978-0-312-34156-5
     1. New Jersey—Guidebooks. I. Gilman, John, 1941–
II. Title.
F132.3.H47 2006

                                2005057704

Third Edition: May 2006

10 9 8 7 6 5 4 3 2 1

Acknowledgments

Editor Tom Mercer, Shannon Twomey, John Murphy, Christine Todd Whitman, Maria Maruca, Don Horn, Stephen "Hoop" Hooper, Jim and Beverly Hans, Vicki Gold Levi—founder of the Atlantic City Historical Museum, Bill Bradley, Jim Fitzgerald, Carol Tooker and family, Madeline Hoffer, Susan Hansen, Doris Dinger, Michael and Gail Coulter, Alma Broedel, Jim and Beverly Caldora, Barbara Baranyay, Timothy Bissell, John Reid Currie, Wendy Lipkind, Alexandra Anderson-Spivy, Linda Jonasch Artalie of Seaside Park, Norma Edgar, Florence Dreml Brown, Alan A. Siegel, Michael Wallis—Route 66, Suzanne Fitzgerald Wallis, Ann and George Harris, Irwin Chusid, Rich Conaty, Philip Cohen, Irene Stella, Chris Weidner, Adele and George Speare, Wren D'Antonio, Robert Ling, Louisa McCune, Mel Camuso Renick, Joseph Lanza, Mary Goldie, Nena Chavarria, Allen C. Perry, Don Rollins, Tom Duncan, Nancy and Donald Newlove, George Bonanno, Glen Craig, Tim Daly, Noam Dworman, Wheeler Winston Dixon, Priscilla, Dan and Ava Sierra, Peter and Laura Gilman, Heidi Gilman, Franck, Claire Sarah, and Marina Walgenwitz, Jeff Painter, Sean Boyd, Lois and John Gilleece, Celeste Holm, Sally and Alyn Heim, Fred and Dan Kanter, Barbara Kulicke, June Kane, Larry L. Lash, William Singer, Mike Loundy, Gillian McCain, Jim Marshall, Maxine and Stuart Evans of 'Tiques, Plaidman Tim McNally, Terry "Lead East" Cook, Sally Kirkland, Jerry Fabris—Edison National Historical site in West Orange, Jerry Ohlinger, Peggy Miller Rush, Ric Cuneo, New Jersey Historical Society, Newark Museum, Montclair Book Shop, Michelle Reutty, the New Jersey Library Association, Irvington Public Library, Newark Public Library, Richard Helfant, Jerry Seinfeld, Joseph Cosgriff, John Pizzarelli, Jr.

Asbury Park neon.

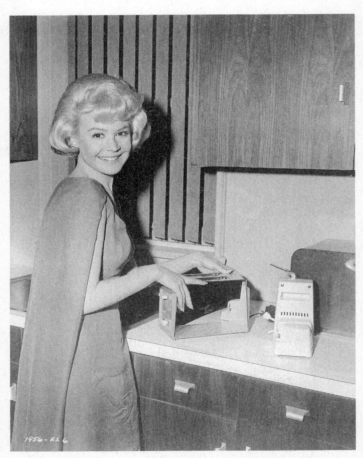

"Sandra Dee" (Alexandra Zuck) of Bayonne, the eternal teenager, with her electric toaster.

Contents

Three New Jersey maps, left to right: Gulf, 1935; Tydol Flying A., 1944; and a New Jersey Esso (now Exxon). These maps were given out to motorists for free.

THE MAJOR ROADS
OF NEW JERSEY

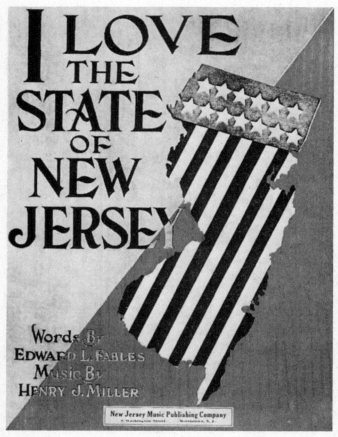

Early 1900s sheet music "I Love the State of New Jersey," words by Edward L. Fables and music by Henry J. Miller, published by the New Jersey Music Publishing Company.

> You go over this fence marked PRIVATE,
> through this gate marked DO NOT ENTER,
> to a lake that has a sign: DO NOT FISH.
> You know, that's the best place for fishin'.
>
> —Stan Laurel to Oliver Hardy
>   in *The Dancing Masters*, 1943.

O' NEW JERSEY introduces the traveler to interesting places to go and journeys to take in a state that many now refer to as "New York's California"—let's face it—it's got everything. For many years now we have chosen to escape the built-up tensions and stress of life in Manhattan by getting into the car, turning on the ignition, and driving through the Holland or Lincoln Tunnel or over the splendid George Washington Bridge, directly into the land of New Jersey. Just-two-guys-on-the-road has been our theme for many happy adventures; and this guidebook sets out to identify and map out for the reader—be they from New York City, Jersey City, Philadelphia, or Los Angeles—the best places to go, explore, and where to experience some good on-the-road food, Jersey style.

For convenience purposes we readily suggest the use of the Garden State Parkway, the New Jersey Turnpike, or the big Highways 78, 80, 280, or 287, but always keeping in mind that the back roads or old two-lane highways (like Routes 1-9) are the most scenic and interesting. Our suggestion is that once you reach a destination, you either park the car and take a walk or drive the back road, stopping frequently to see what's there. Our motto is: "Joy is a back-road adventure." Many of the places in this guide are accessible by public transportation via bus or train. Sometimes it is fun to leave the car home. We also include some of the best "Jersey joints"—bars, diners, pizza hangouts, and a selection of some of the very best restaurants in the state. If it takes awhile to get there, or you just want to relax somewhere and not be in a hurry, stay overnight at a motel, hotel, bed and breakfast, or country inn, sprinkled for your convenience throughout the book.

You don't need to go to Zagreb, Vladivostok, Shanghai, or Havana—or even to Kalamazoo, Altoona, or Cucamonga. It's all here, right in your own backyard, in New Jersey. Though there is no Paris, New Jersey, there is a Berlin and a Timbuctoo; and either of these, both in South Jersey, would make for an exciting, do-it-yourself destination and adventure. While you're out there

"Invaders from New Jersey" T-shirt.

hunting, you'll find that the state is going through a renaissance of its own.

This book will point the way to Newark and Rahway, to Cape May and High Point, but it is also hoped that it will become a blueprint for personal discovery—that the reader will find his or her own niche using *O' New Jersey* as a guide.

Preface

••

> My, look at the sky, wouldya! I'm glad I was born in New Jersey.
> I've always said it was the best State in the Union.
>
> —Ma Kirby from the play *The Happy Journey to Camden and Trenton* by Thornton Wilder.

In the year 2000 we all wondered what the new millennium would be like; and after the shock of 9/11 we came to realize that everything had changed. Many New Jerseyans who commuted to and worked in the World Trade Center towers are among those who perished, and the survivors and family members are still grieving.

We were staying at the Amherst Hotel in Ocean Grove when, on that fateful morning of September 11, the proprietor Madeline Hoffer pounded on the door of our room shouting, "A plane has crashed into the Twin Towers. It's on TV." We bolted downstairs to the parlor only to see another plane hit the second tower. From the boardwalk billows of dark smoke could be seen over the Atlantic and up the coast, to the disbelief of all who had gathered on the shore that terrible bright sunny day.

That evening we stopped at St. Catherine's Church in Spring Lake, where a woman with tears in her eyes and clutching a small child asked, "Have you lost someone too?" Spring Lake, an upscale commuter seashore town, lost many of its residents that day. Throughout New Jersey many memorial sites have been erected to honor the victims of 9/11. We visited one facing Raritan Bay at Union Beach, and another at Eagle Rock Reservation in West Orange with a panoramic view of Manhattan. At Eagle Rock, all of the names of the Jerseyans who died in the attacks are engraved in bronze onto a wall for all to contemplate.

Despite its loss, New Jersey continues to persist in moving forward with optimism and courage. It's as if the state has come forward to help lead the way toward a new and better future for the country. Motion pictures produced by the Edison Manufacturing Company in West Orange as early as 1895 led to the early production of silent films in New Jersey. Today New Jersey is once again a popular place to film, with the state itself often being utilized as an integral part of the subject matter.

Two relatively recent movies were made with the title *Jersey Girl*. One, in 1993, was directed by David Burton Morris, with Jami Gertz, Dylan McDermott, Molly Price, Aida Turturro, and Joseph Bologna. The second *Jersey Girl* flick, filmed in the

Atlantic Highlands, was released in 2004 and directed by Kevin Smith. It starred Ben Affleck, William H. Macy, and Liv Tyler, with a featured special appearance by Jennifer Lopez. Neither of these two romantic comedies fared well at the box office, nor did they capture the feeling of real life as it is lived in the Garden State. Jerseyans are waiting for a Jersey Girl movie that tells the world what it really means to be a hip Jersey Girl.

A Jersey movie that did succeed was *Garden State*, a sleeper 2004 summer movie. Written and directed by Zach Braff, who also serves as his own leading man, this film initially caused a stir at the prestigious Sundance Film Festival in January 2004. Braff created a "coming of age" movie that truly hits the mark in terms of suburban life as it exists today in New Jersey. Born and raised in South Orange, the main character, Andrew Largean, left home to become a struggling L.A. actor. He returns to his hometown after a long absence to attend his mother's funeral. Andrew's detached psychiatrist father is played to perfection by Ian Holm. Andrew meets the disturbed (and unusual) Samantha, played by Natalie Portman, and eventually these two neurotic kids fall in love and clean up their act. The semiautobiographical film is the start of a new career for director/actor/screenwriter Zach, who is proud to be a bona fide Jersey Boy.

Steven Spielberg's *War of the Worlds* (2005), based on the H. G. Wells novel, and following Orson Welles's historic adaptation of the story on the Mercury Theater radio broadcast of October 30,

Cardboard window poster of the 1953 movie The War of the Worlds *based on the H. G. Wells novel.*

1938, depicts a Martian invasion of New Jersey at Grovers Mill (near Princeton). The 2005 Spielberg version stars Tom Cruise, a New Jersey native who grew up in Glen Ridge.

Of course, there are a number of Jersey movies shot in places like Seaside Heights and Asbury Park. Find them at your local video/DVD store. Meanwhile, there is *The Sopranos* television series, which is still going strong. Filmmaker Spike Lee used New Jersey locations for movies set in Brooklyn and the Bronx. Woody Allen made both *Stardust Memories*, set in Ocean Grove, and *The Purple Rose of Cairo*, set in Bertrand Island Amusement Park on Lake Hopatcong.

Since *O' New Jersey* was first published in 1992, and revised in 1998, we've continued our Jersey Jaunts and Jersey Shore vacations, and have found in the State of New Jersey a renewed prominence, fierce pride, stalwart vigor, and a Jersey sense of confidence. New development is happening everywhere in Jersey City and Hoboken, which are on the way to becoming real-estate extensions of Manhattan (but with their own independent view of things, always from a Jersey perspective). Asbury Park is on the way up and "Build-We-Must" is the slogan all over Newark. Historical restoration in towns like Lambertville and Ocean Grove are truly amazing. Historical preservation has always been an important concern in New Jersey, which is proud of being one of the original 13 states.

Some critics continue to focus on what they perceive Jersey to be—just the industrial wasteland close to Manhattan; but meadowlands and estuarial ecology is an ongoing issue among Jersey preservationists and politicians who want to maintain the idea of a Garden State that really has a garden—places like the Pine Barrens and the Great Swamp. Towns like Princeton, Morristown, and Montclair always keep one eye on historical preservation, and signs are posted along the roadsides describing the many battle sites of the American Revolution. Certainly, the presence of George Washington is to be found (and exclaimed) everywhere.

On the promo trail for the '98 edition of *O' New Jersey* we met Jerry Seinfeld having a burger with some pals at the White Manna in Hackensack, and we also hung out with Jersey guy Puff Daddy. Art openings for Tim Daly, who paints big super-realistic canvases of the uninhabited industrial backroads of New Jersey, and Hoop, who specializes in art cars and sculpture pieces made of car parts from salvaged autos, are part of the fun of driving around New Jersey. A documentary film was made by Australian filmmaker Peter Leiss with Hoop, fellow artist Mark Kostabi, and the two of us, called *Cake Walking Babies from Home*, which was shown at many film festivals around the globe. This film focused on diners, art galleries, and the town of Irvington, which has been plagued by continuous gang wars, drugs, car theft, shootings, and crime sprees. (However, of late there is a renewed interest in rebuilding the troubled town, which suffered after the Newark riots of the late 1960s; real estate interests are moving ahead with new housing developments in the works.)

◆

The Sopranos: A Jersey Phenomenon

To say that the Emmy award-winning HBO television series *The Sopranos* has taken New Jersey (and America-at-large) by storm may be the understatement of our time. Set in Jersey, the show features Tony Soprano (James Gandolfini), his wife, Carmela (Edie Falco), and his meddling mother, Livia, originally played by the late Nancy Marchand. *The Sopranos* is the story of a dysfunctional mob family. Lorraine Bracco plays Tony's therapist who only helps to wreak more havoc on the family. Creator David Chase promises more drama in future seasons, and there's also a feature film in the pipeline. In May 2005, after a sixteen-month hiatus, *The Sopranos* began shooting interiors at the Silvercup Studios in Queens for the 2006 season.

City officials in Essex County have banned the show from filming in public locations, claiming that it perpetuates negative stereotypes of Italian-Americans. However, George Bonanno, a Clifton resident and a leading fan of *The Sopranos*, says "it's right on." He adds, "Much of it could easily take place in the North Ward (Newark's Italian district), but the Soprano mansion, which has been said to be in either Glen Ridge or Cedar Grove, has been given a fake address—633 Stag Trail Road, North Caldwell. The house is real if you want to go on a mystery search to find it."

The actual "Sopranos" mansion is a real house in North Caldwell. (Photo by George Bonanno.)

*   *   *

We now often take our breaks from writing assignments by having a picnic and a walk in the woods in the South Mountain Reservation, set between the towns of Millburn, West Orange, and South Orange. This is often followed by a movie at the Claridge in Montclair and a vanilla or black-and-white ice cream soda at Holsten's Brookdale Confectionary in Bloomfield—one of the last old-style Jersey ice cream parlors. We still take our summer vacations at the Jersey shore, either in Ocean Grove, Bay Head, or Seaside Park. Driving a 1954 Plymouth, we can be found in the summer months at car meets in Lyndhurst, Point Pleasant, and Tom's River.

What better way to introduce this new edition than to salute some of our favorite past and present Jersey Girls? One of our all-time favorites is Bayonne's own Sandra Dee, the original "Gidget," who died at age 62 on March 21, 2005. The world's most perfect teenager married singer Bobby Darin and starred, with Troy Donahue, in *A Summer Place*, and, with Lana Turner, in *Imitation of Life*. Sandra, who turned to pills and alcohol after her career ended, said she hit rock bottom in 1988 after her mother's death, guzzling a quart of Scotch every day and weighing in at just 80 pounds.

Other Jersey girls of note must include Annie Oakley and Martha Stewart, both of Nutley; Dorothy Parker of Long Branch; Connie Francis of Newark; Debbie Harry of Hawthorn; Meryl Streep of Bernardsville; Queen Latifah of East Orange; Vivian Blaine, Sarah Vaughan, and Whitney Houston of Newark; author Fran Leibowitz of Morristown; and ex-governor and ex-director of the federal Environmental Protection Agency, the attractive Christine Todd Whitman.

Now even the Jersey Boys are getting into the act with a popular Broadway musical about Frankie Valli and the Four Seasons. According to *Billboard* magazine's calculations, including record sales, radio airplay, and jukebox selections, the five top rock 'n' roll recording artists of the 1960s were The Beatles, The Supremes, Elvis Presley, The Rolling Stones, and, in the fifth place, The Four Seasons.

Jersey Boys, the hit Broadway musical, celebrates the music of the four New Jersey guys who became known as The Four Seasons. The four brash Italian boys who hung out in their home turf of Belleville and Newark's North Ward looking for trouble included Tommy DeVito, Nick Macioci, Bob Gaudio, and Frank Castelluccio. Tommy was the main man and tough ringleader; but it was another neighborhood pal, a short kid named Joe Pesci, who actually brought these guys together in 1959. Nick was a bass player who also could belt out a song. However, the best of the bunch in vocalizing was Frankie, who changed his last name to Valli (some say after the bandleader/crooner Rudy Vallee). When Nick and Tommy were not harmonizing with the group, they did time in the East Jersey State Prison at Rahway for one reason or another. Bob Gaudio, who was the intellectual of the foursome, wrote most of the hit tunes and found his songwriting inspiration in the voice of Frankie Valli.

The Broadway musical tells their story, from growing up in a bad neighborhood to the forming of The Four Seasons, the outfit that hit the top of the charts in the 1960s with original song hits like "Sherry," "Big Girls Don't Cry," "Walk Like a Man," "Dawn (Go Away)," "Can't Take My Eyes Off of You," "Working My Way Back to You," "Rag Doll," and others. Originally appealing mostly to blue-collar workers and diner girls in New Jersey, their songs and their fame eventually took mainstream America by storm. On Broadway, audiences are cheering the cast playing the Four Seasons, including Christian Hoff as Tommy DeVito, Daniel Reichard as Bob Gaudio, J. Robert Spencer as Nick Massi, and John Lloyd Young as Frankie Valli. On Broadway it's "December 1963 (Oh, What a Night)" all over again; and it's a knockout! Shortly after the Broadway opening, John Lloyd Young said he was both exhilarated and surprised to find himself playing the lead role of Frankie Valli in *Jersey Boys*, recalling that the year before he was working as an usher on 42nd Street and just trying to survive. Like Ruby Keeler in the film *42nd Street*, John Lloyd followed the road to become that rare mythic overnight sensation—and a star on the street of dreams known as the Great White Way.

Left to right: J. Robert Spencer as Nick Massi, John Lloyd Young as Frankie Valli, Daniel Reichard as Bob Gaudio, and Christian Hoff as Tommy DeVito in the hit Broadway musical "Jersey Boys," which is based on the group The Four Seasons with a focus on the life of the lead singer Frankie Valli. Here the Broadway cast as The Four Seasons sing "My Eyes Adored You." (Photo courtesy of Joan Marcus.)

Greetings from New Jersey

New Jersey, one of the 13 original states, is just 8,224 square miles, small when compared to most other states; but it is a brilliant microcosm of America. It offers in its grandiose manner skiing, beaches, mountains, lush farmland, swamps, metropolitan landscapes, suburbs, ethnic enclaves, forests, and factories—in short, New Jersey, the land of forgotten time, offers everything. Historic colonial country farmhouses and beautiful Victorian towns are also integrated into the landscape of the state. There are vast tracts of mountainous forests, pinelands and lakes, and a beautiful coastal shore region where you can relax away from the fast lane. There are as well interesting and historical industrialized urban cities that are fun to discover and explore.

The Jersey Bounce

If you don't feel so hot
Go out to some Jersey spot
And whether you're hep or not
The Jersey Bounce will make you swing.

Pine Barrens author John McPhee has referred to New Jersey as a composite of all the other states, and John Cunningham, a New Jersey historian, has written that the incredible variety—the mountain ranges, the vital cities, farmlands, and wonderful white-sand beaches, each of them well defined, unique and nationally known—is the key to the understanding of what attracts both residents and tourists to New Jersey. The secret is out: New Jersey is a wondrous state, a great place either to live or to visit, be it an extended vacation in summertime, or a day trip or weekend at any time of the year.

◆

Jersey Is No Joke!

In the past, New Jersey jokes were a part of the standard repertoire of the old-time vaudevillians, who liked to make cracks about "playing Hoboken," and even today's national television comedians or talk-show hosts have only to mention "Joisey" to get an instant laugh. Example: When drafting the Declaration of Independence one of our forefathers offered the proposition that the British keep New Jersey. Because the state is situated between two major American cities, Philadelphia and New York, and is astride the main transportation routes of the East, it has sometimes mistakenly been thought of only as a pathway from Philadelphia to

One of the main connections between New Jersey and New York is the Holland Tunnel. During Opening Day ceremonies, on November 12, 1927, 20,000 people walked under the Hudson River for the first and last time; at midnight the first car drove through, making the trip in eight minutes. Top: Postcard showing cars emerging from the Holland Tunnel, published by the May Rose Company, 1950s. Bottom: Earliest traffic in what was referred to as the Holland Vehicular Tunnel, 1929 postcard.

Manhattan. This concept began with statesman, inventor, and punster Ben Franklin, who enjoyed making jokes about New Jersey, likening it to "a barrel tapped at both ends." It was Ben Franklin who first wrote about "devils" lurking in the South Jersey pine barrens. Although this was meant to be "filler" in a newspaper article during a summer lull, people took it literally, and thus one aspect of the famous "Jersey Devil" legend was born. The idea of speeding through New Jersey as quickly as possible was concretely reinforced in 1952 when the New Jersey Turnpike first opened, giving travelers from all over the country and the world a clear view of a vast inner industrial belt.

New Jersey has a history filled with political corruption from "Boss" Hague, the ex-mayor of Jersey City, who amassed a fortune of $8 million on an annual salary of $7,500, to Harrison A. Williams, the New Jersey Abscam senator. These scandals have also contributed fuel for more ongoing Jersey jokes. There has also been much reported—and much more rumored—about mobster rule and crime syndicates sprinkled throughout the state, adding further confusion to this funhouse Jersey jigsaw puzzle.

In recent years, however, according to a report from the Eagleton Institute of Politics at Rutgers University, there is evidence of a growing sense of pride in the state. Half of the New Jersey residents polled said they thought New Jersey was a better place to live when compared with most other states, including neighboring states. Eighty percent of the respondents rated New Jersey as an excellent place to live and to vacation. Rock singer Bruce Springsteen, regarded as the country's most admired "working class hero songster" has, according to "The guy from Jersey" Joe Piscopo, a native New Jersey comedian, completely overturned the Jersey joke.

> Question: What is a Jersey jaunt?
>
> Answer: A jaunt is a short journey made just for pleasure. Jersey is a state of mind.

The 15-mile-wide corridor across New Jersey called the "industrial belt" has always been a target for jokesters in the past. Jersey is rich for the taking; pottery and steel from Trenton, the brickworks of Perth Amboy, the locomotive industry in Paterson, textiles from Passaic, diverse manufactories in Newark, heavy machinery from Jersey City. Most of the population, too, is jammed into this corridor between New York and Philadelphia, making it one of the most densely settled sections in the country. By contrast, the rest of Jersey geography, both above and below this notorious belt, is pastoral, covered with beautiful streams and sparkling lakes, gentle rolling hills and valleys, 127 miles of pristine coastline from Sandy Hook to Cape May, the largest wilderness area on the East Coast, the famous New Jersey Pine Barrens, thousands of acres of fertile farmland south and west of the Pine Barrens stretching to the Delaware River, and vast marshes and estuaries on the east side of the Barrens.

New Jersey is proud of its history. Descriptive bronze plaques abound everywhere, in every little park, on every prominent rock, on farmhouses and often even in the middle of a forest region. George Washington and his army spent over a quarter of the Revolutionary War in New Jersey, giving rise to the oft-repeated phrase "George Washington Slept Here." When overnight guests check into one of the state's many country inns, small hotels, or roadside lodgings, they often find this "G.W.S.H." proclamation, intended as a humorous pun, embroidered or handwritten, in the frame hung on the wall over their old-fashioned, creaky bed. In fact, Jack Benny and Ann Sheridan starred in the classic comedy film about country inns, *George Washington Slept Here* (1942).

Atlantic City is famous for its glamorous resort-town past, the Miss America contest, and of course, gambling. Hoboken is famous for the Clam Broth House and Frank Sinatra. Jersey cranberries from bogs in the Pine Barrens are consumed all over the country, and the Jersey tomato is the best grown anywhere. Architectural wonders abound, such as Thomas Edison's towering Menlo Park "lightbulb" memorial and the wonderful Pulaski Skyway, which soars over the Jersey meadows. Jersey "firsts" are legion (see list), and include the invention and production of the moving picture (on the Palisades at Fort Lee).

A fun-filled exploration of New Jersey, using this book as a guide, will hopefully put you into the camp of some of the enthusiastic celebrities who have enjoyed talking up the Garden State. These include: Bruce Springsteen, Joe Pesci, Jimmy Roselli, Whitney Houston, Dionne Warwick, Olympia Dukakis, Jerry Lewis, Sandra Dee, Connie Francis, Vivian Blaine, Doris Duke, Allen Ginsberg, Joyce Carol Oates, Ed Koch, Philip Roth, Anne Morrow Lindberg, Jack Nicholson, Alan Alda, Meryl Streep, Michael J. Pollard, John Travolta, Celeste Holm, Susan Sarandon, Melba Moore, and Amiri Baraka (aka LeRoi Jones).

◆

New Jersey Facts

The state flag, adopted in 1896, is buff with the state seal emblazoned in blue on its center. The colors were selected by George Washington and reflect the insignia of the state's Dutch settlers.

"I Love New Jersey" souvenir pinback button.

The state motto is: "Liberty and Prosperity" (this appears on the state seal and the state flag).

The state flower: the purple violet, adopted in 1913.
The state bird: the eastern goldfinch, also adopted in 1913.
The state animal: the horse, designated in 1977.
The state insect: the honeybee, named in 1974.
The state tree: the red oak, designated in 1950.

Among the 50 states, New Jersey is 1st in average value of farm-lands and buildings per acre, 2nd in per capita income, 8th in value of goods added by manufacture, 10th in population (7,904,200), 29th in gross income per farm, and 46th in size (7,836 square miles).

Some New Jersey "firsts" include:
The first celluloid, invented by John Wesley Hyatt at Newark in 1870.
The first phonograph, made by Thomas A. Edison at Menlo Park in 1877.
The first submarine, built in 1878 by John Holland of Passaic County, and now exhibited in the Pacific Museum at Paterson.
The first motion picture, developed by Thomas Edison at Menlo Park in 1889.

ONE DAY OUTINGS

SPRING EDITION

JERSEY CENTRAL RAILROAD

The first incandescent lamp, made by Thomas A. Edison at Menlo Park in 1879.

The first log cabin, built in Swedesboro in the 1640s.

First brewery in America, in Hoboken, 1642.

First steam engine in America, brought from England in 1753.

First steam locomotive, built by Colonel John Stevens of Hoboken in 1824.

First boardwalk in the world, built in 1870 at Atlantic City.

First American flag from an American loom, made at Paterson by John Rule.

First Colt revolver, developed in Paterson in 1836.

First "condensed" soup in America, cooked and canned in Camden County in 1897.

First saltwater taffy, produced at the Jersey shore in the 1870s.

First cultivated blueberries, marketed by Elizabeth White of Whitesbog in 1916.

First town to be lighted by electricity, Roselle.

First organized baseball game, played in Hoboken in 1846.

First intercollegiate football game, played in New Brunswick, between Rutgers and Princeton, on November 6, 1869.

First Miss America, chosen in Atlantic City in 1921.

First Indian reservation, established August 29, 1758, at an appropriated tract in Burlington County.

First ferry service in the world, operating between Hoboken and Manhattan in 1811.

First road sheet asphalt pavement, laid in Newark in 1870.

First national historical park, created at Morristown in 1933.

First drive-in movie theater, built on a 10-acre plot in Camden County in 1933.

◆

Is New Jersey Really Weird?

The New York Sun columnist Gary Shapiro headlined his January 18, 2005, account of a New Jersey artists exhibition at the Here Arts Center on 6th Avenue and Spring Street in Manhattan "Just How Weird Is New Jersey?" Present at this eclectic art show were Mark Sceurman and Mark Moran, publishers of *Weird N.J.* magazine and authors of the book of the same title, a guide to strange and unusual sites, as well as dark, mysterious events in the authors' home state. The New Jersey artists exhibited at the Here Arts Center included Hoop, a self described techno-visionary who rounds up "techno-trash," which he utilizes in his "art-cars" and sculptural works.

As to whether New Jersey is really weird, we authors—who have traveled and continue to travel the byways and highways of this state extensively—must, after careful consideration, answer with a resounding YES! Since their original publication, the "two Marks" have turned the weird concept into more books with titles such as *Weird Florida*, *Weird Illinois*, *Weird Wisconsin*, and *Weird U.S.*, with more states and more weirdness in the works. So where does all this weirdness end? Now the question to be asked at this time is: "Is all of America weird?" or "Is it a weird world?" Clearly it is no longer just New Jersey. Is it possible that the mythic Jersey Devil started this trend? Not content to spread his wings and fly about and make trouble in his home state, has he taken his act national? There is certainly more to come from the frontiers of the weird.

The following are selected lyrics from the song "I Like Jersey Best," recorded and sung by John Pizzarelli, with words and music written by Joseph Cosgriff (Monster Music—ASCAP).

I Like Jersey Best©

Travelin' down the Turnpike
   heading for the shore
A thought just then occurred to me
   I never thought before
I've been a lot of places
   seen pictures of the rest
But of all the places I can think of
   I like Jersey best.

Bettin' halls and shoppin' malls and
   good old Rutgers U
Forty-seven shoe stores line
   Route Twenty-Two
The Meadowlands, the root beer stands
   Main Street Hackensack
I may leave for a week or two
   but I'm always coming back

Chorus:

   The Pinelands and the Vinelands
Seaside Heights, Margate
   You can have Miami, I love the Garden State
I've been a lot of places, seen pictures
   of the rest
But of all the places I can think of
   I like Jersey best.

New Jersey Classic Car Culture

Since the beginning of the 21st century, and now well into the first decade of the new millennium, a craze for vintage American cars has swept throughout New Jersey and across the rest of the country as well; but in Jersey, like California, classic car meets seem to be happening everywhere. Starting each year in early spring and into the summer vacation months these old-time auto-enthusiast get-togethers continue well into the end of October and include autumnal harvest festivals and Halloween celebrations.

The kinds of vehicles you'll see at a car meet include early pre-1930s bona fide antique vehicles like the crank-up tin lizzy "horseless carriage" produced on Henry Ford's assembly line. Depression-decade autos are also in evidence, including the Chrysler Airstream and Airflow models and specialty hybrids like William Stout's Scarab or Buckminster Fuller's Dymaxion car, which both sport ultra-aerodynamic streamline "teardrop" designs and had a strong influence on the look of today's automobiles. Postwar cars from the late '40s and '50s—including super rocketship models from the late '50s—are a common sight at the auto meets. Many of the design concepts for the innovative cars of the 1950s and 1960s were first displayed at the 1939–1940 New York World's Fair. The fair was halted in 1940 when war broke out in Europe, and production in the auto factories shifted over to tanks, airplanes, and weaponry. Shortly after war was declared in December 1941, civilian auto production ceased and the factories retooled for war exclusively. Auto production resumed in 1945.

Among the "classics" to be found on exhibit at the countless car meets all over New Jersey is a category referred to as "art-cars," which includes custom jobs and hot rods, each more fantastic than the last. Oddball Jersey characters are often in attendance like "Hoop," whose art-mobiles include a Time Machine van covered with clocks, a 1938 Cadillac hearse covered in faux zebra-skin, and a "Can-vertible" made of soda-pop and beer cans. "Eye-Sore" Eddie drives only rusted-out classics that run well but look like wrecks from an automobile graveyard. Fred Kanter, known as Jersey's Packard King, has taken to driving an amphibious vehicle that doubles as a car and a speedboat. Often at these "Cruisin' Nites," there is a section for vintage motorcycles, where leather-jacketed highway macho men trade parts and tell hair-raising stories of life on the road on a motorbike. Various car clubs are formed by bikers and car buffs, who tend to socialize according to the make of their car, whether it's a Buick, a Hudson Hornet, a Plymouth Belvedere, a Mustang, Corvette, or Thunderbird. Vintage pickup trucks and delivery trucks are also an up-and-coming thing at the meets, especially among the younger crowd, who add the glow of neon to the undercarriage or interiors.

Pride of ownership is the key at the car-crazy auto meets, and often classic vehicles are restored to a better-than-showroom state with gleaming replated chrome and with several coats of applied spray-painted enamel. Nothing pleases the driver of a historic car more than a honk-of-the-horn and a thumbs-up from a fellow driver on the highway and shouts at red lights of "What year is it?" or "What make?" or "Super" and "Cool!" Investment is part of the game; but more often than not it is the obsession to recapture and regain some of Lost America when cars were made to stand the test of time. Today when discussing their classic cars owners often like to refer to them as perfect examples of the merging of art and industry, representing a time when automotive designers were functioning at their peak and when the vehicles were manufactured with the idea of being on the road for a decade or two or three or more.

◆

Cruisin' At Lyndhurst

An exciting place to enjoy a classic-car event is in the Meadowlands at **Lyndhurst,** where each Saturday night throughout the warm months, a few miles from the Lincoln Tunnel (just off Route 3), you can see row after row of restored 1950s cars with a sprinkling of pre-war vehicles to boot. A good night at Lyndhurst might bring in as many as 500 vehicles. Owners sit in canvas fold-up chairs, chit-chatting about their car projects, wheeling, dealing, selling and swapping parts. Often a FOR SALE sign is in a car window, and you might find a real bargain this way. Fully-restored

Black 1955 Chevrolet convertible.

autos run high, and the irony is that most of the time a vintage classic is cheaper than a brand-new car—and certainly they are more fun to drive. Once hooked, however, a first time buyer must be prepared for the rituals of the fixer-upper syndrome. This includes finding an old-car mechanic, a body shop, a garage, and a vintage parts supplier; sometimes you'll even join the club of your particular make and model, be it Plymouth, Packard, Edsel, Nash, or Hudson—all makes that are long out of production. *Hemmings Motor News* is the bible for where parts, cars, and mechanics can be located.

The Lyndhurst meet is set in the middle of the Meadowlands, and only minutes away is the Richard DeKorte Park, which has miles of trails through wetlands conservation areas. Check the website of the Meadowlands Commission for activities and scheduled hours of operation at www.meadowlands.state.nj.us. On a warm summer Saturday night, with the moon shining bright, Lyndhurst is a great place to just hang out and have a fun time of it as a golden oldies disc jockey plays Elvis, the Everly Brothers, Ricky Nelson, the Crewcuts, or any number of classic doo-wop performers over the loudspeakers. Coca-Cola, root beer, and hot dog vendors co-mingle with dealers who spread out tables with shiny new exact miniature replicas of '50s Chevys, Fords, Pontiacs, and other earlier old-time buggies. Lyndhurst has a motorcycle section and here you will find "Indians" and custom-jobs galore, some for sale and others that are just there on display and for the purpose of show and tell. The main outdoor event for classic cars, muscle cars, street rods, art-mobiles, custom cars, and motorbikes is Saturday, with special Sunday events. The car show offers up Best in Show and Worst of Show trophies and the hours are 6 P.M. to 10 P.M. There is a separate lot at Lyndhurst available where visitors can park their new cars. Call (201) 939-4889 for directions and

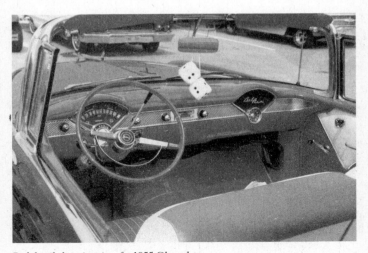

Red detailed car interior of a 1955 Chevrolet.

write **American Cruisers** (c/o Don Nardozza, 430 Thompson Street, Hackensack, NJ 0760l) to register your cruiser in advance or for more information on special events.

The indoor **Whiskey Cafe,** adjacent to the parking lot at 1050 Wall Street, operates from 6 P.M. to 10 P.M., serving good American-style food like burgers and fries or homemade chili and chips or chicken fingers, along with the whiskey or beer of your choice. For dessert the substantial family-style menu offers Chrysler Cheesecake, Mercury Mousse, and T-Bird Tiramisu. All summer long the Whiskey Cafe features what the owners describe as New Jersey's hottest rock and oldies bands, such as Jimmy Dean's Swing Orchestra, the Four Pops, the Be Bops, the Cameo's, and the Soul Cruisers. Check summer dates and times starting Memorial Day and continuing through Labor Day weekend.

Following the Lyndhurst car meet it might be just the thing to visit a classic 1950s diner, and there happens to be one just up the hill called the **Colonial Diner,** 27 Orient Way, (201) 935-3192, that more than fits the bill in terms of period authenticity. It features a stainless steel, glass, brick, and neon exterior; a 1950s-style loud-mouth waitress; and a hash-slinging happy crew cooking things up on the grill. As the lyrics of an old-time Irving Berlin song suggests, ". . . so let's have another cup of coffee and let's have another piece of pie!"

◆

Lead East

Lead East has been described by car connoisseurs as "the world's biggest 1950s party," so for those who want to have a truly retro experience over Labor Day weekend, the place to go is the Par-

Lead East "Participant" window sticker.

sippany Hilton Hotel Complex in Parsippany, New Jersey. The
event is produced by Terry Cook and Linda Naprstek at Appleton
Productions of Long Valley; for more information, check out
www.leadeast.net or call (908) 876-9100 or (908) 876-1672 for
room reservations, car show tickets, vintage car entries, oldies concert tickets, and more. (The same team also produces Spring
Fever, a big car show in May held at the Sheraton Meadowlands
Hotel in East Rutherford.) The Parsippany Hilton is set on beautiful tree-shaded park grounds and has indoor and outdoor pools,
tennis courts, two full restaurants, and a bar. There is also a theater where, on this special weekend, well-known oldies and doo-
wop groups such as the Duprees, Kenny Vance and the Plantones,
The Impalas, The Limelites, Johnny Maestro and the Brooklyn
Bridge, and The Cliftonaires perform. On the premises there are
other oldies bands, a variety of New Jersey Elvis impersonators, as
well as 1,500 classic cars, hot-rods, customized dream cars, movie
cars, celebrity cars, and art cars. Inside the vast lobby of the hotel,
one of the public rooms features 1940s and 1950s jukeboxes.
These fantastic push-button coin-operated machines feature special bubble-blowing water tubes and bright-colored neon trim
with chromium and bakelite details; they play 45 rpm and 78 rpm
records and are for sale. Another room is designated for collectibles, including 1950s retro clothing and jewelry for guys and
gals, hard-to-get '40s, '50s, '60s, and '70s movies on DVD or VHS
for the home TV, and other oldies such as period litho-on-metal
Roy Rogers, Gene Autry, and Howdy Doody lunchboxes. Along
the sides of the lobbies are dealers selling collectible vintage toy
cars and trucks. Rare CDs and tapes for the car are also in abun-
dance. Outdoors there are food stands galore as well as giant tents
that sell enamel-on-metal gas station signs, old motor-oil tins, soda
pop signs, vintage license plates, bumper stickers, and car decals,
special James Dean, Marilyn Monroe, and Elvis license plates,
and the like—some of which are authentic and some that have
been reproduced as faux collectibles.

The excitement outdoors revolves around the people and their
classic cars, which are parked row upon row on streets named
Memory Lane, Nostalgia Place, and Cruisin' Speedway. Families,
groups of friends, and couples displaying their own cars—some
original, some restored, and some super-customized—sit in front
of their cars in deck chairs, the women wearing pink-poodle
bolero skirts with layers of crinoline underneath, while the men
sport gas-station worker outfits, 1950s vintage shirts, the popular
Hawaiian shirts Harry Truman wore, and club T-shirts emblazoned
with the vehicle of their choice. Lead East is all about the real joy
of owning and driving a classic, as well as a reverence and enthu-
siasm for a bygone era. Cars at the show are also often for sale.
Usually these are carefully described in terms of overall condition,
what repair work has been done, what body work was completed,
and what special features were added. For instance, a 1965 ready-

to-go Impala SS recently for sale at a Lead East event is described with a contact phone number or e-mail thus:

> **IMPALA SS 1965**: 65,000 original miles; 3 owners; solid floors, rockers, quarters; stock rebuilt 350 police car motor, 16,000 miles; Edelbrock intake and cams; GM HE1 distributor; TC1 turbo 350 trans; dual exhaust; power brakes; front disc brakes; tilt steering; power steering; air conditioning; new interior from "year one," NOS tail lights, door handles, SS script, hood molding; extra body parts included; all receipts. Sellers offer information on where to obtain replacement parts and where to go for repairs or body work.

Lead East has been in operation for over 20 years and established itself as an annual event car enthusiasts flock to with friends and families. Others are there to marvel at and explore just for the fun of it. Lead East follows the lead of the two other big-time Northeast car events held in Pennsylvania each year: one in Hershey, known for vintage autos from the 1940s, 1930s, and earlier; and one in Carlisle, a 1950s car extravaganza. The Lead East weekend event attracts not just old-timers and their cars, but a younger crowd, some of whom are greasers, car mechanics, and dudes who sport DA (for "Ducks-Ass") dyed black '50s hairdos and wear blue suede shoes, peg pants, and '50s pullovers. It is not unusual to spot a few or more tousled blond Jimmy Dean lookalikes in red jackets and dungarees with their Natalie Wood or Sandra Dee lookalike gal pals who appear to have just stepped out of the 1950s Peggy Sue decade.

Nighttime is the time to turn on the car lights and turn up the car radio to listen to the Beach Boys sing "Car Crazy Cutie" or "Little Deuce Coupe," or Jan and Dean belting out the high notes on "Dead Man's Curve." The parade of old cars and their happy owner-drivers is a wonder to behold. Among the many nighttime events is a big simulated outdoor drive-in movie screen showing classic flicks. *Hot Rod Gang* (1958) is about "crazy kids running wild to a wild rock and roll beat" with jumpin' jack songs that include "Dance in the Street," "Dance to the Bop," "Baby Blue," and "Lovely Loretta." *Dragstrip Girl* (1957) has Frank Gorshin, Fay Spain, and others acting out a "car-crazy, speed-crazy, boy-crazy" scenario with plenty of "thrill-hungry teens on a reckless car crash scramble." *Hot Rod Girl* (1956), with Gorshin again, as well as Lori Nelson and Mark Andrews, has "teenage terrorists on a fast speed rampage." *High School Confidential* (1958) stars Mamie Van Doren and Jerry Lee Lewis. Other movies include *Ghost of Dragstrip Hollow* (1959); *Blackboard Jungle* (1955) with Sidney Poitier and Vic Morrow, which features the hit "Rock Around the Clock," and was called by critics "the first good movie of this kind"; and *Kitten with a Whip* (1964) with Ann Margret. There are triple-features with shorts and documentaries, including sci-fi flicks like *Teenagers from Outer Space* and horror movies such as *The Blob* (1958) or *The Car* (1977), starring a murderous, driverless, beat-up, nondescript black car that chases after and runs over terrified people in the desert. There has even been a Charlie Chan triple-feature festival, for those old-timers who favor the 1930s and 1940s classic cars, including *Charlie Chan Carries On* (1931), *Charlie Chan in Honolulu* (1939), and *Charlie Chan in the Secret Service* (1944).

Since 1960 the famous **Kanter Brothers,** Fred and Dan, at 76 Monroe Street in Boonton, New Jersey, have sold auto parts to classic car owners, including everything from canvas ragtops for convertibles made after the originals to specialty spoked-wire wheels. The business is set in an old Packard factory in the quaint and charming hilltop town of Boonton, which has on its main street the 1950s Boonton Diner, an old-time movie theater, and a number of antique shops. The enterprising brothers drive and restore rare vintage vehicles of their own, and they have an expertise in practically every area within their specialized field. They will supply whatever you need, and if it's not in their warehouse, they'll track it down for you. Some "oldie" parts are newly manufactured to meet the ever increasing demand of car collectors. Engine overhaul kits, exhaust systems, wide white-wall tires, carpeting, headliners, seat-upholstery kits, and chrome accessories are among the many items available from Kanter Auto Products. The Packard was one of America's great automotive achievements, and here you can acquire reprints of original service manuals from the 1920s to the mid-1950s. Chrysler products, Cadillac necessities, or parts for your Kaiser-Frazer, Nash, Ford, or Chevy—it's all to be found here. Call the guys at (973) 345-9575 or 800 526-1096; visit their website at www.kanter.com; or just drop by and visit these legendary New Jersey vintage car experts, who are only too happy to solve your car problems and help you restore that American Dream-mobile.

◆

New Jersey Car Run

Car shows are usually held during the day, and there are often 100 trophies given out, while "cruise nights," most beginning at dusk, hand out only about 10 trophies. Addresses, driving directions, contact numbers, and many more listings can be found at www. njcarshow.com. Check the site for frequency of meets and exact locations and links to other Web sites. Also check the monthly listings for "New Jersey Meets and Cruises" in *Hemmings Motor News*, where you will note that the Garden State has more listings for shows, meets, peel-outs, automotive flea markets, and cruises than any other state in the union. Also, send away for a copy of

Cruising magazine—their motto is "You 'auto' be reading *Cruising* magazine"—and their comprehensive events calendar at 307 A Street, Wilmington, DE 19801, or call (302) 475-CRUZ. You can also visit www.cruisingmagazine.net.

In North Jersey there are great meets in Summit, where you can shop at the antique centers and visit the sublime **Summit Diner,** which was built from an original 1920s railroad car; also, don't miss Clifton's Annual Car, Truck and Motorcycle Show, and check out the deep-fried **Rut's Hut** hotdogs which can't be beat. Other car shows are held in Stanhope's historic **Waterloo Village;** there's Motor Madness in Phillipsburg on the Delaware (in May), Hot Rods and Harleys in Rahway near the East Jersey State Prison; Bergenfield's annual Wild About Corvettes, and the "peel-out" hosted regularly in South Orange by the Royal Devils, the Rusty Relics Car Show in Upper Saddle River, and the annual Cops and Rodders Car Meet in North Brunswick.

At the shore, there are regular meets in Keyport, Long Branch, Seaside Heights, and Smithville (near Atlantic City). Cruisin' with the Oldies is held every spring in the antique town of Red Bank, and they also have an annual car show. Rare Hudson/Terraplane autos rally on Ocean Avenue in Ocean Grove during the summer. Try Bugs and Busses by Barnegat Bay, a vintage Volkswagen car show open to all in Lavallette. In June, July, and August there are classic car cruises in Point Pleasant at Arnold and Bay avenues, which include trucks and motorcycles, live entertainment, and lookalike Elvis sightings from 5 to 9 P.M. Call (732) 899-2424 for more info. Also in June on the boardwalk in Wildwood there is an annual GM Antique Car Show and Parade, and in Ocean City

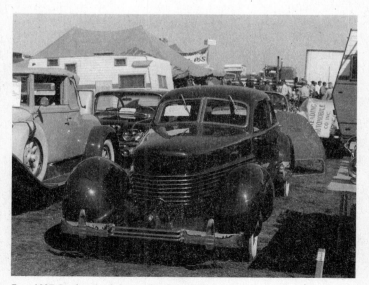

Rare 1937 Cord at Englishtown Classic Car Meet.

in the fall there is "A Day At the Beach—Corvette Style" in which
the cars parade onto the boardwalk. South of the Mason-Dixon
Line, Cape May has frequent meets throughout the summer attracting vintage autos from all over the state, and also from
Delaware, Maryland, and Washington D.C., their owners em-
barking on an ocean voyage from Lewes, Delaware to Cape May
on the Ferry.

In southwest New Jersey there are shows and meets in Berlin,
Smithville, and Vineland, and Trenton has a two-night car show
in June. Princeton University Stadium is host to the Groovy Fête
Annual Car Show, Flea Market, and Auction, an event over 50
years old. There's also the All American Wheels of Steel Car Show
in historic Smithville (Burlington City) at the Village Green, the
Stoztzfus Farm Market Car Show in Williamstown, and the Pa-
triot Window Car Show in Hammonton hosted by the Delaware
Valley Old Goat Club. Also in Hammonton (in the Pine Barrens)
in June is Cruisin' Main Street and the Red, White and Blueberry
Festival and Car Show and Flea Market sponsored by Cruisin'
Classics Auto Club—call Harry Gale at (609) 561-2581 for more
information.

Often there are as many as two dozen "cruise nights" every night
of the week in New Jersey. Good places for cruises (with hours
usually from 5 P.M. to 9 P.M.) are the Galloping Hill Inn in Union
on Mondays and Sundays, and Stewart's Root Beer (Route 9,
Tuckerton) and Rut's Hut (Route 21, Clifton) on Tuesday. There
is also a cruise night at Mugsy's on Tuesday in Tom's River.
Wednesday offers cruising in Keansburg, Bloomfield, and Ocean
City; it's Stewart's Root Beer locations in Point Pleasant on Thursday, in South Amboy on Friday, and in Gillette on Saturday.
Diner locations are often a good car scene on Friday night—
check the Burlington Diner and the Windsor Diner in Clark. On
Saturday in the Meadowlands, from May to October, the fun is at
the Whiskey Cafe on Wall Street in Lyndhurst.
     New Jersey towns and their citizens take pride in classic-car
cruise events. As the craze for vintage American cars continues
through the spring, summer, and fall seasons, these gatherings
continue to get bigger and better as more enthusiasts enjoy getting
together to join in on the good fun.

◆

The Top Ten Jersey Car Meets and Cruises
(Other Than Lead East and Lyndhurst)

Thursday Cruisin' Nites at the Plaza at the Harmon Meadow
parking lot adjacent to the Loew's Theater in Secaucus (through
September 11). Call (201) 272-5403 before 5 P.M.

The annual Englishtown shows: the Great Spring Swap Meet and Auto Show at Raceway Park in April, the Mopar Atlantic Nationals in May, and the Fall Swap Meet and Auto Show in September. Call (732) 446-7800 or visit www.racewaypark.com.

The Great Northern Catskills Festival of Classic and Custom Cars in June sponsored by the Be Bop Cruisers of NJ at Friar Tuck Resort and Spa, 4858 Rt. 32. Call Phyllis Celano at (732) 303-7187 or Bruce Highfill at (732) 701-0829.

Point Pleasant Boro Rotary Club Annual, a one-time night show in late August (6 to 10 P.M.) held at the Crystal Point Yacht Club on Route 70 and River Road. Held to benefit the Vintage Automobile Museum of New Jersey, this show is in a beautiful setting and has '50s and '60s music by Wolfman Jerry. The show features clean and keen machines, rods, trucks, classics, and customs all the way. Call (732) 899-3104.

The Two Kids Foundation Whippany Car Show & Cruise is held the first Sunday of August and features 250 vehicles plus a buffet barbecue. Held at the Birchwood Manor at 111 North Jefferson Road in Whippany, this is a great one, according to Woody, who will answer your questions and set up a space for your motorcycle, car or truck. Call (973) 515-9368.

Toms River holds a great late afternoon/early evening auto meet on tree-lined Washington Street once a month on the second Wednesday in June, July, August, and September. There are dozens of classics and entertainers, including Elvis impersonator Ray Kaminsky, and The Happenings, who sing some of their chart hits like "See You In September." The meets are sponsored by the Toms River Business Improvement District; call (732) 341-8738 for further info.

Twin Brook Golf Center Car Show is held in mid-September at 1251 Jumping Brook Road in Tinton Falls. Call (732) 922-1600.

Wheels in Motion is held at 316 Rt. 15 in Wharton in mid-October with doo-wop oldies on the sound system. Contact Italiano Productions at (973) 328-7900.

In late October Pumpkin Row holds a Halloween event with street rods, lead sleds, race cars, motorcyles, military vehicles, art cars, antique fire trucks, '50s classic antique cars, and steam- and gas-powered tractors and old power and farm equipment and 'dozers, which are the specialty. This annual Pumpkin Run show in Egg Harbor Township (1708 Somers Point Road) takes place in a former automotive junkyard that's been in business since the 1930s. Call Earl Manley at (609) 653-8412; for general information on engines and tractors call Toby Dilks at (609) 653-6868 or Harry at (609) 927-9541. Visit www.oldengine.com.

Morristown's Fall Festival On-the-Green "Antique Auto Alley" in late September offers owners the opportunity to show off their cars to 50,000 attendees who stroll the historic town green and shop in local antique stores. Prizes are given in each category including historic (prior to 1929), 1930s, '40s, '50s, '60s, '70s cars, trucks, imports, custom and street rods, and motorcycles. This show is sponsored by the Morristown Antiques Center at 45 Market Street; for information, call (973) 734-0900 or (973) 455-1133.

Jersey is classic car crazy all during the spring, summer, and fall. Watch for car events at local street and highway diners and at Stewart's Root Beer Drive-In stands held in scenic places like Atlantic Highlands, or in Tuckerton where you can enjoy a "dog" and an ice-cold mug of Stewart's famous root beer, or the Dairy Queen on the Black Horse Pike in Egg Harbor Township, or the A&P and Friendly's parking lot in Old Bridge (Ferry Road and Route 9 South).

If you find yourself in Seaside Heights on Columbus Day weekend you can enjoy a real New Jersey Italian Day parade with classic cars filled with local dignitaries and beauty queens all along Main Street. A recorded Bruce Springsteen is guaranteed to be on the loudspeaker singing "Jersey Girl" and there is literally dancing in the streets—and plenty of authentic Italian food to gobble up at the sidewalk street fair—but watch out for those tough Jersey girls with the big smile and the big hair. They are everywhere in evidence at such events having a hell of a good time. The cruisin' 1950s is still there all over the place in Jersey.

◆

Auto Resources

New, used, and antiquarian books on specific cars are sold on the premises of most car meets. Some of these are beautiful photo coffee-table art books, but the best introduction to the wonderful world of classic vehicles is *Hemmings Motor News*, which has listings of cars for sale, a full section of dealers in old car-parts, and a roundup of monthly New Jersey auto meets and cruises. The same company also publishes *Hemmings Muscle Machines*, as well as other car books and specialty auto magazines. Write to *Hemmings Motor News*, PO Box 100, Bennington, Vermont 05201 for a subscription or call them at (800) 227-4373.

The State of New Jersey is antique country whether you're traveling north, south, east, or west. Collectors are bound to find that treasure they are seeking, and there are always discoveries and surprises in store along the way. When driving through a city, village, or town it is a good idea to check out the county phone book for local shop listings under antiques or vintage clothing; when visiting an antique shop or emporium, be sure to gather up local antique newspapers, maps, and related brochures. Salvation Army stores and thrift shops abound in larger towns. During spring, summer, and fall, as you drive along, it is a good idea to keep a watchful eye open for porch and front lawn sales, garage sales, roadside flea markets, street fairs, bazaars, and festivals sponsored by churches, VFW groups, or volunteer township fire departments. Before taking to the road it is advisable to begin your search on the Internet: go to New Jersey Antique Dealers Directory at www.newjerseyantiques.net. For more information regarding annual indoor and outdoor shows, call **Stella Show Management** at (212) 255-0020 or visit www.stellashows.com. There are annual Stella Shows in Waterloo Village, Cape May, and points in between; the best dealers present a variety of specialty wares from bona fide early antiques, collectibles, primitives, jewelry, modern design, art, photography, mid-50s modern, and Art Deco.

Table-model yellow Marblette radio in lyre shape, manufactured by DeWald, circa 1938.

We once wandered into a junk shop (spelled "junque") on Springfield Avenue in Irvington and discovered a 1940s Leeds China Mickey Mouse Turnabout cookie jar for about $8—a real bargain—and a wooden tabletop radio originally used in rooms at the Robert Treat Hotel in downtown Newark. The lighted glass dial spells out in bold red lettering, "The Robert Treat Hotel." In earlier times, Rexall drugstores and variety and dry goods stores in places like Jersey City or Lakewood or Barnegat would yield great finds that had been stored in the basement for years. These items from the 1920s, '30s, '40s, and '50s might include Art Deco-packaged cosmetic powders covered with yellowing cellophane; tin-litho talcum containers; vintage metal toy cars; old games and novelties; Deanna Durbin and Donald Duck coloring books; Snow White, Mickey Mouse, or Buck Rogers Dixon pencil boxes; aged and brittle Big Little Books; Depression-era movie magazines; cardboard advertising signs with smiling World War II Army WACs drinking Coca-Cola out of a bottle; and die-cut posters of movie goddess Veronica Lake with her 1940s "peek-a-boo" bang hairdo endorsing Lustre-Creme Shampoo.

In the 1970s and '80s, dealers at the New Egypt Farmers Flea Market, housed in World War II Air Force quonset huts, sold fiestaware at 25¢ a plate and Catalin and Bakelite "baby" tabletop radios in working order for $10 to $15. These were the days when Andy Warhol, Bette Midler, Bernadette Peters, Barbra Streisand, and other celebrities haunted flea markets in search of pop-culture artifacts like 1930s Ingersoll Mickey Mouse watches or fanciful 1920s wooden lamps with fabric-fringed shades or chromium Art Deco cocktail accessories to use for decorating their apartments.

1950s plastic Mr. Peanut salt and pepper shaker set could originally be purchased at the Planters Peanut Store on the Boardwalk in Atlantic City.

At one point in our compulsive collecting phase, we had collected over 30 Depression-era blue-mirrored coffee and end tables that were put in storage to be dealt with at some future date. In the 1940s wartime period the cobalt compound used in the blue-mirror process was restricted by the government as it was then needed for the manufacture of atom bombs. Speaking of atom bombs, we also once found a box of a dozen Jergen's Atom Bomb Perfume bottles—yes, the bottle with a red plastic screw-on top in the shape of an A-bomb—in a variety store in downtown Newark. Industrial towns in northern New Jersey were the places where these early and mid-century items were plentiful. Cities like Passaic, Paterson, and Rutherford seemed to still exist in some Depression time-warp where discoveries of future collectibles—what some collectors today refer to as items of a "Lost America"—were to be made.

The nostalgia-producing collecting process seemed to always include products that were mass-produced in the 1920s and 1930s, some created by important industrial designers like Raymond Loewy or Donald Desky. One collector colleague bought a street map of the city of Newark and methodically proceeded to walk up and down every street. On one of these forays he found a 1936 blue-mirrored chrome and ebony wood Sparton tabletop radio designed by Walter Dorwin Teague for the Sparks-Withington Company, a splendid example of Deco-Moderne. In a dilapidated bookstore he unearthed original architectural drawings for the Waldorf-Astoria Hotel on Park Avenue. On one of our own antique trips to South Jersey on old Highway 9, which is filled with antique shops and emporiums, we stopped at a used furniture shop in Tuckerton where we found a porcelain enamel-top kitchen table with four matching wooden chairs all emblazoned with the iconic orange and blue Trylon and Perisphere which were the official logos of the 1939–40 New York World's Fair. This table was later on exhibit at both the New York Art Deco Exposition at Radio City Music Hall in 1975 and at the 50th anniversary of the World's Fair at the Queens Museum of Art. The 1939–40 World's Fair is now recognized as the most important and influential modern fair of the 20th century.

The hilltop town of Montclair, which overlooks the industrial area below and has a splendid view of the New York skyline, has always been a treasure trove for those who have contracted what dyed-in-the-wool collectors call "Antique Pox"—and it still is. We haunted the historic old Montclair Railroad Station in past years where we found a Charlie McCarthy ventriloquist doll, a 1930s Lionel Donald Duck handcar, and an early Edison "electric" toaster. Many collectors who call themselves "archaeologists of the past" feel that they are saving the rarities they find for posterity. Value, of course, is always the name of the game and "What's it worth?" is the question most often asked by those who might have just inherited a Little Orphan Annie Ovaltine Shake-Up-Mug or a

Shirley Temple Depression blue-glass milk pitcher from a deceased aunt or grandmother. When a price is quoted by an expert that is below the expectations of the owner for whatever object it is, the look of shock is all too obvious on the faces of the disappointed. On the other hand, there are the more innocent folk who go onto the television show *Antiques Roadshow* with something they just discovered in their attic or cellar who are equally shocked to find that they have a real piece of history or art that is worth a small fortune.

In some instances experts' appraisals may be either too high or too low; and then there is the question of who to try to sell it to, whether to go the auction route or wrestle with the vagaries inherent in the eBay phenomenon. Many stories of discovery abound, such as the lady who bought a photographic portrait of a bulldog for $5, primarily for the old frame, but when she opened it up she found tucked between the picture and the mat one of the rare copies of the Declaration of Independence worth millions; another recent "big fish" story is of a man who discovered a Bob Dylan *Freewheelin' Bob Dylan* vinyl LP in a dollar record bin—this

This Ferris wheel color lithographed metal wind-up toy was manufactured by the J. Chien Company in Newark in 1947.

mint condition, never-played album had tracks that were cut after just one initial pressing—and on an Internet auction the 33⅓ RPM sold for $35,000 to a collector in Paris. Of course, acquired knowledge is power, but these kinds of finds are rare, like looking for the proverbial needle in the haystack. Still, anything out of the past can pop up in the hunt, and the pursuit and learning are part of what makes it all worthwhile.

Primarily, the sense of fun and discovery is the motivating factor behind it all, since in "The End" no one really owns anything. It just passes on. So the message is: *Get on the Road and Enjoy!* It's okay to be aquisitive and haggle over the price of an item; in New Jersey there are a great many antique trails to follow—and here are some of our best on-the-road suggestions.

By connecting the dots on your highway maps you will find that the following antiques tours (five of them, covering the entire state) link treasure hunters to the towns and regions with the greatest concentration of antiques dealers. Individual shops, large multidealer centers, co-op emporiums, quality antique shows, giant flea markets, and street fairs stretch along the trails. Don't forget to cross-reference the table of contents, the index, and the geographic sections of this book to check out more about the places below. You should try looking up the local yard and garage sales in area newspapers, and for the exact dates and addresses of annual antique events, check with local town chambers of commerce. Information is also available from historical societies.

Litho-on-tin "Dreamboat" hot rod toy was won in a game of chance by author Robert Heide at the Keansburg Amusement Park.

◆
Selected New Jersey Antiques Destinations

There are antique centers, shows, shoppes, emporiums, street fairs, and flea markets in cities and towns throughout the Garden State. Many of these are featurred in other chapters of this book. The following are a few places to get you going.

NORTHEAST NEW JERSEY
Andover: **Scranberry Coop** (150 dealers), 42 Main–Rt. 206N, (973) 786-6414.

CENTRAL NEW JERSEY
Lambertville: **People's Store** (multi-dealer), 28 N. Union Street; **Rado Arts & Auction** Center, 333 North Main Street.

Somerville: **Somerville Center Antiques** (5 centers—220 dealers), 34 W. Main St. and 9–17 Division Street, (908) 595-1294 and (908) 526-3446; **Antiques Emporium,** 29 Division Street, (908) 218-1234.

Summit: **Summit Antiques Center,** 511 Morris Ave, (908) 273-9373.

SOUTHWEST NEW JERSEY
Allentown: **Antique District on Main Street,** (877) 208-1141.

Berlin: **Trackside Treasures Co-op,** 49 Taunton Avenue, (856) 809-1749; **Berlin Antiques,** (856) 753-5559; **Stuff From the Attic,** (856) 753-6450.

Bridgeton: **The Squirrels Nest,** 680 Shiloh Pike, (856) 455-6594.

Burlington: **Historic Burlington Antiques** (85 dealers), 424 High Street, (609) 747-8333.

Pennsville: **Graystone Corner Antiques,** 87 N. Broadway, (856) 678-3234.

Salem: **Market Street Treasures** (40 dealers), 36 Market Street, (856) 935-6699.

Vineland: **Bertoia Auction Gallery** (rare toys), 2141 DeMarco Drive, (856) 692-1881 or www.bertoiaauctions.com.

NORTHERN JERSEY SHORE
Asbury Park: **Antique Emporium,** (732) 774-8230; **Studebaker's and Rumble Seat Tearoom,** 1201 Main Avenue, (732) 776-5565;

Antic Hay Books, 721 Cookman Avenue, (732) 774-4590, www.antichay.com.

Freehold: **Antique District**. For information call Freehold Center at (732) 462-3584

Keyport: **Antique District** (shops on West, East Front, Main, and Broad Street) (732) 203-1001),

Point Pleasant: **Antique Emporium** (125 dealers), corner of Bay & Trenton, (732) 892-2222; **Shore Antique Center,** 300 Richmond Avenue.

Red Bank: **Antique Centers** (three buildings), (732) 741-5331 or (732) 842-3393 or (732) 842-4336.

SOUTHERN JERSEY SHORE (OLD ROUTE 9)
Atlantic City: **"Atlantique City" Show**, the largest indoor antique and collectibles show in the world at the Atlantic City Convention Hall, (800) 526-2724.

Cape May: **Historic Cold Spring Village,** (609) 898-2300; **Tree House Antiques Co-op,** (609) 884-4600.

Tuckerton: **Port of Entry Antiques** (multi-dealer), 147 E. Main St., (609) 294-1527.

Hoboken Day Trip

1. Erie Lackawanna Station
2. Clam Broth House
3. Castle Point
4. Helmer's Restaurant
5. Maxwell's
6. Elysian Fields
7. Hoboken Bookstore
8. Leo's Grandevous Restaurant

Just south of the Lincoln Tunnel and just north of the Holland Tunnel exits in New Jersey, adjacent to the Pulaski Skyway and a spur of the New Jersey Turnpike, lies the old city of Hoboken. In the good old days New Yorkers took rowboats across the Hudson River for afternoon and evening walks in the tree-shaded Elysian Fields of Hoboken. It was the Germans who gravitated to Hoboken in the

Original sign from the Clam Broth House in Hoboken.

1840s (the Irish went to Jersey City to work on the railroads and canals; the Scotch to work in the mills in Harrison and Kearny; the Swiss to West New York and Union City's embroidery industry) and the German beer gardens and Oktoberfests there became legendary. Today the PATH (Port Authority Trans-Hudson) trains whisk passengers from Macy's in Herald Square, from the World Trade Center station in lower Manhattan, from Journal Square in Jersey City, and from Newark's Pennsylvania Station to Hoboken in less than 30 minutes. The PATH system is a cheap, efficient, and pleasant means of travel. Your first big surprise is when you emerge from the PATH into the splendid beaux arts Erie Lackawanna Train Terminal situated atop the Hoboken waterfront. New Jersey Transit trains heading west into New Jersey depart every few minutes from the open-air boarding platforms, and the Hoboken–Battery Park City ferry service is steps away from track 15 at the far end of the station. The recently restored landmark train station, a registered State and National Historic Site, was designed by Kenneth Murchison and built in 1907. It features a brilliant terrazzo floor, Tiffany glass ceiling, and is entirely clad in rich copper work turned luminous green with oxidation.

As you stroll up River Street you will pass on your right what was once the home of North German Lloyd and Holland-America shipping, and the major site for the filming of *On the Waterfront*

An intense Marlon Brando takes a cigarette break during the filming of On the Waterfront, *directed by Elia Kazan and filmed entirely in Hoboken.*

(1954) which utilized Hoboken townspeople in the cast. Halfway up River Street you can either walk through **Stevens Park,** which is fronted by a manicured little league baseball field, or take the low road, a waterfront avenue called "Frank Sinatra Drive." Frank Sinatra Memorial Park was dedicated July 14, 1998 "in memory of Francis Albert Sinatra, Hoboken's gift to the world." The high road, however, takes you up to **Stevens Gatehouse,** built of serpentine rock in 1859 as the home of the woman who tended cows for the Stevens estate, the oldest building on the Stevens 55-acre campus. Walk up through the Gatehouse onto the campus where you will find yourself on an outcropping of rock referred to in the log of Henry Hudson's second voyage on the *Half Moon* in 1609. This is where the Stevens family's "castle" was located until the present-day institute structure was built in 1959. Castle Point observatory terrace features a cannon dating from the Civil War and what is probably the most spectacular view of the entire Manhattan and Hudson skyline from the George Washington Bridge to the Verrazano Narrows and beyond. Turning left and walking upriver you cross a yellow brick street with stately homes formerly lived in by Maxwell House Coffee executives. Turn right down the yellow brick road and you will pass through **Elysian Park,** a remnant of Hoboken's famous Elysian fields. The immense red-and-blue-neon Maxwell House "Good to the Last Drop" coffee cup sign cast a glow over the area at night before the factory closed and the sign was dismantled. When the lights went out Manhattanites mourned, particularly Greenwich Villagers who missed the often discernible smell of coffee wafting across the Hudson River. Recently a 13-foot neon coffee drop from the Maxwell House cup sign was discovered in a Hobokenite's front yard and is now on view at Hoboken's **Historical Museum** at 1301 Hudson Street (at 13th Street). Their telephone number is (201) 656-2240; call for changing exhibits.

Walking out from Elysian Park you'll find yourself at Washington and 11th Streets where a plaque, donated by the Hoboken Indus-

The magnificent view of the Hudson River and Manhattan Island from Castle Point at Stevens Institute of Technology in Hoboken.

The Beaux Arts Erie-Lackawanna railroad terminal, located along the Hudson.

try and Business Association in 1984, commemorates the famous Elysian Fields ballgame of June 19, 1846, the first of its kind in the world. By this time you may probably need some sustenance and **Helmers' Cafe,** a German Restaurant at 1036 Washington Street, only steps from the bronze baseball plaque, will fill the bill. Established at the turn of the century, this highly polished, wood-paneled, exceptionally comfortable restaurant and bar offers a really satisfying dining experience. Sitting in one of the commodious upholstered booths is like taking a voyage on an Art Deco ocean liner like the S.S. *Bremen.* The varied Helmer's menu includes traditional German dishes like Wiener schnitzel or sauerbraten with side dishes of red cabbage and homemade potato dumplings. Hackbraten is a delicious German meat loaf made with veal, pork, beef, and other secret ingredients. Norman Lueders, a commanding presence, dispenses an endless variety of German beers and wines. To secure one of the booths, designed originally for large people who enjoy long dinners, it is best to call in advance at (201) 963-3333. Open Monday and Tuesday 4 to 10 P.M.; Wednesday and Thursday noon to 10 P.M.; Friday and Saturday noon to 11 P.M., closed Sundays. Just across the street from Helmer's is the legendary **Maxwell's** (1039 Washington at 11th), an early haven for bands like R.E.M. and Sonic Youth. Steve Fallon started the place in 1978 and presented the cutting edge of popular music with groups like This Is It, Flying Saucer, Jive Tribe, The Jesus Lizard, The Loveless, Flat Old World, The Mummies, The Toasters, and Dog Eat Dog. If these last two groups make you hungry, Maxwell's serves a full menu from chili con carne to Burger Maxwell (choice of mozzarella, Swiss or colby cheese, served with fries) to "daily fresh specials" like meat loaf dinner with mashed potatoes and vegetable, and black linguine with bay scallops in marinara sauce. A wide selection of tap and bottled beers and premium wines is also offered at Maxwell's, which is open late. Call for the latest industrial rock music schedule, (201) 653-1703. Music entrepreneur Todd Abramson, who presents The Hedons, The Samplers, Blue Channels, and The Butterflys of Love, is now running the place.

Hoboken

An Old-Time Town

Hoboken is just across the Hudson River from New York's Greenwich Village, and like people who live in the Village, Hobokenites have a great deal of pride in local history and landmark buildings. They happily take time to point out historic sites or tell stories about local characters like Hetty Green, the infamous miser who amassed a fortune on the stock market but who chose to live in a cheap walk-up on Washington Street. Despite her wealth she constantly complained to whoever would listen about the nickel bus fare.

It is no coincidence that Hoboken became known as a mile-square gin mill in the years before, during, and after Prohibition. America's first brewery was established there in 1642; and a surge of German immigrants opened up festive beer gardens in the Elysian Fields. Today there is at least one bar per block in "Hoboghan Hackingh" or "Land of the Tobacco Pipe" which is what the Lenape Indians called this area before the Dutch bought it out from under them for a few blankets and some bright trading beads. Colonel John Stevens, who invented the first steam locomotive in 1825, hit pay dirt back in 1784 when he managed to purchase the entire mile-square area for $90,000. He laid out the plan for the "new" city of Hoboken in 1804. In 1870 the Stevens family founded the Stevens Institute of Technology, recognized as one of the great engineering schools in the world.

The first "open challenge" baseball game, organized just for the occasion, is said to have occurred in Hoboken on June 19, 1846, between the Knickerbockers and the New York Baseball Club. It is generally conceded that until this match America's favorite sport was not seriously regarded at all.

For 100 years, between 1850 and 1950, Hoboken flourished as a great shipping and railroad town; but as factories shut down in the 1950s and 1960s and moved elsewhere, all of this business came to a virtual standstill. My-T-Fine Pudding, Cocomalt, Log Cabin Syrup, Newman Leather, and other factories are now converted into commercial lofts, art studios, and residential spaces. The classic 1954 Academy Award–winning film *On the Waterfront*, directed by Elia Kazan and starring Marlon Brando, Eva Marie Saint, and Karl Malden, depicts the heyday of the shipping industry in a Hoboken that is no more. Frank Sinatra, the singer known as the "Chairman of the Board" who belts out "New York, New York," is a hero in Hoboken, the town in which he was born and raised. Sinatra was given an honorary degree at Stevens to the dismay of protesting students. His response to the jeering bunch was "I hope you'll have to listen to my voice forever." The skinny kid who became "The Voice" in the 1940s continued during his lifetime to carry a chip on his shoulder over the tough times he endured growing up on the wrong side of the tracks in Hoboken.

Hoboken is an unusual place to go to. It is isolated from the rest of the world and yet at the same time it's right in the middle of it. The city was originally a tidal swamp, separated from the mainland of New Jersey by the rocky cliffs of the Palisades to the west, the Hudson River to the east, and the vast trainyards of the Erie Lackawanna to the south. When you're there, you're really there. To get the right feel, take a bus from the depot next to the 1908 PATH entrance to the end of town (14th Street). Turn around and walk back down Washington Street (it's only 14 blocks to the train station) and experience what's left of a small-town American backdrop with a city feel. There are charming stores. Try Maureen Kennedy's **Hand Mad** for folk, funk, and fine art at 86 Park Avenue — (201) 653-7276.

Johnny Rockets on Washington Street is a sparkling place that resembles the original White Towers, White Diamonds, and White Castles (note: White Castles still stand all over the tri-state area), but with a difference; here the hamburgers, BLTs, and french fries are first-rate on every level. Malted milk shakes and ice-cream sodas are also top-notch. The whole atmosphere of Johnny Rockets is perfect 1950s, with original '50s rock 'n' roll and vanilla pop music that can be heard by dropping a nickel into one of the vintage tabletop jukeboxes. 1940s Coca-Cola signs decorate the white enamel and chrome-detailed walls, and bright neon is aglow throughout the place. Don't be surprised when the happy young waiters in saddle shoes and waitresses in poodle skirts burst into

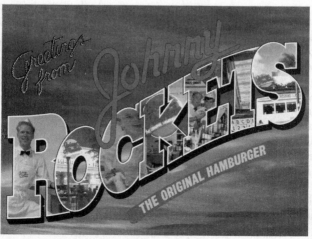

Postcard from Johnny Rockets in Hoboken.

song while dancing away as if they might be auditioning for the Dick Clark Show. Johnny Rockets opened up its first location on Melrose Avenue in Los Angeles in 1986 and it's still standing. To-day "the original hamburger" is served up at locations across the country (and the world) and there are six in New Jersey, in Free-hold, Paramus, the Short Hills Shopping Mall, Woodbridge, At-lantic City, and the aforementioned establishment in Hoboken.

There are little Cuban and Italian counters and sit-down restau-rants, chic watering holes, and even haute cuisine for the younger "in" crowds, old-fashioned ice cream parlors (try **Schnackenbergs** at 1110 Washington Street), bakeries, newspaper and magazine shops, friendly and relaxed people on the street, and a generally pleasant overall atmosphere. In the nineteenth century New York-ers rowed across the river for the spring water and picnics at Sybil's Cave, a legendary spot on the river only rediscovered in 2005.

A good place for a nightcap is the **Elysian Café** at 1001 Washing-ton Street (corner of 10th Street)—yes, another place where scenes from *On the Waterfront* were filmed. This little bar has a nautical motif and retains the full flavor of the 1930s, right down to the "ladies" backroom decorated with spectacular handcarved plaster animals cavorting all over the ceilings and walls. On week-ends there are live blues bands. The **Brass Rail** at 135 Washington Street (corner of 2nd Street) is another landmark bar, with a beau-tiful oil mural depicting Hoboken's history. The place attracts a friendly local crowd, while upstairs a moderately expensive but first-rate restaurant features bubbling onion soup, spicy garlic sausage, steak Diane, and pheasant and duck dishes. Open from Monday to Thursday for lunch and dinner until 10 P.M., Friday and Saturday until 11 P.M., Sundays till 9 P.M.—call (201) 659-7074 for reservations or visit www.thebrassrailrestaurant.com.

Nancy Sinatra's daughter and, natch, Frankie's granddaughter, Aj Azzarto, sings with a group called the New Hoboken 5, and has opened a terrific music bar–lounge with no cover or minimum. There are many drink specials at this fun Jersey hangout, which has a variety of new hot music groups, and Nancy will sometimes drop in for a visit or to do a set of her own in her dad's hometown. (Lately, Nancy performed in concert at a Hoboken street fair singing better than ever and also has had engagements at a num-ber of night spots at the Jersey Shore where her signature song, "These Boots Are Made For Walking," still grabs 'em.) On Fiesta Fridays from 5 P.M. to 10 P.M. they have free chips and salsa and half-price Margaritas. It's all happening now at **The Goldhawk Bar & Lounge** which is at 936 Park Avenue at 10th Street in Hoboken—call (201) 420-7989 for information on entertainment and "special" drink nights, or visit thegoldhawk.com.

As far as history is concerned, you can visit the **Astor Villa** at 128–133 Washington Street (near an original Lenape Indian settlement site), 107 Washington, Ms. Hetty Green's old place, or 601 Bloomfield Street (one block south of Washington) where songwriter Stephen Foster lived in 1854. At First and Washington Streets is the **Hoboken City Hall,** another registered State and National Historic Site built in red brick in 1881 and enlarged in white brick and brown stone in 1911. For stunning laser-color copies of authentic antique Hoboken ephemera, call Hoboken historian extraordinaire Jim Hans for an appointment at (201) 653-7392 or write P.O. Box M-1220, Hoboken, NJ 07030. Burly bohemian Jim and his attractive and exotic wife Beverly, and their cheerful daughter Polly always suggest offbeat walks and interesting tidbits of information, like the exact location of Francis Albert Sinatra's birthplace at 415 Monroe Street (mysteriously torn down; now it is just a brick wall concealing a vacant lot) and his boyhood-teenage home at 841 Garden Street (still standing). Try **El Cuatro Bar,** 87 Jefferson Street between Newark and 1st, for rice and beans, cerveza and salsa favoritas, or **La Isla Restaurant** for a taste of cuba at 104 Washington Street (201) 659-8197, 7 A.M. to 10 P.M. Monday thru Saturday, brunch on Sunday from 10 A.M. to 3 P.M. Tropical milk shakes are made with milk or just blended with ice, and you can bring your own wine. Dishes include ensaladas con aguacate with shrimp, red snapper, grilled salmon, beefsteak, and pork entrees.

Stop at **Carlo's City Hall Bake Shop** for homemade-style crumb cakes and a cup of coffee. A must on any Hoboken tour is a visit to **Leo's Grandevous Restaurant,** 200 Grand Street at 2nd, (201) 659-9467 for a viewing of the Frank Sinatra "hall of fame" exhibition, which includes permanent framed photos of Frank with Major Bowes (when Frank was a member of the "Hoboken Four"), Frank with Governor Thomas Kean and Ronald Reagan (at St. Ann's Annual Feast), Frank with the Hoboken police captain, Frank with the fire chief, Frank with the key to the city, and Frank's high school diploma (a copy). Leo's (since 1939), is only a few blocks from Sinatra's boyhood home and several of the employees as well as many of the patrons remember him fondly. Leo's has got everything: good bar pizzas, salads, minestrone, pasta, chicken, meat, and shrimp dishes with prices that are right. Chicken marsala is $12.50, shrimp parmigiana is $12.50, veal francese is $13.00. Pasta ranges from $6.50 (spaghetti, ziti, or shells) to $10.50 for spinach ravioli alfredo with prosciutto. Shrimp cocktails are $8.00 and antipasto, from small to giant, is $6.50 to $9.50. A regular Leo's salad is excellent for $5.50. Bar pies start at $2.50 for mozzarella, to $5 for double crust, to $6.50—for everything! There is an excellent bar where you're bound to meet someone with reminiscences of Frank Sinatra or Jimmy Roselli (another local favorite and frequent visitor) and more than likely you will be tended by the original founder's successors, Nicholas DePalma or Sergio DeNichilo. Leo's has been cited as one of "The Top 50 Bars in the United States" by *Men's Journal*—try a Berry Berry, Tequila Mockingbird, The Litertini (Absolut citron, peach schnapps, Medori, Blue Curaçao), or just a classic martini, some preferring vodka with a twist or gin with an olive. Leo's is open for lunch from 11:30 A.M. to 2 P.M. Monday through Friday; from 5 until 11 P.M. for dinner. Saturday hours are 5 P.M. to 11 P.M. and Sunday the place is open from 4 until 10 P.M.

Leo's
GRANDEVOUS
Est. 1939

200 Grand Street
Hoboken, NJ 07020
201-659-9467
leosgrandevous.com

Men's Journal's Choice as
one of the **"TOP 50 BARS
in the United States"**

Carlo's City Hall Bake Shop in Hoboken on Washington Street, just across from City Hall.

Paterson Day Trip

1. Paterson Falls
2. Lambert Castle
3. Stewart's Root Beer
4. Argyle Restaurant

One of the most outré cities in New Jersey is the industrial capitol of Paterson. Great poems have unfolded from the pens of Allen Ginsberg, who grew up there, and William Carlos Williams, who practiced there as a doctor and poet, dedicated to this old city of hills, valleys, rivers, and factories. In Williams's poem "The Wanderer" a crazed old hag who reminds him of his grandmother instructs the young man who wants to write poetry:

> Go! she said, and I hurried shivering out into the deserted streets of Paterson.

The city comes to life in a visual evocation from Williams's "The Poor" from his *Collected Poems: 1921–31*:

It's the anarchy of poverty
delights me, the old
yellow wooden house indented
among the new brick tenements . . .
Chimneys, roofs, fences of
wood and metal in an unfenced
age and enclosing next to
nothing at all . . .

How to get to Paterson: To approach the Great Falls, in the center of the city, take the Bergen-Passaic Expressway (Route 80) and exit on Main Street. From the Garden State Parkway, take exit 154, which leads into Main Street. Route 46 also crosses Main. Follow the signs to the Great Falls.

One of the splendid sites to see in Paterson are the famous **Great Falls** of the Passaic River, a natural wonder in the Watchung Mountains with a 77-foot waterfall. During the Revolutionary War, Alexander Hamilton helped to create the Society for Establishing Useful Manufactures to harness the Falls as an energy source. A system of man-made channels was built to provide power to operate cotton, silk, and other industrial mills that are now a part of a National Historic District. This is the only industrial district in the nation designated a National Historic Landmark (by President

This bronze Lou Costello statue entitled "Lou's on First" is the centerpiece of the Lou Costello Memorial Park at Ellison and Cianci Streets in Paterson. "Lou's on First" was Costello's most famous bit as a member of the Abbott and Costello comedy team. (Photo by George Bonanno.)

Gerald Ford in 1976). There are 49 mills still standing in the 119-acre historic district that produced 80 percent of America's loco-motives by 1880, and where in 1927 the Wright Aeronautical Company built the engine used in Charles Lindbergh's plane *The Spirit of St. Louis.* Renovations on the **Paterson Museum,** on the corner of Market and Spruce Streets, in the heart of Paterson's Great Falls historic district, were completed in 1990. The museum, housed in the Rogers Locomotive Erecting Shop, contains the shell of the original 14-foot submarine invented by John P. Holland in 1878, as well as his second submarine (30 feet long) built in 1881. There is also an excellent mineral display and exhibits of the silk and cotton industries of industrial Paterson. The museum is open Tuesday through Friday from 10 A.M. to 4 P.M., Saturday and Sunday from 12:30 to 4:30 P.M. Just west of Paterson is the **Garret Mountain Reservation** and **Lambert Castle,** built in 1893 of brown-and-gray stone, by silk mill baron Catholina Lambert. Garret Mountain Reservation is a 570-acre woodland park on a 502-foot-high plateau with picnic groves and fishing ponds (open all year). Lambert Castle (open Wednesday to Sunday from 1 to 4 P.M.), now a museum of the Passaic County Historical Society, is noted for its rich interiors, paintings and antique collections. Call (973) 247-0085 for further information.

There is a Great Falls Festival every Labor Day weekend, and in the past the Flying Wallendas and Philippe Petit (who once traversed a tightrope between the twin towers of the World Trade Center) have walked over the Falls on tightropes. There is a strange and mysteri-ous commingling of the past and present in the old towns of Pater-son, Clifton, Passaic, Rutherford, North Arlington, Kearny, and Harrison, all in New Jersey's notorious "industrial belt" and just a short distance from Newark. For a glimpse of New Jersey's pioneer-ing past amble down Valley Road to the **Hamilton House Museum** in Clifton at 971 Valley Road where life as it was is re-created at sev-eral annual events. Call (201) 744-5707 for more information. Drive back from the Falls along Main Avenue through Passaic to River Road. Driving south along River Road, turn left at the Belleville Turnpike, crossing the Passaic River into North Arlington, a distance of less than 10 miles from Paterson. Just over the river, at the intersection of River Road and the Belleville Turnpike, you have your choice of two of America's traditional eateries: the 24-hour **Ar-lington Diner,** (201) 998-6262, that has specials like manicotti-parmigiana, corned beef and cabbage, and Italian sausage with linguine, or the Kearny **Stewart's Root Beer Drive-In,** just across the road, which has been specializing in hot dogs and frosted mugs of Stewart's Root Beer for over forty years. Either place is a great spot for a rest. After eating, try a walk in **River Bank Park** for a closeup view of the Passaic. If you're in the mood for something a little more exotic, drive up the Belleville Turnpike to the top of the hill and turn right on Kearny Avenue. Drive south to Bergen Avenue. Here, in the immaculate middle-class town of Kearny, which was originally settled by Scottish immigrants, you can dine as they did in the old country at the wonderful **Argyle Restaurant**—212 Kearny Avenue, (201) 991-3900. Fish and chips is the main order of the day; usually codfish with (french) fries, which comes with crisp coleslaw for $8.22. This is a meal in itself, but the baked tomato at $1.35 rounds it out. Other specialties are Scottish meat pies, fried chicken, or shrimp and scallops. For those in the know (and for the adventurous), the black pudding, made with meat and spices and mixed in blood, with chips and coleslaw is the ticket. An ice cream or shortbread dessert will finish the repast. The Argyle includes a charming Scotland shop where you can take home Scottish jams, shortbreads in tins, canned goods, candies, and other specialty items. Men's Scotch plaid ties, scarves, kerchiefs, or a stuffed Scottie might make for a nice gift for a friend. Hours are Tuesday through Sunday from 11:30 A.M. to 8:30 P.M. Friday until 9 P.M.

A 1938 booklet die cut in the shape of a White Castle restaurant.

The trip to fascinating, historic Paterson Falls and to dinner at the Argyle may be made at any time of year. The mighty Falls are as beautiful in winter as they are in summer. The portions that are frozen over in wintertime become giant icicles.

The Diner Experience

Let's Have Another Cup of Coffee and Let's Have Another Piece of Pie

The roadside diner as we know it today is derived from the horse-drawn lunch wagons of the late 1880s and 1890s. In 1872 in Providence, Rhode Island, one of the first of these, Pioneer Lunch, served a ham sandwich, a boiled egg, and a piece of pie for 5¢. Setting a tradition, the Pioneer baked bread and pies on the premises, including blueberry, apple, cherry, mince, squash, huckleberry, and cranberry pies. The first walk-ins—wagons without wheels—in New Jersey were the Quick Lunch and the Stalwart, in Clifton and Plainfield, respectively. Often open all night and in dilapidated areas, they gained a reputation as rough-and-tumble rowdy houses. After the turn of the century when trolleys and electric streetcars came into play, abandoned and used cars were purchased and refurbished by enterprising restaurateurs.

Separate entrances were made for women, with signs proclaiming LADIES INVITED or LADIES WELCOME. The diner was ubiquitous—manufactured by a dozen companies, such as the Fodero Dining Car Company, On-Site, Silk City, Bixler, Comac, Manno, Mountain View, Swingle, and the big three: Patrick J. Tierney in New York, Worcester Lunch Car and Carriage Manufacturing Company of Worcester, Massachusetts, and the Jerry O'Mahoney

Joe's Diamond diner with coffee cup tower, once part of the White Clock System, Belleville Turnpike, Kearny.

The White Rose diner in Roselle serves hamburgers and eggs to customers 24 hours a day.

Company in Elizabeth, New Jersey. Today two main companies manufacture diners in New Jersey—Kullman Industries, Inc. (since 1927) in Avenel, and Paramount Modular Concepts in Oakland.

The dining car of a train was the inspiration behind the idea of parking an actual railroad car on a plot of land and turning it into a diner that served up steaks, eggs, and homemade pies. Diner design evolved rapidly from the wooden, wagonlike diners of the roaring twenties to the sleek, streamlined moderne style of the Depression Era 1930s, the 1940s, and 1950s. Everything from toasters and refrigerators to cars, radios, and locomotives were streamlined. This modernist style seemed perfect for a fast-paced, fast-food demand, and the numbers of diners increased as more and more people bought automobiles and more paved roads were built across America. These attractive food emporiums ultimately utilized stainless steel, glass blocks, mirrored ceilings, chromium fixtures, shiny tiles, neon signs and with leatherette or Naugahyde booths, recessed Lumalite, Formica countertops, and blue or peach mirror decorative detail added up to an easy-to-maintain establishment. The same industrial designers who created trains, ships, and automobiles also came up with the perfect machine-age diner, some of them called Streamliner, Pullman, Moderne, Zeppelin, or just the word "Diner" preceded by the owner's name—Joe's, Pat's, Gus's, Freddy's, or Katie's on the enameled metal front or on a huge neonized sign atop the roof. By the late 1950s some diners began to look like rocketships with extreme peaks, exaggerated overhangs, and giant tail-fin archways incorporated into an overall zigzag architectural concept. By the 1960s and 1970s they were no longer stylish, streamlined, and practical places, but instead had become plush-deluxe restaurants overly filled up with

White Diamond dinette on Route 27 in Linden.

oddball gaudy crystal or wood and metal "pirate-ship"–style chandeliers, rococco brass bins inhabited by dusty plastic plants, and featuring menus offering a bewildering selection from frozen-patty-style hamburgers, hot dogs, and eggs to fancy shrimp cocktails and lobster fra diavolo. Often a cocktail bar was added, serving up old-fashioneds, Manhattans (made with blended whiskies), or martinis.

With the awareness of a diner culture due to the super-realist paintings of John Baeder, books on diners, and diner periodicals like *Roadside*, the original concept of what a real diner is has come full circle. This does not prevent some enlightened diner owners from remodeling and refurbishing a classic goodie into an eyesore and thus turning the whole affair into an unpleasant Mediterranean hodgepodge dining experience. But take heart, a retro movement is afoot. Known for its elegant Art Deco designs of the 1930s, Kullman Industries has manufactured a new series of classic Blue Comet diners at their factory in Avenel. The aerodynamic angular and curvilinear stainless-steel diner is once again in demand, and having a successful revival. At the same time many vintage diners from the "golden age" are being sold off and trucked out of state or shipped to foreign countries (the Excellent Diner of Westfield now resides in Germany and the Shortstop Dinette of Belleville is in a shopping mall in Cleveland), where they stand as curio-centerpieces to help promote buying in the big chainstores.

Yet, amazingly, many diners are still to be discovered by the side of the road, a highway, or on back-city streets where a weary traveler can stop for a cruller, a piece of pie, waffles, pancakes, a hamburger and a milkshake, or perhaps a big meat loaf special with mashed potatoes all covered with gobs of gravy and served up with canned corn, peas, or string beans and a tall side of white, rye, or whole wheat bread. Put your money in a Seeburg box, drink a cup of coffee, and listen to Elvis, Sinatra, the Inkspots, Glenn Miller, Bruce Springsteen, Patsy Cline, or the latest top fifty. Usually the waiter-gals and high-hat cooks are friendly, tell jokes to customers, and create that necessary sense of a home away from home. Some diners continue to bake their own pies and pastries— and take pride in serving

The unfranchised White Castle System: since 1921.

wholesome, fresh, American-style dinners. New Jersey is pop-culture diner country—and these hangouts are open late, many around-the-clock. Today full-scale diners and smaller dinettes, new and old, attract interesting and sometimes wacky characters like Bible-thumping religious fanatics or leather-clad bikers, fast-lane truckers, and honky-tonk girls; and conversation is usually easy to engage. The diner has been at the heart of the American experience throughout the twentieth century. Unlike downtown single-screen movie theaters, old-fashioned ice cream parlors, or five-and-ten-cent stores (all practically gone), the diner is still a place to hang out, have a motorcycle or car meet, have fun and good eats!

DINER FOOTNOTE: If you see a lonely guy or gal nursing a cup of coffee in a diner booth while staring into space and if the record on the jukebox happens to be a nostalgia-hit like "Eddie, My Love," "Earth Angel," "Big Girls Don't Cry," or "Twilight Time," just give out a cheery "hello." That's called "diner-friendly"—and if they don't offer a "hello" back, well, we know you'll understand that it's okay to just "live and let live" and remember—it's the reality of the donut, the steaming hot cup of coffee, the piece of lemon meringue pie, and the toasted BLT with mayo that really matters in Dinerland. Hungry, anyone? Order up. Chase away those blues—in a New Jersey diner.

Diner Day Trip

....

"Lost" Diner Tour: The Dime-Store Kids in New Jersey

1. Journal Square
2. White Mana
3. Miss America
4. Athens Diner
5. Max's Grill
6. K & K Spanish American Restaurant
7. Stewart's Root Beer
8. The Short Stop
9. Harris Diner

Get in your car, van, or on your motorbike and join the "Dime-Store Kids" (the authors) for a diner tour in New Jersey's beautiful industrial belt. We guarantee a gastric, pop-architectural, and fun-filled adventure to those who are open to the idea of just plain folks and the enjoyment of a cheap hearty meal. We start off at **Journal Square** in Jersey City, New Jersey's second largest city.

This original circular White Mana has been on Highway 1-9 in Jersey City since 1946. The owner is Mario Costa Jr., who worked in the diner during high school and college, saved his money, and bought it from the original owner, who himself had bought it as a prefab at the New York World's Fair in 1939.

The sights to see here include the enormous **Stanley Theater** and the **Loews of Jersey City,** both built in 1928. The Stanley has been restored as a temple by the Jehovah's Witnesses and is an "atmospheric" theater in the Spanish/Alhambra–Valentino Hollywood style. The interior has elaborate stained-glass sconces, Moorish chandeliers, marble columns, and a "moving cloud" ceiling. Next to Radio City, the Stanley, with 4,500 seats, was one of the largest of the great movie palaces. Less ornate, the Loews was designed by Rapp and Rapp and featured a "Morton Wonder" theater organ. The Morton organ is gone now, slated for replacement in ongoing plans for restoration of the 3,200-seat theater at 54 Journal Square; call (201) 798-6055 for movie schedules.

Drive north up Kennedy Boulevard to Leonard Gordon Park— featuring a turn-of-the-century bandshell, two huge stone buffaloes and a bear, with a breathtaking view of the western slopes of the Palisades and the Meadowlands. Turn left by the Park on Manhattan Avenue and coast down the hill to the **White Mana,** 470 Tonnelle Avenue (Route 1-9), owned by Mario Costa Jr., a New Jersey and New York fight manager. Mario worked in the diner during high school and college and bought it from the original owner, who bought it at the 1939 New York World's Fair, where it was on display with another identical prefab fast-food eatery that wound up on Route 1-9 in Elizabeth. Several years ago this latter one disappeared one night and no one has ever seen it since.

Go down Tonnelle (Highway 1-9 South) through the Tonnelle Traffic Circle. Continue on Tonnelle to Sip—make a right on Sip and zip down to West Side Avenue. Turn left on West Side and drive on down to the **Miss America Diner.** This beautiful streamlined diner, 322 West Side Avenue, (201) 333-5468, (see color photo) was built in 1939 and has been in its present location since 1944. Their motto: "The old-fashioned diner with the home-style cooking." Backtrack a few blocks north and turn left on Communipaw Avenue, which takes you past Lincoln Park and onto the old Lincoln Highway (1-9 South). Half a mile past the Hackensack River Bridge, exit at Central Avenue East, Kearny. Turn right at the Fish House Road intersection, following Fish House to the Route 7 West Belleville exit ramp on the right. On Route 7 West, bear left following signs for Harrison. This will become Harrison Avenue. The sights along the way include the PSE&G Generat-

Vanishing diners—this one, a relic of the 1939–1940 New York World's Fair, disappeared mysteriously a few years ago from its location near the East Jersey State Prison.

Interior of the vanished 1939 diner, Route 1-9. Behind the soda dispenser is Claude Bowman (with apron), who now works at the White Rose Diner in Roselle.

ing Plant, a view of the magnificent Pulaski Skyway (1928)—at three miles, the longest viaduct in the world—the moderne-style Coca-Cola bottling plant, and the bulk-mail facility of the U.S. Post Office. The **Athens Diner,** 1002 Harrison Avenue, Kearny, was manufactured by Fodero Dining Car Company in New Jersey. The **K & K Spanish-American Restaurant,** 424 Harrison Avenue, Harrison, used to be called the China Town and before that it was a classic diner. Check it out—this could be exotic diner food at its best. Harrison's shining light is **Max's Grill** at 731 Harrison Avenue, (201) 483-2012, built in 1927 by the O'Mahony Diner Company. Often painted by renowned diner artist John Baeder, Max's Grill,

With its original 1927 railroad wheels still in place, Max's Grill has a maroon-and-deep-cream baked enamel exterior with wood trim.

though not a registered historic landmark, is a diner not be be missed by connoisseurs. Barrel-roofed and with a maroon-and-cream porcelain-enamel exterior and with deco-style lettering that says LADIES INVITED and MAX'S GRILL, the diner now serves Spanish-Portuguese food. Get a Portuguese shell steak dinner or eggs, potatoes, and toast. Max's closes every day from 2 to 4 A.M. but is open at all other times. To get to Max's in a hurry, take exit 15W off the New Jersey Turnpike into downtown Harrison. The PATH train makes a stop here also for diner aficionados on foot.

Leaving Max's continue over Harrison Avenue to Passaic Avenue in East Newark. Turn right and drive north on River Road alongside River Bank Park and turn left onto the Belleville Turnpike. This intersection offers **Stewart's Root Beer** on one side of the road and the **Arlington Diner** on the other. Cross the Passaic River into Belleville up to Washington Avenue. Take a left to Sylvan, which meanders west between Belleville Park and Newark's Branch Brook Park. Drive to Franklin Avenue and turn left. Go to Franklin Street and turn right. Continue out to the Dunkin' Donuts, which was once the **Short Stop Diner,** 315 Franklin Street, Bloomfield. This 18-seat Kullman-Manno-built diner building (1955) is the last of five. There was one in Plainfield, two in Newark, and one in Belleville (now in Cleveland). Dunkin' Donuts bought the property and overlaid their orange vestments on top of the original place. You can still see the colored aluminum details, only now there is nothing to eat but donuts. The stream next to the parking lot is a good place to stop, rest, and contemplate the architecture.

Jerry Seinfeld having a hamburger inside the Hackensack White Manna with a book poster of O' New Jersey *in the background.*

Turn left onto Glenwood Avenue and drive alongside Watsessing Park to Park Avenue. At Park turn right and right again on Washington Street. At the "point" of Washington and North Park, just a few blocks from Main Street, East Orange, is the **Harris Diner,** 21 North Park, (201) 675-9703, built in 1952 by the O'Mahoney Dining Car Company and owned since 1958 by Bill Nicholas and Bill Marmaras. This is a large stainless-steel-and-chrome diner that rates the very highest for original decor and food. It is well-lit with indirect recessed lighting, has a mirrored ceiling, and individual jukeboxes at each Formica-topped table, offering the Mills Brothers and Tommy Dorsey alongside Frank Sinatra and Bruce Springsteen. Connie Francis singing "Who's Sorry Now," alas, is nowhere to be found. The Formica, chrome, steel-and-tile interior of this diner is perfect and is kept immaculate. The Harris Diner waitresses are themselves out of another era, and the food is mighty fine indeed. Try the famous Black Angus Steak Sandwich or a special Harris Diner Dagwood "Sputnik," which—it is promised—"is out of this world." There are many egg specialties for late-night or early breakfast, as well as triple-decker sandwiches, fried seafood, Reubens, and homemade, thick Belgian waffles served with Log Cabin syrup or La Salle ice cream. The Harris Diner, with its friendly atmosphere, is open 24 hours every day. End of tour.

◆

More Jersey Diners

The above tour represents just one possible trip to some of the state's finer diners. Feel free to make your own way, though; the following are some more diner destinations you might consider. The **White Manna** in Hackensack, 358 River Street, (201) 342-0914, is a good example of the 1930s streamlining concept in early eatery chains. This building could almost qualify for the Smith-

HALF CHICKEN in the BASKET	CHUCK WAGON STEAK	BROILED LOBSTER TAIL	"SPUTNIK"
With French Fries and Cole Slaw	Tomato Sauce French Fries and Cole Slaw	Drawn Butter	IT'S OUT OF THIS WORLD! Open Faced Sandwich with Cheese, Bacon and Tomato, Served on Toasted English Muffin with Cole Slaw
4.75	3.30	9.95	3.00

Harris DINER

THE DINER WITH THE *friendly* ATMOSPHERE

HARRIS DINER

Open 24 hours a day

Orders to take out call ORANGE 5-9703

21 n. park & washington streets

EAST ORANGE N.J.

TROPICAL HEALTH PLATTER	OUR FAMOUS "BLACK ANGUS" STEAK SANDWICH	HARRIS DINER DAGWOOD
Creamy Cottage Cheese with a Variety of Cut Fruit and Jello, Served on Crisp Lettuce	Lettuce, Tomatoes and Golden Browned French Fried Potatoes, Mushroom Sauce	A Triple-Decker of Choice Hamburger Topped with Cheese, Lettuce, Tomato, Sliced Pickle and Onion
3.40	Served Only 4.75 As Shown	Served in a Bowl 3.05 with French Fries

Menu from the Harris Diner, showing the streamlined stainless-steel-and-chromium exterior. The Harris serves good food at 21 North Park and Washington Streets in East Orange.

sonian Institute, with its glass blocks and chromed metal front. The **Melrose Diner,** previously located in East Windsor (about 12 miles east of Trenton), is the one that ended up in the National Archives in Washington, D.C. The Hackensack White Manna was also a futuristic architectural feature at the 1939–1940 New York World's Fair. Later it was purchased and transported to its present site, where brothers Ofer and Ronnie Cohen serve up hamburgers smothered in onions, and delicious ice cream shakes. Open Monday through Saturday 8 A.M. to 9:30 P.M., Sunday 10 A.M. to 6 P.M.

The **Summit Diner,** (908) 277-3256, is on Summit Avenue at One Union Place, across the road from the New Jersey Transit Morristown Branch Summit Railroad Station. Legend has it that Ernest Hemingway used to stop off here. This is another spot where the food is cheap and the dinner portions big. Try the Summit Diner meat

This White Manna Hamburger Dinette was originally at the New York World's Fair of 1939–1940 before being moved to Hackensack.

loaf. A heavy, hearty meal! This 1929 Depression-era diner is still 80 percent original and it is an Edward Hopper painting come to life. The place may be an anachronism but it is a gem to be treasured by all. They're open every day from 5:30 A.M. to 8 P.M.; Sundays until 1 P.M.

In addition to the **White Castles,** which are everywhere, the **White Mana** in Jersey City, and the **White Manna** in Hackensack, many early chain eateries still survive in New Jersey, offering up atmosphere and good eats, including the **White Rose System** in Roselle (ask for Claude), Linden, and Highland Park, the **White Circle System** in Bloomfield, the **White Star Diners** in Plainfield and Elizabeth, the **White Diamonds** in Linden and Clark, and the **Blue Diamond** in Pomona. Other old-fashioned treats are the orange-painted **Stewart's Root Beer Drive-in** restaurants, some of which feature carhops and cartray attachments. Usually they are freshly enameled orange and lit with yellow bug lights. The service is friendly and courteous—and the ice-cold mug of root beet and a Stewart's hot dog is good stuff.

There are over 600 diners in New Jersey, more than in any other state. A careful selection of some of the good ones includes the following: **Newark Avenue Diner** and **Tunnel Diner** in Jersey City, the **Liberty** in North Brunswick, the **Americana** in East Windsor, the **Truck Stop Diner** in Kearny, the **Avenel** and **Premium Diners** on Route 1-9 in Avenel, the **Egg Platter Diner** in Paterson, **Chappy's** in Paterson, the **Bendix Diner** on Highway 17 and Williams Street in Hasbrouck Heights, **Tops** in Bayonne, **Kless's Diner** in Irvington, **Betsy Ross** in Elizabeth, the **Mark Twain** and **Huck Finn diners** in Union, the **Tom Sawyer** in Ridgewood, the **Dumont Crystal,** the **Teamsters** in Fairfield, the **Freehold Grille,** and **Tick Tock Diner** on Route 3 in Clifton (built in the "classic" style in 1994 by Kullman), the **Lido Diner** in the center of Route 22 in Springfield, the **State Diner** in West Orange, **Greek Delights** (formerly the **Park Diner**) in Montclair, the **Franklin, Boonton, Bound Brook,** and **Washington Diners,** the **Colonial** and **the Schyler Diner and Cafe** in Lyndhurst, the **Crossroads** in Bridgeville, **Toms** in Ledgewood, **Linda's** in Sussex, **Sue and Bernie's Diner** in Belvedere, **Key City Diner** on Route 22W, Phillipsburg, and the **Five Star,** Route 206, and the **New Royal,** 3331 Route 22E, both in Branchville.

Down the shore, in the Pine Barrens, and in southwest New Jersey's vast farm belt, diners are a mainstay. Some of these include the **Peterpank Diner** in Sayreville (see p. 155), the **White Crystal Diner** in Atlantic Highlands, the **Roadside Diner** in Wall Township (see p. 175), **Captain John's Mr. Breakfast** in Surf City and **Moustache Bill's Diner** at Barnegat Light, both on Long Beach Island, the **Olympic Diner** in Pleasantville, the **Point in Somers Point,** the **Wildwood** and **Big Ernie's** in Wildwood, the **Shore** in Rio Grande, **54 Diner** in Buena, **Angie's Bridgeton Grille, Salem Oak Diner** in Salem, **Mastoris Diner** in Bordentown, **Hammonton Diner** in Hammonton, **Time Out** in Tuckahoe, the **Liberty** in Clayton, **Angelo's Diner** in Glassboro, the **Elgin Diner** in Camden, the **Club Diner** in Bellmawr, and the **Mount Laurel Diner** in Mount Laurel.

If you don't find one of these diners at the location listed, drive on to the next one. Diners sometimes disappear mysteriously, right off the face of a map. For more about diners and a New Jersey diner locator map call the **American Diner Museum** at (401) 723-4342; their address is PO Box 6022, Providence, Rhode Island, 02940; their website is www.americandinermuseum.org. Also go to johnbaeder.com for a display of this famed artist's brilliant diner paintings.

Tunnel Diner in Jersey City outside the Holland Tunnel. Open 24 hours a day, the vintage diner displays a great neon sign, and has a pink, blue, and chromium 1950s style interior.

Newark Day Trip

Cherry Blossom Time in Newark

1. Penn Station
2. Newark Museum
3. Newark Cathedral
4. Portuguese Restaurants
5. New Jersey Performing Arts Center

Penn Station in downtown Newark is a good starting point for this city day trip. It is "the end of the line" of the PATH commuter train from New York, Hoboken, and Jersey City. If you come by car over the Pulaski Skyway into Newark or from south or north on Highway 1-9, all roads lead into downtown Newark and Penn Station. Buses from all locations also head in and out of this station to suburban cities and towns. You can park the car in one of the many lots near the station.

The monumental station itself is an Art Deco masterpiece. Completed in 1933, it was designed by Stanford White and features faces of lions and statues of spread-winged eagles on its limestone facade, while the interior, completely restored by New Jersey Transit, who bought it from Amtrak in 1984, has beautiful bronze ceiling fixtures with astrological signs of the zodiac, glass deco globes, and transportation-theme wall medallions. Outside the station, bordered by Market Street, the McCarter Highway, and Raymond

A terrazzo mural in the lobby of the Bell Telephone Company building in downtown Newark.

Boulevard, walk (or drive) up Market Street past the old **Newark Paramount Theater** to Broad Street, Newark's famous crossroads. Continue on Market Street to the old **L. Bamberger's Department Store** (closed in 1992); throughout downtown Newark original 1920s and 1930s storefronts still exist, their facades clad in vitreous glass or sheets of terra cotta. Newark is the home of the **Prudential Insurance Company** and it maintains several office buildings downtown. On the 13th floor of the **Gibraltar Building** at 153 Halsey Street, near the bank, is the **Prudential Museum,** filled with company memorabilia and early Newarkiana. A main attraction is the Tiffany stained-glass window of the Rock of Gibraltar (the Prudential's trademark symbol) that was originally created by Maitland Armstrong for the Panama Pacific International Exposition held in San Francisco in 1915. While strolling in the downtown Newark areas, take note of the fine old and new

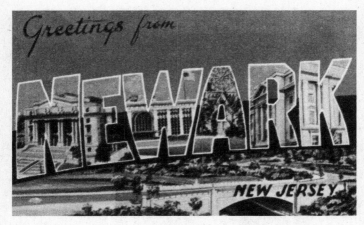

Greetings from Newark—linen postcard made for the Star Stationary Company of Newark by Tichnor Bros., Inc., circa 1930s.

architectural attractions. A spectacular monument to culture (completed in October, 1997), representing a gigantic leap in faith in the city's future is the **New Jersey Performing Arts Center,** adjacent to Military Park. Providing a permanent home for the New Jersey Symphony Orchestra, it also features artists like Isaac Stern, Wynton Marsalis, and famed dance troups like the American Ballet Theater and the Alvin Ailey American Dance Theater, as well as providing creative arts workshops for children and community groups. Leaving the Arts Complex walk past Military Park to the **Bell Telephone Company,** at 540 Broad Street at Lombardy. This magnificent Art Deco building, designed by the architectural firm of Voorhees, Gmelin and Walker is one of the best examples of an early Art Deco skyscraper to be found on the East Coast, and is definitely worth a visit. The lobby, with its elaborate and ornate bronze-work grills in deco-floral patterns, tall bronze Egyptian-style torchère lamps and an artful communication-theme terrazzo mural is exhilarating and awe-inspiring. The cast cement relief sculptures, with operators talking on the telephone and callers listening in, on the building's facade, must be the ultimate in camp Deco-Moderne.

Just across the street from Bell Telephone, through Washington Park, is the **Newark Museum** at 43–49 Washington Street, (973) 596-6550, open throughout the year. Architect Michael Graves has integrated four existing museum buildings, as well as a five-story building acquired from Newark, into one great cultural complex, and the building is a masterpiece. The museum's African and Asian holdings (and one of the most extensive Tibetan collections in the Western Hemisphere; there is a complete Buddhist altar as well as paintings, musical instruments, and intricately woven Tibetan costumes) are well known; less known and a must to visit is the Renaissance Revival **Ballantine House,** restored to complete Victorian perfection in the spacious grounds behind the museum's main building. The Ballantine House, built by John Ballantine, the son of the founder of the renowned Newark brewery, built the house in 1885. Now designated a National Historic Landmark, each room offers a glimpse into Victorian excess; the stained-glass window in the library, based on Mr. Ballantine's design, depicts the family name, derived from the Scottish words *bael*, or fire, and *antin*, a worshipper. The window shows a maiden worshipping the sun as incense rises skyward.

Branch Brook Park in Newark is accessible from East Bloomfield Avenue, spur Route 506; from Park Avenue, Route 16. Not to be missed in the spring (usually early April) are the pink, white, and mauve cherry blossoms opening forth in full splendor. There are 2,700 cherry trees in this 2-mile by a quarter-mile-wide section of the park designed by the famous Frederick Law Olmstead. The magical, sweet-smelling cherry blossom display is larger than Washington, D.C.'s. In the winter there is an ice center for ice skating and ski slopes for sledding. Bicycling is permitted, and there is a boating lake.

Following a visit to Branch Brook Park, the hungry traveler in search of excellent cuisine should go back to Penn Station. The **Ironbound District,** so named because it is surrounded by the rattle of the trains that enter Newark, is within walking distance of the station and is the center of Newark's large Portuguese population. Go out the Raymond Plaza East exit from Penn Station, cross the street, walk right one block to Ferry Street and make a left, walking two more blocks past Edison Street and McWhorter Street. Populated by over 35,000 Portuguese immigrants, this mile-square area, surrounded by the factories and manufacturing sections of Newark, is a lively place by day or night and the restaurants, dozens of them, serving piping hot paella, stewed rabbit, and dried salt-cod specialties, are open late. Most of the establishments serve either a marinara (with shellfish) paella or a Valenciana (with sausage) paella, *gambas al ajillo* (shrimp tumbled in an oil–and–red-pepper mixture with diced garlic), sweet sangria and *papo seco* (cornmeal-enriched loaves and rolls). Other dishes include chicken in garlic, clams in green sauce, *mariscada* (the Spanish version of bouillabaisse), which is a stewpot full of lobster, shrimp, clams, mussels, and scallops with a tangy garlic sauce, and garlicky pork chops served with potatoes and rice. Some of the better restaurants include **Fornos of Spain,** 47 Ferry Street, (973) 589-4767; **Sagres Restaurant,** 71 Ferry Street; **Iberia Tavern and Restaurant,** 82–84 Ferry Street, (973) 344-7603; and slightly-off-the-beaten-path **Tony Da Caneca's** at 72 Elm Road,

(973) 589-6882, and **Poeta Bar and Restaurant,** 97–99 Lang Street. Particularly authentic and charming, Poeta is named to honor Portuguese poet Luis de Camoes. The prices and portions at all of these restaurants are unbelievably reasonable by any standards.

．．．

Newark is one of the oldest cities in America, and in 2006 it celebrates its 340th year. In 1666 Captain Robert Treat, on a foray from Milford, Connecticut, with a band of New England pilgrims, landed on the shores of the Passaic River at the site of what is now Newark. He had to buy the land from the Indians, paying over 850 fathoms of wampum in addition to axes, coats, guns, pistols, kettles, swords, blankets, beer, breeches, and 20 gallons of liquor. Eleven years later, with an additional payment of 2 guns, 3 coats, and "13 kans of rum," the English settlers acquired deed to land stretching to the top of the Orange Mountain. Quite a real estate bargain! Celebrated persons who lived in or are from Newark include writers Philip Roth, Stephen Crane, Amiri Baraka (formerly LeRoi Jones), Washington Irving, Zane Grey, Allen Ginsberg (born in Newark, raised in Paterson), Nick Tosches, and Dore Schary. Entertainers Whitney Houston, Joe Pesci, Frankie Valli, Eva Marie Saint, Vivian Blaine, Sarah Vaughan, Melba Moore, the Ritz Brothers, and Connie Francis are also from Newark. Whitney Houston is active in the revitalization of this great city, investing in new real estate development. Former New York Mayor Ed Koch is from Newark, as was composer Jerome Kern.

Newark's greatest monument is the **Cathedral of the Sacred Heart,** a spectacular French Gothic cathedral, the fifth largest in the nation. The flagship of the Roman Catholic Archdiocese of Newark, at the corner of Clifton and Victoria Avenues, it is noted for its 9,500-pipe organ, its massive gargoyles, and the largest rose window in the Western Hemisphere. Architectural tours are given on the first Sunday each month after noon Mass; at other times you can tour the cathedral yourself. The entrance is at 89 Ridge Street; call (973) 484-4600 for further information.

Another Newark landmark, Newark's 2,800-seat **Symphony Hall** at 1020 Broad Street, hosts year-round programs of plays, concerts, and other performances. Built in 1925 as a Shriner Temple, its sculptured limestone facade is a sight to behold. Call (973) 643-8009 for tickets or go to www.newarksymphonyhall.org to be put on their mailing list. Another fascinating section to visit in Newark, and one that will give you renewed faith in the city's future, is **St. Joseph's Plaza**—a complex that includes a medical clinic, a sandwich shop, a spa, and a restaurant, all housed in the historic 19th century priory at St. Joseph's church. The **Priory Restaurant** features made-to-order waffles, hot-and-cold selections, and other treats—brunch is Monday to Friday from 11:30 A.M. to 3:00 P.M.;

Three New Jersey hometown gals also happen to be international recording stars. Top: The Divine Miss Sarah Vaughan, now buried in a cemetery in Belleville, New Jersey, near her beloved Newark. Middle: Whitney Houston, a major force in the development of new housing in the City of Newark. Bottom: Glamorous Dionne Warwick, native of East Orange, now resides in a posh Newark suburb.

Two more Jersey Girls of note. Top: Queen Latifah, whose real name is Dana Owens, was born in 1970, and grew up in East Orange where she worked at a Burger King. Her 1988 debut single in the jazz-soul tradition was "Wrath of My Madness," and she chose for herself the name "Latifah," which in Arabic means "delicate and sensitive." As a movie star, she scored the role of a prison matron in the Academy Award–winning film musical Chicago. (Photo by Randee St. Nicholas.) Bottom: Martha Stewart was born Martha Helen Kostyra into a Polish family who lived in Jersey City. When Martha was three years old, her family of seven moved to Nutley, New Jersey, the same town that gun totin' Annie Oakley had lived in. Although she's moved to a farmhouse in Connecticut, Martha remains a down-home Jersey Girl at heart, and she still keeps in contact with her old chums and attends high school reunions in her hometown of Nutley.

Newark city subway system, WPA tile mural showing men at work, 1935.

This extraordinary "Turkey-Deco" terra-cotta panel was on an industrial building at Washington and Linden Streets in downtown Newark.

The Nave in the Cathedral of the Sacred Heart, Newark.

dinner is Wednesday to Saturday 5 P.M. to 10 P.M.; champagne brunch is 10 A.M. to 5 P.M. The Priory Restaurant is just a part of the "New Community," a development corporation founded by Monsignor William J. Linder (a MacArthur Foundation Award winner), which provides guidance to inner-city residents for housing and jobs, financing for fast-food franchises, a day-care center, and other services. Father Linder was also instrumental in bringing a Pathmark supermarket into Newark. St. Joseph's Plaza is in the University Heights district of Newark at 233 W. Market Street, (973) 242-8012.

According to lifelong resident and historian Michael Immerso, by 1910 Newark's First Ward (a half-mile square between Sixth Avenue and Nassau) was home to the fifth largest Italian population in the country. Immerso claims a 1910 Italian business directory lists 63 grocery stores, 4 macaroni manufacturers, 17 bakeries, 23 shoemakers, 40 barbers, and 88 saloons in the old First Ward. In the 1950s the First Ward's "Little Italy" attracted celebrities like Abbott and Costello and Jayne Mansfield and performers Billie

Holiday, Gypsy Rose Lee, and Jackie Gleason, who performed in Newark's large downtown theaters. After the riots of the 1960s what was left of that teeming population finally fled to the North Ward, out Bloomfield Avenue. Pizza and other Italian restaurants on either side of Bloomfield Avenue are all bound to be authentic, as this vicinity, though it is more spread out than New York City's Italian restaurant section, is now known as Newark's new "Little Italy."

Dickie-Dee Pizza, 380 Bloomfield Avenue, (973) 483-9396, is a favorite of Joe Pesci, who comes in often for a pie with friend Robert De Niro, who likes to hang out on Bloomfield Avenue. The pizza here has been rated number one by many culinary periodicals, and it does not disappoint. Dickie-Dee features one size of pie, which is $7.00. Extras like sausage or pepperoni are $1.25; a slices is also $1.25. Recommended is the Special (everything on it) at $10.55. Pizzas fall into the categories of regular, Sicilian, or deep dish, and there are "gourmet" pizzas like spinach and ricotta that are very tasty indeed. Connoisseurs of "the best" pizza arrive from everywhere to have a pizza or a Dickie-Dee antipasto, which includes rolled ham, black olives, and anchovies.

The Belmont Tavern and Restaurant, 12 Bloomfield Avenue, (973) 759-9609, *is actually in* Belleville on the border between Newark and Bloomfield. It is presided over by attractive Helen Churchill, who runs a tight ship. Everything is cooked from scratch, so you must be patient. This is fine Italian food in a small family-style setting. "Stretch's Chicken Savoy" is a specialty cooked in wine and olive oil and Helen's secret spices. Two can enjoy a meal with salad and wine here for about $25. The spaghetti and ziti dishes are also first rate. The tangy sauces are home cooked and fresh whether made with ground meat, cheese, or sausage. This is a bustling, fun place to go. You will not have trouble parking your car on a side street here, and like New York's Little Italy, the streets are safe. There is a middle class feeling to the Belmont, and a homey atmosphere. It's a dinner-only place; hours are Monday, Wednesday, and Thursday from 5 until 10 P.M.. Friday and Saturday they are open until 11 P.M., Sunday until 9:30 P.M. Closed Tuesday.

Driving up Bloomfield Avenue through Newark's North Ward Italian district, which is immaculately maintained, you will arrive in Bloomfield. A notable stop-off is an old-fashioned–style ice cream parlor called **Holsten's Brookdale Confectionery** that serves its own homemade ice cream and sells quality homemade chocolate candy, all made on the premises. Holsten's is run by Ron Stark and Chris Carley and specializes in French ice cream cakes and ice cream logs for parties and events, to order. A luncheon-style menu serves a variety of relatively inexpensive American sandwiches, in-

Ron Stark, behind the candy counter, is co-owner with Chris Carley of Holsten's Brookdale Confectionery and Old Fashioned Ice-Cream Parlor, which has been in business in Bloomfield for over 50 years.

cluding peanut butter and jelly, which is $2.25. Grilled cheese and tuna is $4.70, double-decker clubs are $4.95 to $6.25; and naturally, there is a terrific selection of ice cream sodas—French-style with real whipped cream, $3.75, special sundaes (some with four scoops of ice cream), $5.75, selected from 15 flavors, and malted milk shakes, $4.50. In summer try a fresh-fruit orange or lemon fizz at $4.75. **Holsten's,** which also offers eggs and omelettes and delicious coffee, is at 1063 Broad Street at the corner of Watchung Avenue, (973) 338-7091. Store hours are 11 A.M. until 11:30 P.M. and Sundays till 10 P.M. The service and old ice-cream-parlor decor make this a friendly stop, and well worth a trip in itself. Just across the road is beautiful **Brookdale Park,** where you can enjoy your ice cream cones either on the grass or on a park bench.

If, after too much good ice cream, you need a walk, there is the lovely **Town Green Historic District** that has 229 Queen Anne, Federal, Greek revival, and Italianate Victorian buildings surrounding it. This is New Jersey's largest "town green" and a self-tour guide pamphlet is available from the **Historical Society of Bloomfield,** 90 Broad Street, Bloomfield 07003. The Historical Society itself is open September through June (Wednesdays from 2 to 4:30 P.M.; Saturdays 11 A.M. to 3 P.M. or by appointment in summer).

Garden State Parkway, exit 148, at Bloomfield Avenue. Up the hill along Bloomfield Avenue, just before coming to Montclair and as you leave the town of Bloomfield, is Glen Ridge. There are many fine old New Jersey homes to view in this gaslit town; and if you turn left or right off Bloomfield Avenue, the main thoroughfare, you will drive down wonderful tree-lined streets that will immediately give you a feeling of serenity and well-being. One of the great houses here belonged to singer Connie Francis—the "Empress of New Jersey."

The city of Montclair is set on a high ridge of the Watchung Mountains, overlooking the New Jersey and Manhattan mega-

Miss Connie Francis, the "Who's Sorry Now?" girl of Bloomfield, who was often referred to as "The Empress of New Jersey," courtesy of MGM.

lopolis. West Bloomfield wanted a rail link to New York City and Bloomfield did not so in 1868 the two towns separated, the former renaming itself Montclair. Once you're in town you should park on a side street or in the many metered public parking lots. It is fun to walk up the hill in Montclair, beginning at the old, restored Erie-Lackawanna railroad station designed by William Hull, an architect who perished at the age of 26 on the *Titanic*. Montclair, of course, is accessible by train: Take the Montclair Branch of NJ Transit from Hoboken to Bay Street Station. Bay Street is a block away from the old train station, which is now part of a minimall shopping complex; its great waiting room a fast-food eatery. Several very fine antique stores abound in this elegant old town as well as some interesting bookstores and boutiques. Much has happened in the happening town of Montclair ("Bright Mountain" in French) in recent years. The 1950s **Hahne's Department Store** has been torn down. A new **Rascals** nightspot has opened; the Park Street Diner has become the wonderful **Greek Delights** (14 Park Street, (973) 783-9100); and new entertainment venues range from the soprano (not *The Sopranos*) performances of Karen Lundry at the **Luna Stage Cabaret** (695 Bloomfield Avenue) to the bluesy jazz singing of chanteuse Jan Loe at **Trumpets** near the Grove Street train station. The guitarist-vocalist and harmonica player Enrico Granafei headlines and the address is 6 Depot Square. Call (973) 744-2600 or log on to www.trumpets jazz.com. To hear the latest from the Jersey punk/metal scene pop into **The Bloomfield Avenue Cafe** at 347 Bloomfield Avenue. Call (973) 783-2100. There is also a fun time for adults and kids to be had at the **Soda Pop Shop** (558 Bloomfield Avenue) with retro décor and memorabilia; they feature scrumptious Hershey's Ice Cream in their Super Soupy Sundae (created by Soupy Sales) and good burgers like the Herman Muenster or Huntley Brinkley burger. Pop parfaits are called Elvis Presley, Gilligans Island, the Green Hornet, and Hawaii Five-O, and you might also want to try the Egghead Salad Sandwich which is egg-cellent! They're not yolking.

The menu changes daily and no reservations are needed at the casually elegant Art Deco **Raymond's,** 28 Church Street, (973) 744-9263, open 6 to 10 P.M., Tuesday to Saturday, 5 to 9 P.M. on Sunday. BYOB. For fantastic one-of-a-kind New Jersey photos by Andy Foster cross the street to his **Gallery 51** at 51 Church Street. Call (973) 744-4484 or 632-8000 for special exhibitions, and look at his web at www.gallery51.org.

Antique and book shops are most likely to be open from Tuesday to Saturday with closings at 4 or 5 P.M. Start at the **Montclair Antique Center** at 34 Church Street, (973) 746-1062. Try **Stations West Antiques** on Glen Ridge Avenue (just off Bloomfield in town center), (973) 744-9379, which is chock full of whatnots, pop-culture artifacts, oddities, and bona fide antiques. A charming

The Montclair railroad station at Bloomfield Avenue, which has been turned into a minimall (top). The famous Hinck Building (above) shopping and office complex, which also houses the Claridge movie theater, and is still functioning to this day. This is 1931, but Montclair continues to be a gracious town that values its past.

lady, Shirley Shaller, operates this co-op shop. Down the hill a few steps is the **Montclair Book Center** at 221 Glen Ridge Avenue, (973) 783-3630, which carries a large selection of books, paperbacks, magazines, and comics. The best New York antique dealers look upon Montclair as a good town to buy in, since many of the shops purchase their goods right out of nearby mansions that periodically have garage sales or estate auctions. Several shops carry crystal, silver, 18th- and 19th-century furniture, oak pieces, wicker sets, rugs, lamps, and other household furnishings, as well as paintings and prints. A Church Street shop called **Beans,** run by Stefan Peters since 1974 (he arrived in Montclair as an actor with the Whole Theater Company, founded by a Montclair celebrity, actress Olympia Dukakis) sells freshly ground coffee, tea, condiments, jellies, honey, and other culinary gift items; (973) 783-7175. A local Salvation Army band often plays on the streets of town, lending an old-time musical biblical air to the gracious surroundings. The 1930s **Trinity Apartment** buildings, one block off Church, with their bevelled-crystal glass doors, add to the town center's charm. The entire top of the hill shopping area, with its

Mega-superstar sex symbol Tom Cruise, a New Jersey native, grew up in Glen Ridge.

brick sidewalks, is centered around the terra-cotta-clad **Hinck Building** and has an aristocratic feeling about it that bespeaks a slower, easy pace for shoppers or casual strollers. If a movie is in order on your Montclair sojourn, try the **Claridge** in the Hinck Building, which now houses three theaters as well as several shops.

Stefan Peters in his gourmet coffee store, Beans, at 42 Church Street in Montclair.

A note of historical interest: The Montclair Historical Society maintains a historic house-museum at the **Israel Crane House** at 110 Orange Road, (978) 783-1717. This 1796 Federal-style mansion depicts the life of the wealthy in Colonial times. The Montclair Junior League offers tours and a cooking demonstration featuring the use of old utensils, utilizing a fireplace oven and an old reflector rotisserie. There is a country store on the premises. Israel Crane House is open Sundays only from 2 to 5 P.M. It is closed during July and August because no air-conditioning is used. The **Montclair Art Museum,** South Mountain and Bloomfield Avenues, (973) 746-5555, has a good permanent collection of 20th-century prints and art, as well as many excellent changing exhibitions. Open Tuesday–Sunday 11 A.M. to 5 P.M.; Free Fridays between 11 A.M. and 1 P.M.

A beautiful drive in Upper Montclair is along Mountain Avenue. Turn right off Bloomfield Avenue if you are driving downhill, left if you are going up, onto Mountain Avenue. Along this drive you will see the huge mansions with their manicured lawns and landscaped grounds that are the grand homes of many New York and New Jersey corporate executives and millionaires. Eventually you will find yourself in the tiny Upper Montclair hamlet where there is a charming old wooden railroad station, a movie theater called the **Bellevue,** a popular "good time Charlie" restaurant and pub, and a handful of interesting shops. Just down the hill is **Applegate Farm** at 616 Grove Street, (973) 744-5900, where you can park and line up at a stand for delicious homemade ice cream served in cones, elaborate cup sundaes, and malted drinks and shakes. Applegate was established in Upper Montclair as a dairy farm in 1848. They began selling homemade ice cream at their roadside stand in 1930. The current owner, Jason Street, says it has always operated at this location only. "Accept no substitutes," he adds. Hours in spring, summer, and fall are 9 A.M. to 11 P.M., and in winter from 9 A.M. to 10 P.M. There are no booths or tables (perhaps a couple of benches), so you must enjoy your ice cream standing around the farm's parking lot or in your car. There is ample room for parking here. The farm also sells milk, butter, and double-yolk eggs.

A nice place to walk is just over the ridge along Bloomfield Avenue in nearby Verona, the next town west. **Verona Park** will be on your left off Bloomfield Avenue on Pleasant Valley Way. This beautifully landscaped park, which actually evokes the feeling of old Verona in Italy, has charming walkways and bridges and surrounds a large lake with wild ducks and chirping frogs. There is a planned exercise regime around the park and you can also rent a boat and row across the lake. Nancy Reagan, when she was known as Anne Frances Robbins, spent her formative childhood years in Verona. This was before she was adopted by her "second" father, Loyal Davis, who made the adoption when Nancy was a teenager. Connie Francis, who moved from Glen Ridge to Verona, and finally to Florida, was often seen on the paths and bridge in Verona Park.

The Sound of Edison

In 1888, Thomas Alva Edison developed the cylinder phonograph, and in 1889, he pioneered the process for motion pictures at what is now the **Edison National Historical Site** in West Orange, at Main Street and Lakeside Avenue, not far from Montclair. The unique revolving "Black Maria" building, originally constructed in 1893 and replicated in 1954, is the movie studio where some of the first celluloid films were shot—actual one-minute movies that can be viewed on kinetoscope. The great inventor of everything from the incandescent lamp—a light bulb that could burn for 13½ hours—to the automatic repeating telegraph machine, lived in a mansion called Glenmont in Llewellyn Park with his wife Mina and their three children. Although he was born in Ohio, Edison became one of New Jersey's favorite sons, with invention factories in Newark, Menlo Park, and West Orange. He was awarded 1,093 patents in his lifetime, his first at age 22 in 1869 for an electric vote recorder. Edison's factory site and nearby Glenmont can be toured. For more information, call (973) 736-0550 or visit www.nps.gov/edis.

Thomas Edison's Attic is a radio show emanating over the airwaves from WFMU (91.1 FM) in Jersey City and East Orange on Tuesday evening from 7 to 8 P.M. Hosted by Jerry Fabris, the one-hour program focuses on old recordings from Edison's own collection, which includes rare Edison 78s, as well as early cylinders. Tune in or write for further information to Jerry Fabris, "Thomas Edison's Attic," c/o WFMU, PO Box 2011, Jersey City, NJ 07303. The show is on the air every other week; on alternate Tuesdays in the same slot is Mack Cumella's Antique Phonograph Music Program. Mack plays his original 78 rpms on an old machine, scratches and all.

For over 25 years Rich Conaty has been the charming, witty, and informative host of "The Big Broadcast" on 90.7 FM. Station WFUV, which beams out of Fordham University in the Bronx, can be heard all over the greater New York/New Jersey area each Sunday evening from 8 P.M. to midnight. An erudite musicologist of the first order, Mr. Conaty plays from his vast collection of 78 rpm platters the popular music from the teens, twenties, and thirties. You can call him to make a request at (718) 365-9070 while the show is on the air or e-mail him at richconaty@wfuv.org. You can also listen to the show on the web at www.wfuv.org. Upbeat Depression songs like "Keep Your Sunny Side Up," "The Bluebird of Happiness," or "There's A Rainbow On My Shoulder" are all part of the Sunday night fun, with a sprinkling of early blues, jazz, and some oddball classics.

An original 78 rpm lateral Edison record for a needletype electric phonograph, courtesy of Diamond Cut Productions.

Contact **Diamond Cut Productions** for original Edison Laterals on CD, such as one that features Vaughn De Leath, "The Original Radio Girl" who was also known as "The First Crooner" who "crooned" softly to save radio tubes. (In the early Edison days, tenors and high-pitched sopranos literally could break the sensitive tubes.) Write Diamond Cut Productions at PO Box 305, Hibernia, NJ 07842-0305 or call (973) 316-9111 for a CD catalogue.

Archeophone Records produces perfect digitally remastered CDs of Edison's early electrical style music from the 1920s and a good many rarities from the turn-of-the-20th century. They can be reached at 2244 Jeffery Drive, St. Joseph, IL 61873. You can also call owner Richard Martin for a chat about these early musical gems at (217) 469-7331. Digitally-enhanced CD sets of "Hit Of The Week" 1930s recordings are a collector must-have. Re-recorded with great care, the original crude 78 rpm "Hit Of The Week" were made of unbreakable Durium resin on one side and cardboard on the other. In the Depression years, new releases were sold at dime stores and newsstands each week for 15 cents. The sound reproduction of the originals was not of the best quality. Now collectors who listen to these Archeophone CDs say they are of such a high standard of sound emission that even Edison would jump for joy if he heard them. A two-CD collection of great historical importance is *Lost Sounds: Blacks and the Birth of the Recording Industry 1891–1922.*

This Depression-era Jersey lampshade was found in the Stations West Antique Shop in Montclair.

WFMU 91.1 F.M. is one of Jersey's best radio stations. One of the top mainstay programs is hosted by Irwin Chusid, who is heard on the air every Wednesday from noon to 3 P.M. The music Irwin presents on his show is of the esoteric oddball variety, including New Jersey novelties that often focus on the worst Jersey pop songs ever heard, as well as calypso, jazz, the music of Django Reinhardt, International, Vanilla Pop, and early vaudeville singers such as the Cherry Sisters—the worst singing group of all time. Mr. Chusid excels as "The Old Codger," a crazy cranky character he invented who only plays scratchy 78 rpm records as he rants and raves against a technological world he believes has gone over the edge. A truly inspired comic character in the tradition of Fred Allen and Jack Benny, this is "old time" radio at its best.

Some say that the ultraswank show-spot restaurant of New Jersey—**the Manor**—is the most popular dining spot in the state. Ronald and Nancy Reagan, George and Barbara Bush, Richard Nixon, and other major public figures have elected to dine here over the years. The Manor, hard by the **Montclair Country Club,** at 111 Prospect Avenue, West Orange, (973) 731-2360 (www.themanor restaurant.com), in addition to using Limoges china and crystal-and-silver place settings, serves excellent food. Culinary awards include nine consecutive Holiday Awards for Dining Distinction, the National Restaurant Association's Great Menu Award, and the International Geneva Association's Restaurant of the Year Award. Set on 22 acres, the 11-room Regency mansion can accommodate up to 3,000 people a day, 7 days a week. The Villa d'Este waterfall and gardens and the rococo decor and outside twinkle lighting must be seen to be believed. It resembles an EPCOT Center restaurant and is Disney all the way, ostentatious yet grand. If you are looking for an intimate hideaway to meet that other woman or man, the Manor is not the place. But if you want to impress a client, date, uncle, mother, or show your designer clothing off to the world, this is the restaurant in which to be seen center stage. There is dancing under the stars in **Le Dome,** the sophisticated nightclub, Wednesday through Saturday evenings. Buffet meals are specialties at the Manor; luncheon buffet is served in the Manor Room Wednesday from noon to 3 P.M.; lobster buffet is Tuesday to Saturday from 6 until 9:30 P.M. Sunday dinner buffet is from 11:30 A.M. to 6 P.M. À la carte luncheon in the Terrace Lounge is served Tuesday, Thursday, and Friday from noon to 3 P.M. À la carte dinner on Sunday is served 4 to 7:30 P.M. As a cold appetizer try avocado stuffed with seafood ($16), Maine lobster cocktail ($17), or one ounce of Oregon caviar ($28) or *osetra caviar* (one ounce) at $34. Hot appetizers that are delicious include grilled farm quail with herbed orzo or Maryland crab cakes. Classic main courses are: filet mignon with truffle sauce, $33; roasted duck with sun-dried black cherry sauce, $30; a special (service for two) at $35 per person plus tax includes chateaubriand and rack of lamb served with a bouquet of seasonal vegetables. In a mood for seafood, try the Manor's softshell crabs, or roasted lobster stuffed with scallops and shrimp. From the Lincoln Tunnel, take Route 3 West to the Garden State Parkway South, exit 145. Follow signs for 280 West, exit 8B. The Manor is on the left-hand side of the road, straight ahead one mile. You can't miss it.

South Mountain Reservation Day Trip

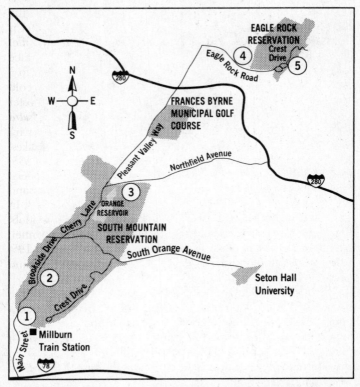

1. Paper Mill Playhouse
2. Elmdale Picnic Tables
3. Turtleback Zoo
4. Pal's Cabin
5. Highlawn Pavilion

South Mountain Reservation, a 2,048-acre preserve bordered by the townships of Millburn, Maplewood, South Orange, and West Orange, situated on the first and second of the three Watchung ridges of New Jersey, affords spectacular views of Newark and Manhattan to the east, less than a half-hour drive away. But once within its wooded, secluded confines, hiking the **Lenape Trail** or picnicking by the side of the upper reaches of the Rahway River, you can forget the hustle and bustle of modern civilization. To preserve the long wall of the Watchung (Lenape Indian for "high hills") ridges, the Essex Park Commission, established in 1895, consulted with the renowned Frederick Law Olmstead, creator of New York's Central Park. The plan conceived by Olmstead comprised 3 reservations and 23 parks, the middle and largest of which is the South Mountain Reservation. Eagle Rock Reservation to the

A vintage rumble-seat Ford parks by the side of the road in the South Mountain Reservation (Millburn area).

north and the Watchung Reservation to the south, across Route 24, together with 2,000-plus green acres in between, throw off enough oxygen to more than offset all the bad effects rising up out of the urban-suburban morass lying below.

To get to South Mountain Reservation, go to the little town of Millburn; take Route 78 to Route 24, exit at Route 527 (Millburn Avenue). To get to the Reservation by public transportation, take the Gladstone or Morristown NJ Transit trains from Hoboken or Newark's Penn Station. They all stop at Millburn, right across the street from the Reservation. Millburn sits at the base of the South Mountain Reservation.

Driving, take Brookside Drive, just beyond the railroad tracks, out of Millburn Center, pass the Papermill Playhouse, and enter the preserve. The Rahway River, dammed at various spots, flows by the side of the two-lane road. There are several picnic groves along the way, equipped with tables, fireplaces, and garbage cans, and places to park for fishing, wading, or walking. Elmdale, the first picnic area, features two large wooden tables and two fireplaces. The little stream separating the parking area from the picnic spot fills with fresh watercress every spring, which is a treat to eat. If you're feeling like a hike, cross the road and the river beyond, jump from rock to rock and climb the hill until you reach the broad trail. Used for bicycling, horseback riding, and walking, it meanders for miles through the secluded valley, culminating beneath Hemlock Falls. Stand under the falls for a wet nature experience, turn around and hike on back to your car. Pack up your picnic things and drive through the reservation, cross Orange Avenue and continue to Brookside Drive. The Orange Reservoir, surrounded by pine trees, will be on your right. When you come to Northfield Avenue, turn right and drive to the **Turtle Back Zoo,** New Jersey's largest. It's located at 560 Northfield Avenue in West Orange. The hours are 10 A.M. to 5 P.M. weekdays and Saturdays in summer, 11 A.M. to 6 P.M. on Sunday. In the winter it's 10 A.M. to 4:30 P.M. daily. There are about 800 animals at this zoo, featuring native New Jersey species including cougars, bobcats, wolves, bears, otters, bison, and deer, as well as birds, fish, reptiles, and amphibians. Call (973) 731-5800 for information on train rides, picnic facilities, etc.

Walking, the **Lenape Trail** begins at the Locust Grove parking lot next to the Millburn train station. Cross the road and enter the woods, following the yellow-marked trail out to the **Oakdale Trail,** marked in red, and return on a different part of the Lenape Trail and the **Cascade Trail,** marked in white. A quarter of an hour from the parking lot you will be at the top of the ridge, opposite historic **Washington Rock.** Here you can see New York City, Newark Airport, and the entire megalopolis. Naturally George Washington slept here, while keeping his eye on the British who were foraging down in the valley. You can continue your hike through the South Mountain Reservation or opt out by hiking *down* a trail leading to the village of South Orange. You can catch the train here also, the advantage being that it's cheaper because you're closer to your departure point (providing that was Hoboken or points east), and also you don't have to double back over territory you've already seen. Another advantage is that it is a much shorter walk this way. As an incentive to keep you going, there are some fun singles bars and restaurants in the village of South Orange. For terrific Italian cuisine and pizza, don't miss **Reservoir Pizzeria & Restaurant** at 106 West South Orange Avenue, (973) 762-9795 and 763-1488 (see also p. 96).

Millburn

···

Short Hills Shopping Mall, Pal's Cabin, Eagle Rock
Reservation, and Highlawn Pavilion

To get there: From Route 78, take Route 24 and exit at Route 527 (Millburn Avenue) into Millburn. For Short Hills take Route 24 to the intersection of JFK Parkway.

Millburn and the adjoining town of Short Hills have the charm of old New Jersey Revolutionary towns. "Mill-on-the-burn" comes from the Scotch-Presbyterian people who settled there when the town was first incorporated in 1857. During the industrial revolution, Millburn was known for its cloth mills, sawmills, hat mills, and paper mills. In fact, the beautiful **Papermill Playhouse** on Brookside Drive in Millburn is on a site that served as a paper mill from 1795 to 1926. In 1934 the mill was converted into a theater by Frank Carrington, an actor, and Antoinette Scudder, a patron of the arts, as a home base for their Newark Art Theater. It was established with the help of none other than Eleanor Roosevelt, and it has become the oldest continuously operated nonprofit theater in the United States. It became the official state theater of New Jersey in 1972. After a disastrous fire in 1980, it was completely rebuilt, combining the old and the new and featuring glass-enclosed promenades on the second floor, looking out into the South Mountain Reservation, and including a stark-white art gallery and a modern wide fanlike design for the theater itself. The emphasis at this theater is and always has been musical; a staple of operettas from Rudolf Friml to Jerome Kern has been the entertainment since the 1940s, and today there are 26,000 subscribers. The average annual attendance of 250,000 makes it the largest performing arts organization in New Jersey. Estelle Parsons starred in the musical, *Harold and Maude* in 2005. The box-office telephone number is (973) 376-4343.

Millburn itself, just down the road from the Playhouse, has an exquisitely landscaped park, perfect for a nice walk in spring during the full floral bloom and an assortment of interesting gourmet shops, boutiques, bakeries, ice cream parlors, coffee shops, and intimate restaurants for before or after the theater are to be found in the village on Main Street and Millburn Avenue. **Buncher's** hardware store is an old-style hardware supplier carrying everything but the kitchen sink—but it is the shopping mall at Short Hills, just over the ridge on Route 24, where it intersects with the JFK Parkway at Chatham, that is a "shopping" must. Some of the major department stores at **The Mall at Short Hills** include **Bloom-**

ingdale's, **Macy's, Neiman Marcus, Saks Fifth Avenue,** and
Nordstrom. Some of the other shops include **Brooks Brothers,
Louis Vuitton, Godiva Chocolatier, Sbarro, Polo/Ralph Lau-
ren, Roots, Saint Laurent, Rive Gauche,** and many others. There
are also sit-down restaurants, including **Legal Sea Foods, Au Bon
Pain,** and **Johnny Rockets.** Hours at the mall are 10 A.M. to 9 P.M.;
call (973) 376-7350 for weekend and holiday hours. Speaking of
malls, the **Livingston Mall** in nearby Livingston features all the
major department stores as well. It is much larger in scope than
the Short Hills Mall but it is by no means as unique or intimate.
Shopping in New Jersey is not only diversified and pleasant, but
cheaper, as you save on taxes on many items.

One of the best restaurants in the area is **Pals Cabin,** 265 Prospect
Ave. in West Orange. This famous landmark restaurant first
opened as a small roadside refreshment stand–cabin in 1932 serving hamburgers, franks at 10¢, and orange soda for a nickel. By
1934 Martin L. Horn and Bion LeRoy Sale—the two pals—were
offering a charcoal broiled steak for 50¢. By 1936 the enterprise
grew—in the true American style right in the middle of a Great
Depression—into a full-fledged restaurant serving the special
steak for 75¢ and a filet mignon for $1. A sirloin choice-cut char-
broiled steak was $1.50 and a sirloin for two was $2.90. A broiled
half chicken was 85¢, all served with french fried potatoes and a
chef's salad served in a wooden bowl. By 1941 the two pals, Marty
and Roy, could afford to hire a cocktail pianist named Liberace
(yes, the same) who was then paid $50 a week and all he could eat.
The two men subsequently opened another restaurant called the
Mayfair Farms, just a stone's throw from Pals; this is considerably
more formal than Pals, however. Pals has three dining areas; a sit-
down counter, a bake shop, and a room for special occasions such

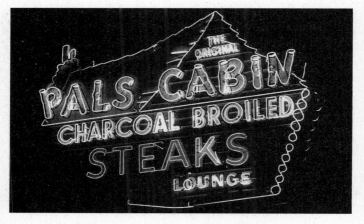

*The original Pals Cabin neon sign. Pals opened as a roadside stand in 1932 and
still serves excellent food at Prospect and Eagle Rock Avenues in West Orange.*

In his rise to fame, Liberace pounded the ivories at Pals Cabin in West Orange. His salary: $50 a week. The famous Liberace piano is still on view in the cocktail lounge.

as birthdays, anniversaries, or catered business meetings (lunch or dinner). The clean, stainless-steel kitchens and brick charcoal grill are wide open for all to see. If you sit in the first dining area, which has comfortable leatherette booths, your picture-window view is a gas station across the roadway and cars whizzing by, which seems to suit the delicious charbroiled American fare. The "Winchester Room," decorated with oil paintings of cattle and cattle ranches, is a jacket-and-tie affair, and reservations are accepted there.

The service at Pals is swift and they have the best naturally aged beef in New Jersey. If you are not in the mood for a big steak there are hamburgers, Welsh rarebit, or hot gravied white-meat turkey sandwiches. Pals's cold, crisp salads with croutons are still served in a large, wooden bowl and are excellent. A Caesar salad—made right at the table—is also a specialty. Pals does not offer meat or fish that is frozen and does not use artificial tenderizers. Jackie Gleason and Babe Ruth were two guys who were regular customers. Though the two pals are no longer around to enjoy the fun they have created at Pals, the tradition of "good food for good health" is carried on by the Horn family sons Marty Jr. and Don (and their children) who are all earnest about maintaining the top standard set by the founders. Pals has a good wine menu and offers tempting mixed drinks of all varieties. They are open daily from 9 A.M. to 10:30 P.M., Friday and Saturday until midnight. Call (973) 731-4000.

To get to Pals: Located on the corner of Prospect and Eagle Rock Avenues in West Orange, Pals can be approached from the south by driving from Millburn over Brookside Drive (though this road does not change its direction, it does change names: from Brookside Drive to Pleasant Avenue and finally to Valley Way). When you hit Eagle Rock Avenue, turn right and drive to Prospect Avenue. From the metropolitan area exit onto 280 West either from the Turnpike or from the Garden State Parkway. Exit 280 at Prospect Avenue.

Route 280 West (exit Prospect Avenue, left onto Eagle Rock Avenue) will also take you, within minutes from the metro region, to **Eagle Rock Reservation,** a gem of the Essex County Parks system. The lookout area here provides the best view anywhere. It also has picnic tables, walking trails, bridle trails, and birdwatching sites. It's a magnificent spot, ideal for giving you a sense of the height of the Watchung Ridge and a geographic "feel" for the region. It's also an excellent place for a walk after dinner at Pals. The parks' architects, the Olmstead brothers, said in 1902 that from this spectacular overlook "you see all the intervening country as from a balloon." The Knowles family, who run the **Manor Restaurant** as well as the Ram's Head Inn in Absecon, (609) 652-1700, opened a new place in 1986 on the site of a pavilion built on the outlook in 1908 as a refreshment stand. The Northern Italian, Mediterranean architecture of **Highlawn Pavilion** blends perfectly with the old restored Florentine pavilion—muted corals, terra-cotta, and deep blue-green colors in the high-ceilinged rooms, a splashing fountain and the riveting view make this a wonderful dining experience—a French rotisserie, wood-burning Italian brick oven and char-grill whet the appetite with specialties including roasted baby chicken, honey-glazed duckling, baked oysters, gourmet pizzas, and grilled veal chops. Call (973) 731-DINE for reservations, or log onto www.highlawn.com.

A "Memory-Image" by Robert Heide

The small town of Irvington (population 60,000) was a wonderful place to grow up in. It had been settled by German immigrants at the turn of the century. My father, Ludwig, had a bakery with a man named Schmaltz in Newark and later got into the tool-and-die-making business manufacturing needles for the Singer Sewing Machine factory in Elizabeth. We lived at 34 Franklin Terrace and then moved to 214 Elmwood Avenue, just two blocks away. Today the neighborhood and the houses my father owned are exactly the same. The orange-brick Second Reform Protestant Church where I went to Christian Endeavor and where I was confirmed is unchanged. My favorite teacher in the fourth grade, Ada Schwab, lived on the block on Elmwood Avenue near where the church stands. The Florence Avenue School seems also to be just as it always was. The majestic Frank Morrell High School that I graduated from in the 1950s looks the same, with its high cement columns in the Greek Revival style. Right in the center of town, on Springfield Avenue, the five-and-dime stores I loved to go into

Robert Heide on the steps of the very same house at 34 Franklin Terrace where he lived as a child. The wood-frame house and the neighborhood in Irvington remains virtually unchanged.

back then have disappeared. Gone are the old movie theaters, the Sanford, the Liberty, and the Rex. The Castle, listed as an important architectural landmark by the Theater Historical Society, is still intact, however. Merkhin's ice cream parlor, with its wood-paneled booths and stained glass is, alas, no more. Whatever happened to the Wurlitzer jukebox, where as a teenager I first heard Elvis shouting out "You ain't nothin' but a hound dog!"? I used to love to take the Springfield Avenue bus to downtown Newark with my mother, Olga, who couldn't get enough of the great department stores there, mainly Kresge's, Hahne's, and L. Bambergers.

The most famous place in Irvington, though, was Olympic Park, one of the greatest of the old-time amusement parks. It became the prototype for the Disney theme

parks; but they are only a slick imitation of the original. When I talk
to many of the New Jerseyans who
went to Olympic Park, they are
usually ecstatic. Some remember
Palisades Amusement Park; but all
agree that Olympic Park was bigger and better. I considered myself
lucky to live only two blocks from
the great park that usually opened
on Memorial Day and closed
right after Labor Day. Trolleys and
buses up Springfield Avenue deposited visitors at the magical entrance to the old park that first
opened as a tree-shaded beer garden in 1887. The first thing you
saw was the white stucco archway;
after you paid your entrance fee of
10¢ you passed through to the
geyserlike fountain with a revolving rainbow of colored light. To a
child, a visit to Olympic Park was
like going over the rainbow and
landing in Oz. A real brass band
led by Captain Joe Basile featured

A 1943 souvenir Olympic Park
calendar. The graphic was used on
gigantic billboards that advertised
the same Irvington amusement
park.

blond singer Bubbles Ricardo. She was a former trapeze artist who
lost an arm in a fall from the high wire. The Guenther family, who
operated the park on land in both Irvington and Maplewood, built
"the world's largest" swimming pool, where many of us learned to
swim. There was a sandy beach, a restaurant on the side, and a jukebox for dancing. The pool had an opening-day ceremony on July 4,
1924 and featured that day a star performance by athlete Johnny
Weissmuller. The wooden roller coaster, called the "Jack Rabbit,"
brought screams of sheer terror the minute you hit the first incline,
and was a favorite for years with roller-coaster aficionados. Amidst
the games of chance, which offered painted plaster Popeyes, Lone

Painted felt Olympic Park souvenir banner.

Newark Sunday Call *rotogravure showing girls emerging from the tunnel of love in the Old Mill, Olympic Park, 1942. The blonde is author Heide's cousin Doris Dinger of Flemington.*

Rangers, or Betty Boops, were an array of rides like "the Whip," electric "Dodgem" cars, "the Caterpillar" (with a green canvas top that opened and closed), "the Tunnel of Love," a giant Ferris wheel, and a spooky and musty walk-through called "the Haunted Castle." There were penny arcades on the midway, a real live circus featuring Hildy's Midget Troupe, some of whom were the Munchkins in the film *The Wizard of Oz,* aerial artists and animal acts; but it is the merry-go-round, with its ancient calliope and beautifully carved wooden horses that will remain as an image in my mind forever. The Guenthers had purchased the carousel with 80 hand-carved horses, 4 chariots, and 3,000 lights in 1928. The merry-go-round is now in Disney World, Florida.

My parents would meet many of the members of our large German family in the open beer garden on a summer Saturday night. Great-Aunt Gussie, Aunt Emma, Aunt Alma, Aunt Martha, Aunt Bertha, Uncle Adolph, Uncle Freddy, Uncle Albert, and others would sing along with Bubbles and the orchestra. I remember them singing the songs of World War II — "The White Cliffs of Dover" and "When the Lights Go On Again All Over the World." Bubbles would usually end with a rousing version of "The Star Spangled Banner" while the crowd cheered. Sometimes fireworks would explode in the night sky while she was singing. Now they are all gone; and so is Olympic Park. But the memory lingers on.

Note: The Guenther family decided not to reopen the park for the 1966 season. Today, if you drive by the old site of Olympic Park,

Memory image, Irvington. Top: Author Robert Heide's mother Olga, grandmother Amelia Strafehl, the author himself (center), and sister Evelyn (with flowers) sitting on the steps of the house at 34 Franklin Terrace. Middle: Back row, left to right— Billy Burlew, Richard Edgar, Lois Hausmann, Norma Edgar; front row, left to right—Cousin Georgie Reiman, Robert Heide, Cousin Herbie Reiman, at author's birthday party, all neighborhood kids. Bottom: Robert's parents Ludwig and Olga, and great-uncles Adolph and Louie on the front porch at 34 Franklin Terrace.

on Chancellor Avenue, you will see not shaded tree gardens or glittering lights but drab boxlike buildings that comprise an industrial park. If you listen carefully, though, you might hear the sound of the brass band, the calliope, or the organ from the old roller rink. The great Olympic Park served Newark and its suburban environs from 1887 to 1965, when it was shut down. Area bookstores sell copies of *Smile—A History of Olympic Park* by Alan A. Siegel (New Brunswick, NJ: Rutgers University Press).

What used to be the **Old Homestead** in Irvington, just a couple of blocks from the grounds of Olympic Park, still stands at 1133 Stuyvesant Avenue. It is the oldest building in Irvington (1833) and was originally a stagecoach stop. It was the only tavern right next door to a church, the Mount Zion Primitive Baptist Church. Next

The Old Homestead Restaurant-Tavern, "the only bar next door to a church," in Irvington.

to the church is a 1950s drive-in Dairy Queen. The anomalous juxtaposition of these three peculiar places achieved historical trivia status by several mentions in *Ripley's Believe It Or Not*. Unfortunately the legendary historic Old Homestead closed with the passing of its owner, a colorful character named Johnny Metropolitan who drove a . . . what else . . . Nash Metropolitan. The Dairy Queen is still there, and now there is a Dunkin' Donuts, too. Nearby in Irvington you can go to the terrific 1950s-style 24-hour **Kless's Diner** at 1212 Springfield Avenue. Kless's (you can't miss the giant neon sign) has good home cooking and endless steaming cups of hot black coffee. They also offer free home-baked cookies at the cash register, which is a smart alternative to their giant cakes, pies, and pastries.

Union Day Trip

Going into the town of Union is almost like entering the twilight zone, circa 1950. Even the friendly townfolk seem to have come from another time, another place. It has been called the "most typical American town" because of its melting-pot population ratio of Polish, German, Hispanic, Italian, African-American, Asian, and other nationality groups. Presidents come to visit; George Bush in 1989 and Bill Clinton just before his second inauguration in 1996. Clinton returned to stump for presidential hopeful John Kerry in 2004, but with lesser results. Road signs proclaim WHAT HELPS YOUTH HELPS UNION. To be sure. This flag-waving town would never be confused with the colorful, predominantly Spanish-speaking town of Union City, on the edge of the Hudson River, just above the Lincoln Tunnel, famous for its raucous nightlife and bars.

(Indeed, Bergenline Avenue, stretching through Union City and West New York, has become a microcosm of Central and South American cultures. There are excellent Cuban and Ecuadorian restaurants, food markets that sell Caribbean products like frozen papaya pulp and bricks of guava paste, upholsterers who specialize in clear-vinyl furniture coverings and shops selling painted plaster Catholic and Santeria saints, many life-size.)

Getting to Union is easy: Route 22 borders Union Township and exits 140 and 142 from the Garden State Parkway lead directly into town. You can also take Highway 78, which has an exit marked Union-Vauxhall. Stuyvesant Avenue is the main street that runs through Union Center.

Park your car and walk down Stuyvesant Avenue, which is a great place to shop. A famous landmark is **Lutz's Pork Store** at 1055 Stuyvesant Avenue, (908) 688-1373. Here you can stock up on the best in homemade bolognas, bloodwursts, liverwursts, potato salad, German rye breads, and German import mustards and pickles to go along with it. Likewise, you will find just up the street, on Morris Avenue, which crosses Stuyvesant, **Gaiser's Pork Store** with its neon pig glowing in the window. This is a large specialty butcher delicatessen of the type that used to be found in the German Yorkville section of Manhattan. Today, Russian and Polish products are also available here. Take home some of these goodies for sandwiches and you will not be disappointed. **Union Center,** which has ample and convenient parking was, like many "main streets," in decline until energetic locals protested the encroach-

A one-time furniture store in the shape of a ship on Route 22 in Union was a night-club where the big bands played in the 1930s and 1940s.

ment of the shopping mall. Now it is bustling with shops and places to go. All on Stuyvesant Avenue are **Here's The Story— Books and Video,** owned by Joe Leo, (908) 688-2665, **John & Mary's Luncheonette, Mr. Nino's Pizza and Restaurant, Perkin's Pharmacy, Van Gogh's Ear Cafe,** and **Blue Ribbon Bakery.** A cozy place for cocktails and fine food is **Spaeter's** on Rosemont— or hustle over to **Michael's Roscommon House,** 1871 Vauxhall Road, (908) 687-7777, for burgers, steak sandwiches, boardwalk pizza, and malted milk shakes, not to mention a terrific liquor bar.

Summit is just a hop, skip, and jump out of Union Center (take Route 82 West—Morris Avenue—to Broad Street), and the charming town center is worth a visit. One of the finest dining experiences anywhere is **Fiorino Ristorante,** 38 Maple Street, (908) 277-1900, Summit. Legendary restaurateur John Bitucci (the former owner of the Minetta Tavern in Greenwich Village) and his son and general manager serve first-class Italian dishes in a cozy atmosphere that features artful murals of Italian scenes. Bitucci has assembled his best chef and waiters from Minetta Tavern. Their website is www.fiorinoristorante.com. Summit also offers antiques and gifts galore (try **Christopher's Books and Gifts,** 338 Springfield Ave., co-owned by Rayma Moor and Joan Papio) and the renowned **Summit Diner** (see p. 57), across from the Summit train station, which is still serving Jersey's best BLT's and Navy Bean soup.

Union, Maplewood, and South Orange Village

One of the highlights of the Union area is the **Connecticut Farms Presbyterian Church** (at Stuyvesant Avenue and Chestnut Street), which was founded in 1730. Visiting the church and the adjacent graveyard, you can imagine General George Washington tromping around as he did during the Revolutionary War when he commandeered the place as a temporary headquarters. The ghosts can make you hungry, so head on out on Chestnut Street to the **Galloping Hill Inn** at 325 Chestnut, Union. Situated in a mind-boggling intersection called "Five Points," where five different rural roads cross each other, driving into the parking lot of this drive-in–type place feels oddly like berthing a ship, out of the flow. Order terrific roadside hamburgers, hot dogs, or french fries with special relishes. A small, nostalgic restaurant with sparkling painted red tables and knotty-pine walls lined with antiquarian calendars and yesteryear photos (there are even some old menus from the time when a complete chicken dinner was only 35¢ and coffee a nickel), it is intimate and fun in the family style. Diners can order special American meals of stuffed capon or flounder, fried shrimp, or large beef hot dogs and potato salad. Hours are 11 A.M. to 8 P.M. every day, Friday and Saturday until 9 P.M. (in the summer they stay open an hour later on weekends); telephone (908) 686-2683. Still in Union, but over on Springfield Avenue (at Millburn Avenue), is another legendary eatery called **Joe's Famous Pizzeria,** which has been serving up mouth-watering tomato pies, hot dogs, sausages, and such Italian specialties as lasagna, calzone with pizza toppings, and mozzarella sticks since 1948. To take home food, stop in at **DiPietro Italian Specialty Foods,** 1701 Springfield Avenue, (973) 762-4077, hours 7:30 A.M. to 5 P.M. (closed Monday), just across the road from beautiful Maple Crest Park.

To get to the Hamlet of Maplewood, drive over the hill from Maple Crest Park to Valley Road, past the lush golf course and country club, the town library and beautiful Maplewood Memorial Park. Across the road from the top of this park is the Maplewood train station, and the charming hamlet is just beyond. Shops and restaurants line both sides of the curving, hilly Maplewood Avenue. There is a choice of several movies at the **Maplewood Cinema.** Try the **Maple Leaf Coffee Shop** at 165 Maplewood Avenue, which features fifty gourmet flavored coffees, a showcase of dessert sensations, and food with low-fat ingredients. **Robin Hutchins Gallery,** also at 165 Maplewood Avenue, (973) 762-4714, features changing art exhibitions.

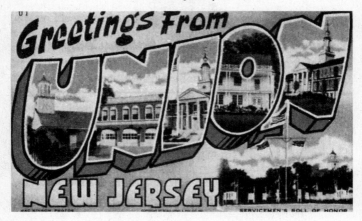

Greetings from Union, New Jersey, postcard.

The hilly outlying streets and roads of South Orange are all lit by old-fashioned gaslight—in the higher elevations on the mountain there are astonishing views of Manhattan and the metropolitan region. **Seton Hall University,** famous for its basketball team, is located in South Orange. South Orange Village has a charming railroad station and brick firehouse and tower. Located at the steps to the train on South Orange Avenue is the new 1950s-style retro diner **Blue Moon. Town Hall Deli,** up the street, is sheeted in 1930s black vitreous glass. There are some "Good-time Charlie" hangouts for the college kids, but the place to go for pan pizza is the **Reservoir Pizzeria & Restaurant** at 106 West South Orange Avenue, (973) 762-9795 and 763-1488. Try one of Tony's immense salads, too! Old-timers remember this place when it was located down next to Newark's old reservoir. A legend then, a legend now. Ask for Bill or Barbara, the brother-sister team that runs the place.

1. Passaic Township Grange
2. Boardwalk Swamp Walk
3. Minuteman Family Restaurant
4. Wick House
5. The Old Book Shop
6. George Washington's Headquarters
7. Rod's 1890s Ranch House
8. Museum of Early Crafts and Trades

To get to the **Great Swamp,** located just to the south of the little town of Chatham, take Route 24 off the Garden State Parkway or the Jersey Turnpike. In Chatham, turn left into Fairmont Avenue and drive up the hill until the avenue doglegs onto Meyersville Road. You'll pass a good produce farm on the hill to the left and the **Passaic Township Grange** farther down the road on the right. Beyond the Grange, turn right on New Vernon Road to enter the Great Swamp. Posted signs direct you to various locations inside the Swamp; park headquarters is on Pleasant Plains Road. Fifteen thousand years ago a glacier receded across the Passaic Valley, creating a 30-mile-long, 10-mile-wide lake that gradually drained off to leave behind 7,400 acres of swamp, hardwood forests, marshland, and open fields, now known as the **Great Swamp National Wildlife Refuge.** Ideal to visit September through May, when there is no humidity or mosquitos, the Great Swamp was saved by residents of Morris County from developers who were planning on turning it into a jetport.

This incredible swamp has 30 species of mammals, 24 of fish, 21 of reptiles, 18 of amphibians, and more than 200 varieties of birds. Open daily from dawn to dusk, the 3,600-acre core of the refuge allows no motorized vehicles or equipment, and there are no man-made structures to block the view. The National Wilderness Preservation system provides a primitive "outdoor experience" for the public — 10 miles of trails at the northeast end of White Bridge Road and Laurel Trail — and 5½ miles of walking trails on the western border as well as a wildlife observation center off Long Hill Road with a mile of trails and blinds for observing wildlife. To exit the Great Swamp continue on New Vernon Road, up Long Hill to Logansville Road. Turn right on Logansville to Glen Alpin Road. Turn left on Glen Alpin and drive to Route 202 (Mt. Kemble Avenue). Turn left on 202 and drive south to the 145-acre **Wightman Farm,** Route 202, (201) 425-9819, owned and operated by the Wightman family since 1923. At the farm's produce store you can pick up fresh cider, apples, homemade doughnuts, jellies, pickles, relishes, smoked hickory bacon and ham. Pumpkins and farm-grown mums are the big fall specialty.

If you are looking for a lunch stop in the area, the **Minuteman Family Restaurant and Pie Shop,** (973) 425-9798, on Mt. Kemble Avenue (Route 202) as you head back toward Jockey Hollow is just the spot. This is a knotty-pine place with comfortable booths and a relaxed atmosphere. Under "burger brigades" on the menu you'll find the Ethan Allen, a burger on a toasted bun with french fries, coleslaw, lettuce, and tomato. The James Madison is a burger covered with pizza sauce and mozzarella cheese. The Nathan Hale has Old English cheese and Russian dressing. There are others, including the Ben Franklin, the John Adams, the John Hancock, the Thomas Paine, the Thomas Jefferson, and the Alexander Hamilton. The Ichabod Crane is a diet special, a burger on toast with lettuce and cottage cheese. Other patriotic American fare includes triple-decker sandwich deals, homemade apple, sour cherry, blueberry, fresh peach, or strawberry-rhubarb pies. The delicious pies may also be taken home; but served with Welsh Farms ice cream and Minuteman's strong coffee, they should be eaten on the spot.

After fueling up at the Minuteman, drive up to Tempe Wick Road at the traffic light, turn left, and drive through the densely wooded area known as **Jockey Hollow,** part of Morristown National Historical Park. Reconstructed quarters that housed our Revolutionary-era soldiers yield sobering insights into the harsh realities of winter during

Wick farmhouse where Tempe Wick hid her favorite horse for three weeks (in her bedroom) to prevent its seizure by British soldiers during the Revolution. Linen postcard from Tichnor Brothers.

the Revolution—huts chinked with clay and held together with wooden pegs. There are over 900 wooded acres in this designated wildlife sanctuary, with miles of hiking trails.

The **Wick House** is restored and furnished and set next to a fascinating Colonial kitchen herb garden where something edible seems to grow year-round. Quince, gooseberry, and currant shrubs are prominent in spring. This is a lovely farm site with wooden fences enclosing a pasture and apple orchard where deer and horses gambol in proximity. The Wick House, field headquarters for Washington's

The man who slept around—George Washington's Revolutionary War headquarters are in Morristown, but Washington himself apparently camped out all over the state during the war, as well as having slept the night in many country inns and farmhouses.

Major General, Arthur St. Clair, during the Revolution, is located in the Jockey Hollow encampment area and has parking, an information center, and rest room facilities. An interesting bit of historical trivia associated with the Wick House during the Revolution is the story of Tempe Wick, a strong-minded farm woman who was the daughter of the owner. Everyone was away, and soldiers, as usual, were rampaging through the area. Tempe Wick, in order to prevent the seizure of her horse, secreted the animal in her bedroom for three weeks.

Morris County

Madison—Morristown—Mendham

Worth looking into in the Morris County area, home of the Great Swamp and the Morristown National Historical Park, are the grounds of **Drew University.** Drew University is a Methodist college with a liberal attitude, located in the town of Madison, which is called the "Rose City" (from the turn of the century through the 1950s, Madison was the center of the commercial rose-growing industry), on Route 24. Park the car inside the 186-acre forested campus grounds, which are entered through a stone arch just to the left as you drive west from Madison center. Beautiful plantation-style mansions such as the administration building, Mead Hall, the manor house of the Gibbons family, built in the neoclassical style with Greek revival decor in 1836 and listed on State and National Historic Registers, abound. The New Jersey Shakespeare Festival, a not-for-profit professional (Equity) theater group is in residence at Drew each summer; and they alternate the plays of Shakespeare with modern classics like *Long Day's Journey Into Night* or *A Man For All Seasons.* The town of Madison is sparkling clean, with a 1920s architectural style. It is filled with inexpensive luncheonettes, antique and boutique shops. **Time After Time Clothing From the Past** at 81 Main Street, is run by a vivacious woman named Bette Moore. Bette likes to dress up in vintage silk dresses and 1940s platform pumps. Check out her stock of 1930s, 1940s, and 1950s shirts and jackets for men, and dresses, blouses, undies, hats, and accessories for women. The college crowd keeps the glad rags moving but Bette is constantly restocking. Hours are Monday through Friday, noon to 6:30 P.M., Tuesday until 7:30 P.M., Saturday 10:30 A.M. to 5:30 P.M. Call (973) 966-6877.

Also on Main Street at Green Village Road is the **Museum of Early Crafts and Trades,** located in a stone church and open daily from 10 A.M. to 5 P.M. and Sunday from 2 to 5 P.M. The museum houses reconstructed shops of the early trades and presents the life of the early settlers in this historical region, with seasonal crafts exhibited at corresponding times of the year.

Drew is not the only college in the Madison area. Farther out on Route 24 is the **Fairleigh Dickinson University** Florham–Madison campus, situated on 187 acres of what was once the 900-acre estate of Florence Vanderbilt Twombly and centered around a 100-room replica of Henry VIII's Hampton Court Palace, designed by Stanford White. Here, as in many other places in New Jersey, the parklike grounds were designed by Frederick Law Olmstead. A few miles west is the **College of St. Elizabeth,** a Catholic college for women at Convent Station. At this spot, still on Route

24, is the **Madison Hotel,** 1 Convent Rd., (973) 285-1800, www.themadisonhotel.com, a 195-room hotel run by Motor-Hotel Management Company. **Rod's 1890s Ranch House,** owned and operated by the Keller family, which also runs the building housing the Madison Hotel, is right next door, serving breakfast, lunch, and dinner and featuring a beautifully decorated (in period) cocktail lounge. Call (973) 539-6666 for reservations.

Route 24 rambles on into the business district of Morristown, the shopping center and "hub" for more than 300,000 people in three counties. The town is also on Interstate Highway 287 (north-south) and U.S. Route 202.

Morristown made the iron and gunpowder used in the Revolutionary War and because of this the town was subject to many attempts by the British to capture it. Its high-perched location and defensibility made these attempts futile, however, and Washington consequently decided to make it his headquarters. There are two major department stores, a half-dozen large office buildings, banks and two movie theaters, several beautiful historic churches, and dozens of retail shops situated around the large town green. During the 1960s small bands of hippies congregated here; now it's more or less a ragtag group of mild-mannered homeless men. At Christmas time the "green" becomes a fantasy of Santa Claus's North Pole headquarters, in honor of the famed cartoonist Thomas Nast, who lived in Morristown and created the character of Santa Claus as we know him today. The town decorates the square with elves' houses, castles, and giant, brightly colored Christmas packages. Santa and his reindeer, crêches of the Madonna and Child and other yuletide exhibits make this a "must stop" for the kiddies during the Christmas season, particularly if there is snow on the ground.

The **Old Book Shop** in Morristown, run by Virginia Faulkner and Chris Wolff, specializes in Americana and New Jersey history. Their total stock of over 30,000 books, on a great variety of subjects, includes several thousand volumes of fiction, many with their original dust jackets intact, as well as maps and a good selection of paper ephemera. From the train station, pass under the tracks to Ridgedale Avenue (near the Gulf station). Turn left on Ridgedale, drive one-half mile to John Street, turn right; they are at 4 John Street. Hours are Monday through Saturday, 10 A.M. to 5:30 P.M., (973) 538-1210.

Twice a year the **Morristown National Guard Armory** hosts a splendid antiques show, which is well worth a visit, if only to view the fine antique wares exhibited by as many as 100 top quality dealers in the lofty premises of the regimental headquarters. Call Wendy Show Management, Westchester Enterprises, Inc., (914) 698-3442, for the exact dates, usually in late January and again in late April.

Washington's Headquarters, Morristown, New Jersey.

Morristown is steeped in Revolutionary War history and is quite proud of the restored **Jacob Ford House** (Washington's headquarters during the tough winter of 1779–80) and other preserved and restored historic structures, many of which, it is rumored, George slept in. The Ford House (230 Morris Avenue), built in 1772 and furnished with period pieces, is part of the Morristown National Historic Park that includes Jockey Hollow, the Wick House and Farm, and Fort Nonsense, the latter on a high hill on the western outskirts of town, which has a fine vista. The **Schuyler Hamilton House** (5 Olyphant Road) where Alexander Hamilton met his future wife, Betsy Schuyler, is now the headquarters of the Morristown DAR. **Acorn Hall** (68 Morris Avenue) is a fine example of Victorian Italianate architecture with a beautiful Victorian garden. It is also the headquarters for the Morris County Historical Society, (973) 267-3465, and has a complete Victorian research library.

Proceeding southwest out of Morristown on Route 24 is Mendham, home of the **Black Horse Tavern and Pub,** opened in the farmhouse of Ebenezer Byram in 1742 and in continuous operation for well over 200 years as a tavern for travelers. A sign at the rear door proclaims: PURVEYORS: BRING THROUGH THESE DOORS ONLY THE FRESHEST, FINEST TOP QUALITY MERCHANDISE OR BE PREPARED TO TAKE IT BACK! The pub has a fine old bar decorated with old Lowenbrau casks and kegs, copper kettles, and knotty pine. They serve Bass Ale, Grolsch, and New Amsterdam beers. Call (973) 543-7300 for reservations, or log onto www.blackhorse nj.com. The Tavern is open for dinner six nights a week (closed Monday) and the Pub for lunch and dinner seven days a week. **Sammy's Ye Old Cider Mill Inn** on Route 24, Mendham, (973) 543-7675, has no signs and you wouldn't know it was a place of any kind if it weren't for the Mercedes, Jaguars, Bentleys, Rolls-Royces, and Cadillac Coupe de Villes parked in the back. The simple white farmhouse is the setting for wonderful family-style meals featuring large steaks, thick lamb chops, and 2-pound lobsters, served with complete meals. You have to bring your own wine, dress simply but nicely, and be patient while waiting to be served. This is the place that Bill Bradley told us was one of his favorites for the first edition of this book.

Between Chester and Long Valley (see *Chester/Long Valley Day Trip*) on Parker Road, off Route 24, just beyond the grist mill, is the beautiful and mysterious **Hacklebarney State Park,** situated in a gorge along the brooding Black River. There are dozens of picnicking areas with tables and fireplaces, with running water and rest room facilities within easy walking distance. There is also very good fishing and hiking. Stop at the Jacobson family farm—**Hacklebarney Farms,** phone (908) 879-6593—established in 1851 on the winding road to the park, and stock up on apples, peaches, home-baked goods, and fresh apple cider pressed in their own mill, and sold by the quart and gallon to take along on your picnic. The Jacobsons also give tours of their beautiful farm by appointment.

Chester/Long Valley Day Trip

The historic (1799) township of Chester (west of Mendham) is at the junction of Routes 24 and 206. Settled in 1713, sawmills, grist-mills, and distilleries utilized the industrial possibilities offered by the waters of the Black River. Later woolen mills and iron mines operated here. Today all that remains of this busy past are the peach orchards southwest of town. The bustling town has more than 40 shops and almost a dozen restaurants. The old-style shops, in restored 19th-century buildings, have humorous names like **Chester Drawers, Bare Necessities, Geppeto's Workshop, Party Parrot, Spiced Apple,** and **Pegasus.** Take a peek into the last and browse through the past—there are Mickey Mouse toys, Jer-seyana, and other antique goodies for sale including 20th-century pop-culture collectibles, advertising signs, toys, furniture, and Fi-esta ware. For vintage and antique clothing, jewelry, and more fur-niture and collectibles, try Tom & Jacqui Crowe's **The Beauty of Civilization,** 30 Main Street, Suite 6, Chester. Call (908) 879-2044 or check out www.ilovechester.com.

Chester goes all out several times a year with events and celebra-tions such as the arts and crafts show in the spring, an Oktoberfest, and a Christmas open house. Cabin fever weekends and sidewalk sales and special antique shows abound. **Larison's Turkey Farm** on the hill used to be the largest restaurant in the area, where fam-

One of the many farms in the Long Valley region.

ilies could walk across a sloping lawn under a spreading oak tree to visit the turkeys, peacocks, ducks, goats, chickens, rabbits, and donkeys in the paddocks. At press time, though, the restaurant has been closed and sold to new owners who intend to try a "fresh concept." Stay tuned. This legendary restaurant was a true family enclave for Jersey folk and for New Yorkers, as well.

From the crest of a hill on Route 24 (west of Chester) one looks down upon the length of **Long Valley,** a tributary of the Raritan River running through the center, and the **Schooley's Mountain** forming a backdrop to the northwest. Long Valley is a rich farm region (stop at **Ort Farms** just off 24 on Route 625 as you cruise down into the valley) and though the town itself is not much more than a crossroads, it is well worth a long stop for "on foot" investigation. There is a general store that juts over the stream at the back, a gas station, an ancient tavern, and a very good family-style restaurant. The Zion Lutheran Church has a sign out front declaring that Long Valley was originally called German Valley before the First World War. Behind the church is a miniwilderness area with miles of walking paths meandering alongside a fast-moving stream. This is an excellent (and relatively unknown) place for spotting large, rare birds. There is also a dairy and other farm-related operations, including a distributor for delicious Welsh Farms ice cream and milk. There is an ancient cemetery with headstones dating from the late 18th and early 19th centuries, quite open for walking. In the center are the ruins of an old stone church. Back at the **Long Valley Pub and Brewery,** 1 Fairmount Ave., (908) 876-1122, at the crossroads, you will find huge framed sepia-toned photographs of the days of the horse and buggy in German Valley. There is bold American fare and they serve quality handcrafted ales. Live entertainment on Thursday, Friday, and Saturday nights

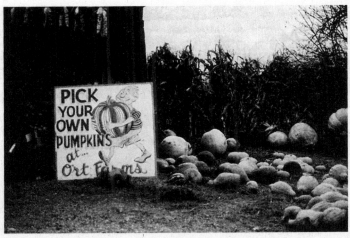

At Ort Farms in Long Valley you can pick your own pumpkin right off the vine at Halloween.

livens up the scene. Another good place is **Apgar's 1778** at 1 West Mill Road, (908) 876-9307.

Route 24 takes a northerly turn at Long Valley, and a very steep ascent up Schooley's Mountain, before it connects with Route 46 in Warren County. Schooley's Mountain has a 2-gas-pump general store with a potbellied stove and penny candies in glass jars (and 100 post office boxes lined up side by side). **Schooley's Mountain Park** and the 1½-acre Lake George are located on Camp Washington and Springtown Roads, just off Route 24. There is a unique floating bridge that separates the swimming area from the fishermen and boaters. Swimming on a hot summer day is a pleasure and there are many picnic sites, hiking trails, an amphitheater, and scenic overlooks.

Traveling southwest through Long Valley from Long Valley Center on Route 513, you drive through Lockwood Gorge where **Voorhees State Park** is located. There is a magnificent view of the **Spruce Run State Park** region in the western distance from here. There are picnic facilities and fireplaces. Refresh yourself and drive down the steep road to High Bridge, where Highway 31 will connect you to quick connections at east-west 22 and 78.

Doris Duke's Gardens Day Trip

To get there: Take Route 287 South. Exit at 13, Route 206 South, to Somerset Shopping Mall. The **Duke Gardens** are a mile and a quarter south as you head in the direction of Princeton. From midtown Manhattan take the Lincoln Tunnel to the NJ Turnpike to Interstate 78 West. Exit at Pluckemin onto Route 287 South. From lower Manhattan take the Holland Tunnel to the Pulaski Skyway to I-78 West. From New York City the trip to Somerville should take about one hour. Buses from New York Port Authority leave every day for the estate.

Drive through the great iron gates of the Duke estate and park your car. Once inside you will have that very special feeling of quietude and grace usually offered only to the wealthy and privileged members of society. The 6,000-acre private estate was created out of the low, flat farm country south of Somerville, the county seat of Somerset. Doris Duke's father, James Buchanan Duke, the tobacco and electric-power mogul, spent $10 million in the days when a dollar went a long way, creating a magnificent series of lakes and 25 miles of paved roadways that wind around the lakes, through wooded hills, lagoons, grandiose fountains, waterfalls, cottages, stables, and greenhouses. Doris Duke, the late tobacco heiress and sole owner of the place, kept up the formal greenhouses, originally built for family use, opening them up to the public for the first time in 1964, by appointment only. The gar-

Among the fourteen Victorian hothouse gardens open to the public on the Duke Estate in Somerville, the formal French Garden was one of tobacco heiress Doris Duke's favorites.

dens are open Wednesday through Sunday and have seasonal
schedules. Check out the website at www.dukefarms.org. In 2005
the Duke Foundation added a tour of the magnificently landscaped estate, including the picturesque lakes, waterfalls, bridges,
and historic buildings. For estate or garden tour information and
reservations, call (908) 722-3700 at least one week prior to making
this trip. There is an admission fee of $10. From the parking lot in-
side the gates a van takes about 10 people through the estate, offering glimpses of manicured meadows and gigantic trees, to the
formal gardens. The walk through the garden is never rushed; but
you may not wander, take photographs, or eat snacks or sandwiches during the tour. Once deposited at the visitor's center, a
tour guide will take you through the eleven 19th-century glass-
enclosed Victorian hothouses. The entire walk-through with a
guide takes about one hour.

The first garden you enter is a very romantic Italian garden filled
with rare Italian statuary and fountains. Luxurious plants include
birds of paradise, bougainvillea, and mimosa. Stepping through
an archway you find yourself in the American Colonial garden
featuring clipped hedges, camellia bushes and magnolias, all in
an early-American setting. The Edwardian garden beyond houses
a vast assortment of rare orchids, palm trees, and rubber plants
with extra humidity pumped into the atmosphere. The other gardens that follow include the formal French garden, an English
garden, a desert garden featuring giant cacti from the Southwest,
a traditional Chinese garden with a mysterious "grotto among the
stones," landscaped Japanese gardens, an Indo-Persian garden that
contains the atmospheric beauty of the Taj Mahal and its gardens,
an African rain forest garden that assimilates the jungle plants one
might also find in the Amazon regions of South America, and finally, the Mediterranean semitropical garden.

Once this exotic tour is over and you are brought back to your car
you will feel as if you have actually had a miniature trip around the
world; a truly enchanting experience. These types of gardens were
extremely popular among the wealthy at the turn of the century;
but few private ones exist today. Certainly, none of such magni-
tude. Once outside the great gates and driving around the stone-
walled estate on Duke's Parkway, one can appreciate the extent of
the late Ms. Duke's personal desire for privacy, as the trees are
posted with signs that read, NO TRESPASSING — PROPERTY OF DORIS
DUKE. The great mansion itself is hidden from view behind a forest of pine trees. It has over 100 rooms, a huge indoor swimming
pool, indoor tennis courts, a theater, and among the many wonders on the grounds is a miniature version of the Black Forest of
Germany.

After a visit to the Duke Gardens, take a picnic lunch and drive to **Duke Island Park.** If you are adventurous, in the winter months or early spring, bring along a hot thermos of coffee and another filled with soup. Bring along a pair of ice skates too, because you can ice-skate on the lake during very cold weather at the park, which is upstream from the Duke Farms. It is located on grazing land donated by the Duke Foundation, between two branches of the Raritan River (just off Highway 22 on Old York Road). This large park, just south of North Branch Park (site of the Somerset County fairgrounds) has a loop bike and hiking trail, a fine new boat pavilion, canoeing, rowboating, fishing, and playgrounds. There are large picnic areas for family groups.

Nearby Somerville, the county seat, is an active antiques shopping center with dozens of dealers; a good start would be the **Somerville Antiques Emporium,** 29 Division Street, (908) 218-1234. The hours are 11 A.M. to 5 P.M.

If you don't bring your own picnic or winter thermos, you will find plenty of diners and eateries on nearby Routes 202, 206, or on Highway 22 heading east to New York or west to Clinton. The **Lido Diner,** a nifty fifties diner, sits in the middle of Route 22 in Springfield, its tricolor neon sign blinking at motorists speeding both ways on the busy highway. Try it out for atmosphere and coffee on the way home.

High Posh

••

Somerville—Far Hills

Somerville, county seat of Somerset County, was very respectful and protective of its premier millionairess, Doris Duke, whose 6,000-acre estate, Duke Farms, came closest to being a real "home" for the heiress of the American Tobacco Company. After she inherited $79 million from her father in 1925, 13-year-old Doris, then known as "DeeDee," was hounded by the press and labeled the "richest girl in the world." Tom Valentine and Patrick Mahn, the authors of the book *Daddy's Duchess*, worked as accountants for Ms. Duke and commented thus, "Shall we say—the richest *person* in the world." Her reported wealth, the authors claimed, was only the "tip of the iceberg." Publicity-shy and single (her two marriages, to James Cromwell and playboy Porfirio Rubirosa, ended in divorce), Doris Duke spent her time in Somerville caring for her extensive collection of Oriental art, studying such alternative lifestyles as yoga and vegetarianism, and keeping up with the horsey social set. A few years before her death, she and some friends threw a lavish party for King Farouk at a Far Hills estate, for high-posh society invites only, complete with outdoor tents and pavilions and a real live elephant. In her later years, adding to her eccentric image, Doris offered much needed sanctuary at her estate for such beleaguered high-profile celebrities as Betty Hutton, Pee-wee Herman, and Imelda Marcos.

One of Doris Duke's husbands was the playboy Dominican ambassador to Argentina, Porfirio Rubirosa, shown here on his wedding day with a glamorous Doris in the late 1940s.

Jacqueline Kennedy Onassis maintained an estate in Peapack in the fox-hunting countryside of Far Hills.

Morris County, traditionally the home of New Jersey's largest number of millionaires, has given way in recent times to the area a bit farther south, known as Far Hills in Somerset County. Route 202 traverses this beautiful section not too far off the beaten track from the late Jacqueline Kennedy Onassis's 10-acre hideaway weekend escape estate in Peapack. Jackie O. bought the estate after renting in the area and staying at the Far Hills estate of Charlotte Ford. Bernardsville, the largest town in this rural area, has long been the center for wealthy estate dwellers who have their Rolls-Royces and Bentleys serviced in the many auto garages and service stations. Far Hills itself, west of Bernardsville, is no more than a small village with a handful of shops and a train station. The population is about 800. One of the best ways to see this rich (scenerywise) countryside is taking the train. The newly rebuilt and electrified commuter trains on the Morris and Essex Line of New Jersey Transit (out of Hoboken) take you through middle-class communities, open farmlands, and rolling woodland hills to

WARNING
NO TRESPASSING

THIS IS PRIVATE PROPERTY
Hunting, Fishing, Trapping or
Tresspassing for Any Purpose is
Prohibited Under Penalty of the Law

DUKE FARMS
Doris Duke, Owner

A sign from along the Doris Duke Parkway.

Gladstone, the end of the line, with stops at Bernardsville, Far Hills, and Peapack.

It would seem that this is a special train just for millionaires and their families and friends, like the Dillon family (Douglas Dillon was chairman of New York's Metropolitan Museum) who have holdings in the NCR Corporation and other investments worth conservatively $300 to $500 million. The Dillon family has an elegant estate in Far Hills, as does Jane Engelhard, widow of the prototype for James Bond's nemesis, the main character portrayed in Ian Fleming's *Goldfinger*, Charles Engelhard. Mrs. Engelhard, once New Jersey's wealthiest woman, lived at Cragwood, a fantastic Rhine-like turreted castle on a 172-acre estate overlooking the lush hunt country where, as a young girl, Caroline Kennedy was taught the symbolic meaning of the traditional (and bloody) foxhunt. Newcomers to the sport are smeared with the blood of the dead and mangled fox that is supposed to imbue them with a life-long understanding and appreciation of "the excitement of the kill." Another Far Hills home belongs to the Forbes family, publishers of *Forbes Magazine*. The family also owns a 20,000-acre ranch in Montana, a 260 square-mile ranch in Colorado and New Mexico, a castle in Tangier, and a mansion in London (plus 10 other spectacular homes around the world).

Princeton Day Trip

HOUSES OF THE STARS IN PRINCETON

MOUNTAIN AVENUE

Svetlana Stalin

206

NEW JERSEY

287

78

New York
City

ATLANTIC
OCEAN

Robeson
Place

Paul
Robeson

Grover Cleveland

1

Princeton

Brooke Shields

0   10

Miles

ELM ROAD

Trenton

F. Scott Fitzgerald

T. S. Eliot

Aaron Burr

John F. Kennedy

27

NASSAU ST.

Albert Einstein

Woodrow Wilson

Jimmy Stewart

MERCER ST.

COLLEGE RD.

Princeton
NEW JERSEY

PRINCETON
UNIVERSITY

WASHINGTON RD.

HARRISON ST.

J. Robert Oppenheimer

ALEXANDER ST.

ELM
DRIVE

OLDEN
LANE

SPRINGDALE
ROAD

Lake Carnegie

To get there: Princeton is at the junctions of Route 206 and Route 27, just a few miles west of Route 1, which traverses this middle section of New Jersey like a straight arrow, from Trenton to New York. The Turnpike is not far; take exit 8 onto 571 West directly onto the campus. Signs along the road will point the way from any direction and from all of the scenic back roads. All autos are barred from the actual campus so once there, park the car and walk. Buses also depart regularly from Port Authority in New York and from other points.

The great Gothic architecture and hallowed halls of Princeton University and the old Revolutionary-style town with its quaint shops and interesting restaurants make Princeton a great place to go on a day trip. The university's many acres are enclosed by stone and iron fences and intricate sidewalk paths are provided for the stroller. Autumn and spring are good times for this day trip. Summer is also a lovely time, when the campus is most peaceful and quiet, as there are few students. Princeton is particularly enchanting during and after a snowfall, so if you choose to go in winter, it might be fun to do a snow walk.

Whig Hall, built in 1893, designed in marble by A. Page Brown in the ionic style of a Greek temple.

Princeton University was founded in 1756. **Nassau Hall,** in the center of the campus, was built in 1756 and is still in use as university administrative offices. In 1783 the Continental Congress met there. The Gothic **Princeton Chapel** is an architectural wonder and should not be missed. Built in 1928, it is a strange mixture of Gothic gargoyles and Art Deco stained-glass windows. There are fine examples of Greek Revival architecture and an excellent art museum. A map of the campus and the walkways, and Princeton proper, is available at **Maclean House.** The map will also direct you to the former homes of Svetlana Stalin, Paul Robeson, Thomas Mann, Woodrow Wilson, and Albert Einstein, who worked and lived in Princeton (at 112 Mercer Street) for 20 years at the Institute for Advanced Study. If you are interested in the Princeton football games, call the Princeton switchboard at (609) 258-3000 for tickets. You might also want to ring up the **Historical Society of Princeton,** (609) 921-6748, for further information or a brochure. There is also the **McCarter Theater,** (609) 258-6515, which mounts professional productions of thoughtful, exciting plays like those of Edward Albee, Tennessee Williams, or Eugene O'Neill—the latter a Princeton attendee. Other writers who were either students or teachers at Princeton include F. Scott Fitzgerald, John O'Hara, Joyce Carol Oates, Philip Roth, John McPhee, Russell Banks, and former publisher Nelson Doubleday. Some other points of interest on the campus are the Princeton cemetery, with stones dating back to pre-Revolutionary times, and the **Firestone Library,** which has over three million books. If you want a

Albert Einstein, shown here with fellow genius Charlie Chaplin, lived at 112 Mercer Street in Princeton. Chaplin married Jersey girl Oona O'Neill, whose mother, Agnes Boulton, lived in the seaside town of Point Pleasant, New Jersey.

guided tour with an escort, this is also available by calling (609) 258-4820 for a reservation.

When you are finished with the walk on the grounds and are going into some of the buildings to examine their interiors, you may want to look at some of the shops in town. Antique stores, bookstores, university clothing shops, a Brooks Brothers, and gourmet shops are part of the fun of Princeton. The place to stay in town is the **Nassau Inn** on Palmer Square, just across the street from the main entrance to the campus. The inn, which originated in 1756, moved to its present location in 1937 and has 217 attractive rooms for overnight accommodations from $215 for a single to $235 for a double, not including special discount rates. If you are in the mood for a weekend, it is a gracious place in which to stay over. Call (609) 921-7500. The **Tap Room Restaurant** in the Inn serves breakfast, lunch, and dinner until 11 P.M., and inside there is a giant and spectacular mural painted in 1938 by Norman Rockwell of Yankee

Nobel prize–winning playwright Eugene O'Neill attended Princeton University and lived for a time in Point Pleasant with his wife Agnes Boulton, who wrote about their life together in New Jersey in a book entitled Part of a Long Story.

Doodle Dandy. The place to dine is **Ichiban** at 66 Witherspoon, (609) 683-8323, which is close to the Princeton Library. Graced by beautiful bamboo gardens, the restaurant serves traditional Japanese tempura noodles, sushi, and teriyaki, with entrees ranging from $10–27. Lunch specials are also offered. Hours are Monday to Thursday from 11:30 A.M. to 10 P.M., Friday and Saturday until 11 P.M. and Sunday 2:30 P.M. to 10 P.M.

A good inexpensive meal in Princeton can be had at **Mexican Village** at 42–44 Leigh Avenue, (609) 924-5143, where the food is truly Mexican, fresh, and well prepared. The delicious Mexican dishes served include *flautas* (a long, crispy tortilla shaped like a flute) with guacamole and stuffed with melted cheese, chicken or beef; burritos, tamales, tostadas, enchiladas, or tacos served with rice and refried beans, *chile relleno, carne a la tampiqueña, bistek a la Mexicana,* enchiladas *Jalisco* or *chalupas.* The hot Mexican salsa with warmed taco chips served at each table is prepared fresh daily. Also available is *salsa verde* and *salsa mole.* There is also a full range of vegetarian dishes and delicious margaritas and other drinks and Mexican beers. The motto here is: ¡*Comer bien es vivir bien!* (Translation: To eat well is to live well!)

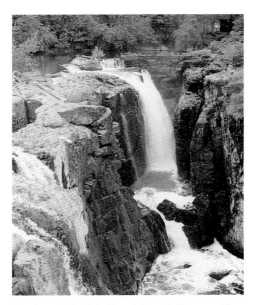

The Great Falls of the Passaic River in Paterson. Photo by "Hoop."

Illustrated map–printed linen-and-cotton kitchen towel; map tablecloths are prized pieces among collectors of Jerseyana.

The 131-foot Art Deco Edison Memorial Tower, with a massive, glowing fourteen-foot lightbulb at its top, casts a beam of light visible from highways and byways throughout the area. A small Edison Museum is located on the grounds of this unique place, atop a hill off Route 27 in Menlo Park.

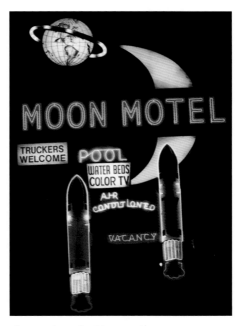

Spectacular rocketship neon sign—MOON MOTEL— beckons motorists on the Route 9 motel strip in Lakewood.

Fred's Diner, 188 Stuyvesant Avenue (corner of 18th Avenue), stood next to a gas station in the Vailsburg section of Newark. Proprietor Fred Steinke was also the cook and baked pies on the premises. This 1940s "memory image" snapshot is from the family scrapbook of Evelyn Heitke, who worked as a waitress at the diner.

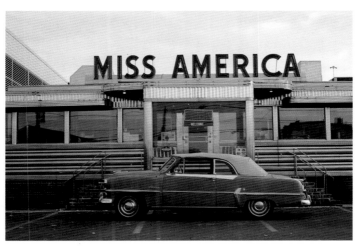

Classic 1954 pink Plymouth Belvedere convertible parked in front of the Miss America Diner, 322 West End Avenue, Jersey City. This stainless-steel streamliner was manufactured by the Jerry O'Mahoney Company in Elizabeth in the 1950s.

Stainless-steel, blue-enamel, and glass-block Truck Stop Diner on Hackensack Avenue and Scout Street, South Kearny. Owner Sam Kolokithas is always on the premises of this New Jersey-built Kullman diner.

The classic 1929 enamel-fronted Summit Diner, Summit Avenue and Union Place, Summit.

1941 Packard Hearse covered in faux or "fun" fur with applied mosaic pattern at Lambert Castle in the Garrett Mountain Reservation. Art Car owned by "Hoop."

Plaidmobile: Owner Timothy J. McNally in plaid pajamas atop his 1985 classic Buick Skyhawk Art Car. (Photo by Harrod Blank)

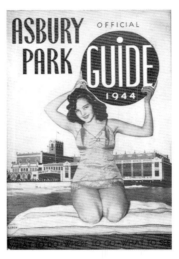

A 1944 Asbury Park seashore guide features attractive beauty contestant Bette Coe, posing in front of the Convention Hall and the Paramount Theater (both recently restored) at Asbury Park's Boardwalk.

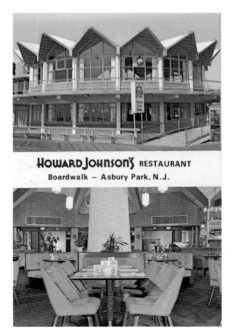

The round 1950s Howard Johnson's space-port-style restaurant with zigzag roof pictured in this souvenir postcard is on the boardwalk across from the Paramount Theater in Asbury Park. It is still serving fried clams, hamburgers, ice cream sodas, coffee, and cocktails—with an ocean view.

Curteich-Chicago, "C.T. Art Colortone" vintage linen postcard, showing beach girls on a portable merry-go-round at Manasquan.

Seaside Heights Casino Amusement Center at night. The boardwalk and the ocean amusement piers at Seaside boast sensational action rides, games of chance, bars, nightclubs, Berkeley's homemade candies, Johnson's caramel popcorn, Kohr's frozen custard, Marucca's Pizza, and more. Vintage Tichnor linen postcard.

*"Old Barney"—Barnegat Lighthouse—Long Beach
Island. Vintage Tichnor linen postcard.*

*This automobile window decal for Point Pleasant
Beach could also be used as a luggage sticker. This is
from the 1940s.*

Jersey Country

It's great fun and very relaxing to take drives into the countryside outside Princeton. In nearby **Hamilton Grounds for Sculpture** (18 Fairgrounds Road), at the former location of the New Jersey State Fair, is a beautifully landscaped sylvan setting for monumental and small scale works by renowned artists, including James Dinerstein and Yuyu Yang. J. Seward Johnson, Jr., an heir to the Johnson and Johnson pharmaceutical fortune and an accomplished and well-known sculptor himself, is the founder of **Grounds for Sculpture,** and the oddly named but highly praised **Rats Restaurant** which is on the grounds. The **Toad Hall Shop and Gallery** hosts photography and art exhibitions; there are artists' lecture series and photography workshops as well as poetry slams and musical concerts year round. Call (609) 586-0616 for further information or log onto www.groundsforsculpture.org. The following country towns can all be reached by major roads, but "back country" routes are recommended to give you an idea why New Jersey is called "the Garden State."

Hopewell is at the junction of Route 518 and route 569 (about midway between two major roads, Route 1 and Route 202). From Princeton take the Rosedale Road north to the Hopewell–Princeton Road (569) to Hopewell Borough. Hopewell, not to be confused with Stanhope, New Hope, or Hope, was the home of Charles Lindbergh in the 1930s. The famous Lindbergh baby kidnapping was perpetrated by Bruno Hauptmann in Hopewell, though he was tried and convicted in the neighboring county at Flemington. In October 1991 Anna Hauptmann returned to the Union Hotel on Main Street in Flemington for the first time since February 13, 1935, the day her husband was sentenced to death in the electric chair. "From the day he was arrested, he was framed, always framed," she said at a press conference where over 50 years later she still proclaimed his innocence. "It is my duty to fight for my husband as long as I live," she added. Interesting footnote: The lead investigator in the case was New Jersey State Police Superintendent H. Norman Schwarzkopf, father of the commander in the Persian Gulf war, General H. Norman Schwarzkopf. Today Hopewell is antique country, and is an excellent place for browsing and shopping for country antiques. Notable for antiquers is the **Hopewell Canning Company** (two blocks off Route 518), a restored factory building housing the **Tomato Factory Antique Center** with 35 shops on two floors, (609) 466-9833. Worth a stop in Hopewell is the **Hopewell Museum** at 28 East Broad Street, considered an excellent small museum, with collections of early costumes, china, and a Native American room containing Navajo handwoven rugs and baskets, as well as stone artifacts and tools made by local Lenape Indians.

Flemington (at the junction of Route 31 and Route 202, or take Route 569 to Route 514 from Hopewell) is another great old farming town and tourist attraction not far from Princeton. It is set on 105 acres and contains fine old Victorian homes. It is famous as a factory outlet town for such diverse items as designer jeans, active sportswear, shoes, lingerie, decorator fabrics, curtains, lamps, silver, bags, shoes, sneakers, and much more. There are hobby centers for toy-train enthusiasts, and doll collectors. New dishware sets from Royal Doulton, Corning glass, and Pfaltzgraff stoneware can be found at **Liberty Village,** a Colonial shopping center. Stangl pottery, Fulperware, and Flemington cut glassware was originally produced here, but is now found in antique shops, notably **Popkorn Antiques** at 4 Mine Street, (908) 782-9631, near Main. Bob and Nancy Perzel, who run Popkorn, have a huge selection of Stangl pottery as well as Fiesta ware and other popular pottery from past decades. They also carry advertising signs, cameras, and toys from the 1920s, 1930s, and 1940s. Bob is also at the nearby **Somerville Antiques Emporium** (see page 110). The **Flemington Cut Glass Company,** 156 Main Street, has a showroom of the most beautiful pieces produced over the years and presents free glass-cutting demonstrations. The showroom is open daily from 10 A.M. to 5:30 P.M. Call (908) 782-3017.

Other stores in downtown Flemington include the **Hunterdon Exchange** at 155 Main Street, offering handicrafts and antiques to benefit the Hunterdon Medical Center, and **The People's Book-**

Bob Perzel of Popkorn in Flemington holds up a rare 1939 New York World's Fair tapestry made in Belgium.

shop, which is at 160 Main St. in a big red barn. There are other antiques shops and emporiums as well as restaurants to explore on foot up and down Flemington's Main Street, and there is plenty of parking. To stay over and explore the country, stay at a bed and breakfast like **The Cabbage Rose Inn,** (908) 788-0247, or **Jerica Hill,** (908) 782-8234, or any number of motels and hotels in and out of town. You can fuel up for your shopping benders at **Jack's Pizzeria** at 55 Main Street, "where you're treated like one of the family," for Sicilian and gourmet pizza, lasagna, grilled hoagies, pasta dinners, and specialty Italian platters served up by Salvatore Mannino and family since 1972. Jack's delivers; call (908) 782-4266.

Particularly engaging and a fun adventure-ride is the 11-mile round-trip on the **Black River and Western Railroad** plying between the center of Flemington Township to Ringoes. You can take this farmland journey on a steam-locomotive train on Saturdays and Sundays and holidays, with trains departing every 1½ hours (between 10:45 A.M. and 4:45 P.M.) from mid-April to November 30. During the summer months of July and August a Tuesday–Friday schedule includes trains leaving every hour between 12:30 and 3:30 P.M. Call (908) 782-9600 or log onto www.brwrr.com. The 1870 **Union Hotel** at 76 Main Street in the downtown center of Flemington, just across the street from the county courthouse, has a restaurant serving traditional American food, a lounge, and many historic displays echoing the folklore of those Depression days when Lowell Thomas, Damon Runyon, Adela Rogers St. John, and Dorothy Kilgallen reported the sensational developments in the famous Hauptmann case. The hotel number is (908) 788-7474. Flemington is also the site of the New Jersey agricultural fair, a wonderful event to attend, which runs for 10 days toward the end of August every year.

Just a few miles east of Flemington is **Neshanic Station,** which holds a regular weekend farm, flea, and antiques market (take Route 567 or Pleasant Run Road at Centerville off Highway 202). The pleasant road meanders casually for three or four miles through a hilly farming and grazing valley along the scenic banks of the south branch of the Raritan River, which meets the Neshanic River at Neshanic Station. It's a lovely spot for a spontaneous alfresco swim or fishing under the old bridge and abandoned railroad trestle. The preserved train depot is now an ammunition and gun supply store, featuring the latest in hunting equipment. The market itself is always diverse, with vegetables, baked goods, and general country flea market merchandise with the occasional good antique dealer. This is a beautiful setting and interesting local characters make this stopoff worth a trip. Sunday is the best day in spring, summer, and fall; but go early as many start packing up by 3 P.M. The homes and the farmlands in this country area make for a nice Sunday drive.

Lambertville Day Trip

1. Lambertville House
2. Flea Market
3. Ferry House Tavern
4. The Old Barracks

To get to Lambertville: Enjoy the road and take a scenic drive in spring, summer, or fall on Highway 29 South from Frenchtown to Lambertville or drive from Trenton, the state capital, north on Route 29 to Lambertville. This highway parallels the Delaware River, and it is an enjoyable tour through many old villages along the route. This is also true along the Pennsylvania side where from Easton, Route 611 south turns into Route 32 at Kintnersville. Traveling along Route 32 you will find bridge river crossings from Uhlerstown, Pennsylvania, to Frenchtown, New Jersey, and New Hope, Pennsylvania, to Lambertville, New Jersey. Both roads are among the most beautiful drives to be found anywhere. From New Jersey there are many approaches to the Lambertville–New Hope area, including Highway 22 West out of Newark, which spurs off of Route 1-9. Route 22 leads into Route 202 West to Flemington; from there take Route 179 South into the town of Lambertville. You may also take the New Jersey Turnpike to Trenton and pick up Route 29 North into Lambertville. There is regular bus service into Lambertville and New Hope from the Port Authority Bus Terminal in Manhattan and from all points in Philadelphia.

Lambertville was settled in 1700 midway on the old road between New York and Philadelphia. It is a Victorian city located in a highly rural area, and the only official "city" in Hunterdon County. Listed on the National and State Registers of Historic Places, there are many charming inns and restaurants and a variety of unusual and inexpensive antique shops. Once in Lambertville, park the car and walk around for an architectural treat that includes Queen Anne, Gothic, Italianate, Victorian, Federal, Georgian, and 19th-century factory buildings. One of the buildings you should see is the **James Wilson Marshall House** at 60 Bridge Street. Built in 1810, this Federal-style house now incorporates a museum that shows photos and objects from Lambertville history. It is open from 1 to 4 P.M., Thursday to Saturday, April through October, (609) 397-0770. Another historical place to check out is the **Lambertville House,** built in 1812 at 32 Bridge Street, (609) 397-0200 or www.lambertvillehouse.com. This was a stagecoach inn for travelers of note like General Ulysses S. Grant and General Tom Thumb, the renowned midget who stayed there with his circus troupes in 1867. Lambertville was not only on the east-west stagecoach line and the Delaware River, but was also located on a feeder-canal leading to the Trenton–New Brunswick canal system (now the Delaware and Raritan Canal State Park). It was once a bustling mill town, which produced paper, flour, lumber, hairpins, spokes, iron, sausage, bricks, linen, rubber, and crackers. In the 1920s most of the city's mills went out of business or moved south to Trenton. The factories are still there, but they now house art galleries and crafts boutiques. The city is attracting a number of artists who are restoring the factories and interesting row houses, in addition to many antique dealers who have traditionally operated in this area. Chief among these is the **People's Store** (since 1859), (609) 397-9808, Lambertville's oldest and largest antiques center. At 28 Union Street (at Church), the building was once a dry goods and furniture store. Now housing antique and collectible dealers and several artists studios upstairs, and the fine **Left Bank Bookstore,** (609) 397-4966, People's Store is open every day from 10 A.M. to 6 P.M. **Phoenix Books** at 49 Union Street has floor-to-ceiling shelves filled with new, old, and rare antiquarian books. You can browse for hours in a homey atmosphere; and the shop is open every day from 11 A.M. to 5 P.M.; Friday through Sunday, until 6. **Seventh Heaven,** specializing in *deco-nouveau-moderne* "heavenly" artifacts, vases, mood lamps, and wall sconces, is operated by Richard Golden at 18 Church Street (weekends and by appointment, [609] 397-8419).

Lambertville has many good restaurants—and one of the largest is housed in the newly renovated **Lambertville Railroad Station.** This is an elegant Victorian-style restaurant with a dance floor and casual pub downstairs. Built in 1867, the 2½-story stone station house was the headquarters of the Belvedere Delaware Railroad,

Antique shop on Church Street in Lambertville.

serving local passengers traveling up and down the river. The rail line, called the **Black River and Western Railroad,** has a real steam-driven locomotive and now offers a 45-minute train ride for tourists and shoppers with stops at Flemington, Ringoes, and Lambertville; call (908) 782-9600. The **Inn at Lambertville Station,** a 45-room hotel behind the station and overlooking the Delaware River, offers antique-filled decor with cozy fireplaces and whirlpool baths. Special winter weekend rates make it an attractive destination for overnight guests; call (609) 397-4400 for both the inn and the restaurant. For a casual or cozy dinner in a rustic setting, walk or drive up to **Bells Tavern** at 183 North Union Street, which was established in 1938 and remains the way it was then. Great food for healthy appetites is prepared daily, including innovative pastas (from Paul R. Eschallier, the chef), fresh grilled fish and meats, and there is a big oval bar. Call (609) 397-2226 for lunch and dinner hours. This is in a quaint residential Victorian neighborhood and a walk before or after dinner is recommended.

An excellent place to stay in Lambertville for an authentic feel of the past is the **Bridgestreet House** at 75 Bridge Street. The house was built in two sections, the back part dating from 1790 and the front addition dating from 1860. There are four guest rooms on the second floor of the house, a two-room suite with a narrow swirling staircase that leads to the old attic, now a bedroom; and other special rooms—some with baths—named after former occupants of the house. For reservations and information, call innkeeper Donna Herman at (609) 397-2503.

For a walk to New Hope, Pennsylvania, across the bridge, you should leave the car in Lambertville. New Hope is filled with interesting boutiques, antique shops, bars, ice cream parlors, bookstores, cheese shops, and restaurants and inns. The famous **Bucks County Playhouse,** the state theater of Pennsylvania, is also in New Hope, with spring, summer, and fall productions of professional Broadway musicals like *Annie, South Pacific,* and *Hello, Dolly.* Call (215) 862-2041 for tickets. New Hope is a touristy town, but it is a colorful place to explore. It is more populated than Lambertville, and is kind of like New York's Greenwich Village, with its population of swinging singles and gays all mixed up with stretch-pants-suited older couples. In fact, Lambertville and New

Hope have somewhat of a kinship with Provincetown, Massachusetts, in the sense of its oddball yet interesting population mix, including its fair share of resident artists, ex-hippies, and bike-boys.
Places to eat in New Hope include **Mother's Restaurant** at 34
North Main Street, which has a bakery attached selling sinfully
delicious cookies and cakes. For a quick food fix there is an excellent Mexican eatery/take-out place with tables called **El Taco
Loco,** 6 Stockton Avenue, next to the railroad tracks up the hill in
New Hope. Under $5.00, open until 8 P.M. on weekdays, week-
ends until 10, (215) 862-0908. This is not like the fine organized
sit-down dinners served along the river in Lambertville, but it is a
great snack place as you walk and shop in the hilly little river town
of New Hope. Don't miss **Gerenser's Exotic Ice Cream** at 22
South Main Street. Family-owned since 1947, they serve over 50
homemade flavors, including French Pink Champagne, Hungar-
ian Tokay, India Mango, Oriental Green Tea, Spicy Caribbean
Tree Bark, and Sunflower Seed and Honey Ecstasy. To get a view
from the water, book a one-half-hour tour of the Delaware River
on **Coryell's Ferry Historic Boat Rides** at Gerenser's at (215) 862-
2050 or www.spiritof76.biz.

Lambertville Antiques

Washington Crossing

New Jersey is antique country, whether north, south, east, or west, and you are sure to find what you want somewhere amongst all the flea markets, antique shops and centers, special antique shows, roadside sales, and country auctions. If you haven't found it, you haven't tried hard enough. A good place to start looking is in the **Golden Nugget Antiques Flea Market,** open every Wednesday, Saturday, and Sunday all year long. This is one of the oldest antique markets in the New Hope/Lambertville area and is considered one of the major antique centers in the country. Located about three miles south of Lambertville on Route 29, this market and the market at Lahaska (five miles southwest of New Hope) have long been favorites of New York and Philadelphia antiques dealers. Many who are in search of antiques and collectibles at the huge Lambertville market get up at the crack of dawn; but you can drop by any time up until 4 P.M., when the many dealers begin to pack away their wares. Sunday seems to attract the most dealers, and you will find among them many rural folk who are still emptying out the treasures from that proverbial grandma's attic of yore. There are inside shops and an enclosed, roofed rotunda for rainy days. The market has two pleasant refreshment stands with sit-down tables to rest the weary feet, where you can enjoy hot dogs, crullers, and other American foods with coffee or cider. The market is set just across the way from the Delaware River; and if you get tired of looking at or buying goods, you can cross the road and take a walk in the green.

The area of Lambertville and New Hope is rich with open-air markets and highly individualized antique shops, craft shops, art galleries, bookstores, and shops devoted to singular pursuits like old magazines and newspapers or fine frocks from yesteryear. You can easily spend a day or weekend here without covering the territory. Surely it will be a time well spent. A fascinating place to stay, even though it is not in New Jersey, is the **Black Bass Hotel** on Route 32 in Lumberville, Pennsylvania, seven miles north of New Hope on the Delaware River. This establishment, reminiscent of an English pub and Colonial tavern was, as a matter of record, loyal to the Crown during the Revolution and would not let George Washington in for the night. There is a veritable museum here of British royal family memorabilia, the dining rooms have wood-burning fireplaces, and the tables are made out of old-fashioned tavern planks. The food is very good; there is a good wine list, and the service is excellent. There are seven rooms with shared baths ($65 weeknights, $80 weekends) and two suites ($125–$150, $25 additional weekends). Call (215) 297-5770 for the restaurant or (215) 297-5815 for rooms, or visit www.blackbasshotel.com for daily menus and more info.

One of the best restaurants on the Delaware, and one of former New Jersey Senator Bill Bradley's favorite places, is the **Frenchtown Inn,** 7 Bridge Street, Frenchtown; (908) 996-3300. This old family-run country inn features a New Jersey tomato filled with shrimp for starters in their famous prix-fixe Saturday night dinner, which might feature rack of lamb and a flageolet bean ragout with garlic sausage; the whole thing finished off with a complimentary chocolate truffle with your coffee.

Washington Crossing State Park at Washington Crossing, New Jersey, (609) 737-0623, is the site where in the winter of 1776 General George Washington and his 2,400 troops crossed the Delaware into New Jersey and raided the Hessian garrison at Trenton. This historic park features the **Ferry House Tavern** where Washington conferred with the locals, a unique and beautiful outdoor open-air theater, seating 1,000 spectators, where they have summer musical and theatrical events, (609) 737-1826, plus nature trails, fishing, and camping, all situated on the banks of a broad and beautiful section of the Delaware River. Picnic tables and fireplaces for cookouts or barbecues are provided here. The park is just south of Lambertville on Route 29. The park's visitor center and museum, (609) 737-9303, was established to commemorate the U.S. Bicentennial Celebration in 1976. Its main theme is the interpretation of the "Ten Crucial Days"—December 25, 1776 through January 3, 1777—during which the Continental Army crossed the Delaware and achieved its first major victories against the British at the Battles of Trenton and Princeton. Washington Crossing State Park extends into the Pennsylvania side of the river, and you can cross over from Route 29 in New Jersey to Route 32 in Pennsylvania. Both towns at this point of the bridge crossing, in Pennsylvania and New Jersey, are called Washington Crossing.

George Washington crosses the Delaware.

Trenton

Over the Trenton-Morrisville Bridge, which crosses the Delaware River from New Jersey to Pennsylvania (and vice versa) there are the words, in giant letters: TRENTON MAKES THE WORLD TAKES. Famous for industry and manufacturing, the legend of Trenton has been enhanced by some of the very finest chinas made by Walter Scott Lenox or the Trent Tile Company, manufacturers of fancy mosaic and bathroom-kitchen tiles, or the New Jersey School Furniture Company, established by L. H. McKee & Company, or the American Steel and Wire Company, or the John A. Roebling Wire Rope Company, which produced the rope used on suspension bridges like the Brooklyn Bridge, the Niagara Bridge, and the Golden Gate Bridge.

Trenton, also famous as the New Jersey state capital, was once thought of in 1784 as the spot that might make a good permanent capital for the United States. Rich in history, Trenton is the place where George Washington attacked the Hessian troops, taking them by surprise on the snowy Christmas night of 1776. Some of the Hessians were fast asleep while others, having drunk too much from their wassail cups, were too ossified to know what was happening that historical night. At Christmastime, citizens of Tren-

Washington victorious at the Battle of Trenton.

ton, in Revolutionary attire, enact the entire battle of Trenton, from Washington's crossing of the Delaware to the siege of the garrison.

The **Trenton City Museum** in Caldwalader Park (designed by Frederick Law Olmstead) on Parkside Avenue is something you will want to see. The museum is a restored 1850 mansion called Ellarslie, designed by John Notman; and it is listed in the National Register. There are picnic grounds, concert bandstands, cherry trees surrounding a duck pond, and "swamp angel," which is a Civil War cannon. The **New Jersey State Library** is at 185 State Street. Call (609) 292-6220 for tours or special programs or write to the Bureau of Archives and History, New Jersey State Library, P.O. Box 1898, Trenton, NJ 08625. The **New Jersey State Museum** at 205 West State Street offers special exhibits in decorative and fine arts, natural science, history, government, archeology, and astronomy, weekdays from 9 A.M. to 5 P.M., weekends from 1 to 5 P.M. For more information on tours and special exhibits, call (609) 292-6464. A beautifully restored 18th-century house once owned by Isaac Watson has a parlor, dining room, kitchen, and bedroom complete with the original furnishings, lamps, and period objects. The **Watson House** is at 151 Westcott Avenue. Call (609) 888-2062 for a reservation and a free tour. The two-story Queen Ann–style brick **William Trent House** is at 15 Market Street. The handsome house with Colonial furniture and attractive gardens was built in 1719 by William Trent. Trent devised the plan for the region he named "Trent's Town"—later becoming Trenton. Call (609) 989-3027 for information.

The **Old Barracks Museum** on Barrack Street, built between 1758 and 1760, housed the Hessians, German mecenaries who fought for the British. The two-story stone barracks contains firearms, Colonial furniture, and period china and silverware. These barracks are regarded as a fine example of Colonial archi-

New Jersey State Capitol building, Trenton.

tecture and are rich in history. Call (609) 396-1776 for information. Nearby is the **War Memorial Building,** at Barrack and Lafayette Streets, which recently underwent a complete restoration to its Italian Renaissance–revival and Art Deco luster. In the lobby of the **First Trenton National Bank** at One West State Street (now it's a Wachovia Bank) is an immense mural painted by N.C. Wyeth of George Washington's reception at Trenton on his 1789 inaugural journey to New York. The bank building was built in 1930 with a Venetian ceiling. Magnificent Art Deco murals created in the 1940s depicting modern interpretations of mythological stories can be found at the **Town House Restaurant** at 39 West State Street.

If you want to view this general region, where Washington and his troops camped out and did battle, you should visit the **Trenton Battle Monument,** built to honor the Battle of Trenton. To view the capital city and its surroundings you can use an elevator to the top of the 150-foot observatory. Call (609) 737-0623 for information.

Trenton proper, other than its grand array of impressive governmental and administrative buildings, some old, some new, has, like many capital cities, many middle-class neighborhoods, as well as some that are just plain poverty-ridden slums. Chambersburg, the Little Italy of Trenton, is worth a tour for its Italian restaurants. For food, try **De Lorenzo's Pizza** at 1007 Hamilton Avenue, (609) 393-2952, and **De Lorenzo's Tomato Pies** at 530 Hudson Street, (609) 695-9534. Both are family-owned (since 1947) award-winning pizza parlors serving Trenton-style pizza and Italian specialties from the town of Biselli, in the heart of Umbria, like bruschetta with sausage and wild mushroom or a Neapolitan ragu. For a fancier sit-down meal, try **Biselli da Baldassari,** at 145 Morris Avenue and the corner of Division Street, (609) 392-2934.

• •

The Campbell's Soup can was famous long before Andy Warhol began painting it, marketing great numbers of them over the years as subjects for his pop art paintings. Warhol, who was originally a highly paid advertising artist, ostensibly painted Nunn-Busch shoes for the ads. He once said that he hated painting the ubiquitous bowl of fruit every art student was required to copy in art school. In his memory bank he most remembered the image of a can of Campbell's tomato soup (his favorite) from his mother's pantry. When he was little Andy Warhola living in Pennsylvania during the Great Depression, this held more significance for him than the bowl of dime-store wax fruit on the family dining room table.

The Campbell's Soup Company was begun when Joseph Campbell, a fruit merchant, and Abram Anderson, an icebox manufacturer, became partners to can Jersey tomatoes, vegetables, mincemeat, jellies, and condiments. Their first plant opened in Camden in 1869. Anderson left the partnership in 1876. Arthur Dorance and Joseph Campbell then formed a new company called the Joseph Campbell Preserve Company. In 1897 the concept of canned, condensed soup was originated; and in 1898 the first red-and-white label (from Cornell football colors) was introduced.

Joseph died in 1900 and the Dorance family took over. This same year Campbell's soups won a gold medallion for excellence at the Paris Exposition, and this medallion has been featured on

Three booklets from The Optimist, *which was published monthly by the Campbell Soup Company in Camden. Left to right: A Campbell's Kid in the kitchen tasting (what else?) a hearty Campbell's soup, March 1932; back cover showing the famous Campbell's tomato soup can which always used Jersey red-ripe tomatoes in its recipes, August 1926; back cover with the two Campbell's Kids saying their prayers in thanks for the bowls of piping-hot tomato soup in front of them, March 1930.*

the soup can label ever since. In 1905 Campbell's introduced its famous pork and beans, competing with the Heinz company.

Also in 1905, Grace Gebbie Drayton created the wonderful Campbell Kid trademark characters. These kids, who somewhat resembled the cherubic kewpies of Rose O'Neill, are among the first early advertising cartoon characters (others were Buster Brown and the Yellow Kid) to win wide appeal with magazine readers and consumers. Over the years many premiums and special "Campbell Kids" products such as recipe booklets, school tablets, dolls, spoons, salt-and-pepper shakers, and the like have been produced; these are highly prized as advertising collectibles in today's nostalgia marketplace. Ads with the kids usually contained some kind of poem that might link up a child going back to school in the fall while mother prepared a hot bowl of Campbell's chicken noodle soup to be served at suppertime. The idea was that children—and the rest of the American family, too—wanted a bowl of Campbell's soup all year long.

Families passed on the tradition of Campbell's soup from generation to generation; and immigrants coming to America used Campbell's products as they became associated with Americanism. An ad in *Good Housekeeping* magazine in 1905 declared: "21 kinds of Campbell's Soup—16 million cans sold in 1904." By 1911 Campbell's entered the California market and achieved national distribution. In 1915 Franco-American spaghetti with tomato sauce in a can was added to the line. In 1922 the company officially adopted the name Campbell's Soup Company; and by 1929, the year of the Crash, a second major soup plant opened in Chicago. The idea of a can of Campbell's Soup in mom's kitchen actually gained momentum in the 1930s during the Great Depression with Campbell's advertising on radio shows like "Amos 'n' Andy." In 1932, Campbell's tomato juice was introduced, and in 1934 cream of mushroom appeared. During the Depression, a can of mushroom soup with a can of tuna fish and with elbow macaroni was a favorite recipe for a cheap meal during hard times throughout America. Another Depression dinner staple was Campbell's baked beans served with frankfurters.

By 1942 sales topped the $100 million mark; and by 1947 a third plant opened in Sacramento, California. V-8 vegetable juice cocktail was added to the company product line in 1948. By 1955 Campbell's entered the frozen food market by acquiring C. A. Swanson & Sons, who originated the TV dinner. Some social critics of the time regarded the TV dinner as marking the beginning of a decline in food ethics for the American family. During the 1950s and 1960s, with sales of over $500 million, Campbell's plants opened everywhere—in England, Australia, France, and Mexico. Pepperidge Farms, Inc., also became an affiliate of the company. In 1970 Campbell's introduced their line of "chunky, ready-to-serve" canned soups and also added pet foods to supermarket shelves. Also in 1970 the Campbell's World Headquarters opened in Camden, New Jersey, which is the place that will forever be known as the home of Campbell's Soup. By 1979 sales topped $2 billion, and in 1981 Campbell's was chosen "food processor of the year." One can see how this company became a symbol of the American dream.

Next time you reach for a can of Campbell's soup on the grocery store shelf, remember it all started in the Garden State and probably was inspired by the Jersey tomato, the reddest, ripest, juiciest, and most delicious of all. A famous French chef once listed the "secret" ingredients of his special French "soupe" as:

1 can of Campbell's cream of mushroom condensed soup
1 can of Campbell's tomato soup
2 soup cans of light cream
2 tablespoons sherry
½ teaspoon melted butter

Heat and garnish with parsley and *Voilà!* You have *ze soupe Supreme de Paree!* On a *Nightline* television news "special report," Ted Koppel interviewed Robert Rauschenberg. The artist stated on the show that he had happily just sold his Andy Warhol soup can oil painting for a million dollars. Art, industry, commerce, television, and the Campbell's soup can managed to become one and the same.

Though the original Campbell's Soup plant, a mammoth relic of the industrial age on the Delaware River in Camden, was blown up in 1991, Campbell's Soup world headquarters, located in an L-shaped quadrangle known as Campbell Place, will continue on in downtown Camden as it has since 1876. The soups and other products manufactured by Campbell are now being processed in huge factories in Napoleon, Ohio, and Paris, Texas, and several other locations, in factories so huge that they accommodate the entrance of freight trains. The **Campbell's World Headquarters** on Campbell Place, (856) 342-4800, features an extensive collection of European soup tureens in ceramic, china,

The original Campbell's Soup Company plant in Camden.

and silver, and exhibitions travel all over the world, wherever Campbell's soup is sold. There is also a "pop" exhibition in the lobby with vintage storefront signs, advertising merchandise, and premiums from Campbell products. Hours are Monday to Friday, 9 A.M. to 4:30 P.M.; closed holidays. The admission is free.

> "Camden was originally an accident, but I shall never be sorry I was left over in Camden. It has brought me blessed returns."
> —Walt Whitman.

The **Walt Whitman House** on 328 Mickle Boulevard is the house where the poet who wrote *Leaves of Grass* lived. Three of the rooms are furnished with his belongings. There is also a library of Whitman's writings including his manuscripts and original photos. Hours are Wednesday to Saturday 10 to noon and 1 to 4 P.M., Sunday 1 to 4 P.M. only. The admission is free. Tour groups may call (856) 964-5383 to schedule an appointment.

Camden has a number of **White Tower** hamburger chain restaurants. These white, tiny castlelike structures serve tasty hamburgers, eggs, and coffee and, of course, you can get your choice of Campbell's soups right out of the can at any one of these establishments—served hot.

Camden, practically an adjunct to Philadelphia, somewhat akin to Queens or Staten Island to Manhattan, has a recently built aquarium and is hoping to attract crowds from the teeming metropolis just across the Delaware. **Adventure Aquarium,** which was a lead project in Camden's attempted revitalization, is built on an acre right on the waterfront on the site of a ferry terminal that closed more than 40 years ago. Ferry service between Penn's Landing in Philadelphia to the Aquarium was reinstituted to coincide with the opening in spring of 1992. A visit here is an ideal family expedition; there are 60 species of fish native to New Jersey, including striped bass, and the Aquarium features the second largest open ocean tank in the United States (EPCOT Center in Florida has the largest). So, pile the kids in the car and head for Camden; road signs point the way. It's open 9:30 A.M. to 5 P.M. Admission for adults is $16.95, less for seniors, students, and younger children. Call (856) 365-3300 or toll-free (800) 616-5297, or visit www.adventureaquarium.com.

*Burlington, Bordentown, Mount Holly, Timbuctoo,
Clementon, Swedesboro, Mullica Hill, Glassboro, Salem,
Bridgeton, and Vineland*

Four New Jersey counties—Burlington, Gloucester, Salem, and Cumberland—comprise the "garden spot" of the Garden State. One-third of all New Jersey's farms, which produce 70 percent of all New Jersey vegetables including sweet and processing corn, cabbage, lettuce, summer potatoes, eggplant, peppers, squash, and soybeans, 75 percent of all Jersey tomatoes (New Jersey is fourth nationally in the production of fresh market and processing tomatoes), and 95 percent of New Jersey's asparagus, are located here. South Jersey is second in the country in blueberry production, a bumper crop reaching as high as 30 million pounds; and cranberry production in this area (third-ranking producer in the United States) often exceeds 250,000 barrels annually. The whole adds up to more than $500 million a year of produce trucked

"Defy the World" brand choice Jersey tomatoes were packed into the can in Salem.

from Garden State farms, predominantly from southwestern New Jersey.

Of the tomatoes grown in the flat terrain and sandy soil of South Jersey 86 percent of them end up in processing plants run by canneries such as Campbell's, Progresso, Heinz, and Hunt. The rest, called fresh-market tomatoes, are sold to vegetable brokers at produce auctions held in Vineland and Swedesboro, in the heart of this rich farm country. The big business farmers offer a tomato plucked from the vine while still green, with thick skin and dense walls, a tomato able to withstand sorting, packing, refrigeration, repacking, shipping, and which ideally turns red by the time it reaches the supermarket shelf. Unfortunately, the flavor of these tomatoes leaves a great deal to be desired. In fact, it is missing. The reddening process of a tomato is accomplished by a natural plant hormone, which as it grows red on the vine, develops a corresponding taste in the ripe tomato. Developments in the automation of "rush-to-market" farming practices include a chemical called *Ethrel* that enables farmers to spray "mature-green" tomatoes in the field, causing the entire crop to redden at once. Unfortunately again, this practice does not help the taste of a tomato.

The only thing to do, of course, is to go to one of the 500 or more roadside stands where summer tomatoes are generally grown in the immediate area. These tomatoes are allowed to mature and ripen on the vine, and are picked daily. Many roadside stand operators are members of New Jersey Certified Farm Markets, a volunteer organization that has developed guidelines for quality produce, courtesy, and honest packaging and merchandising, i.e., what you see at the top of a bushel should be what you get at the bottom also. You may be lucky enough to score a few pounds of the rare and glorious low-acid yellow Jersey tomato, known far and wide by true connoisseurs of the Jersey tomato to be the most savory of them all.

Burlington, about 18 miles south of Camden on Route 130 up the Delaware, was once the busiest port in America and served for a while as the capital of West Jersey during the early Colonial days. The town is filled with historic structures including the **James Fenimore Cooper House** (at 457 High Street), where the first of America's great novelists was born (and lived for a year) in 1789 and the **Captain James Lawrence House** (right next door at 459 High Street), birthplace in 1781 of the hero of the War of 1812 who yelled, "Don't give up the ship!," a statement that later became the slogan of the United States Navy. Also on High Street is the **Bard-How House,** an unusually large, for the period, and beautifully proportioned frame house built in 1705 and enlarged in 1725, furnished with early 18th-century antiques. The number to call for information about touring all of these historic houses owned by the Burlington County Historical Society, which also has a museum and library, is (609) 386-4773.

Burlington contains many more Colonial structures still in use, such as **Burlington Pharmacy** at High and Union Streets, built in 1731, in the historical district located on West Delaware, Wood, and Broad Streets. Call (609) 386-0141 for information. The town is also home to many discount factory-outlet shopping centers like those in Secaucus and Flemington, for untaxed, name-brand clothing, and furniture bargain shopping.

Bordentown, 10 miles north of Burlington and just south of Trenton on Route 130, was a prosperous village settled in the late 1600s. It was, among other famous historical personages, the home of Benjamin Franklin, Clara Barton, and Joseph Bonaparte, brother of Napoleon, who had a 1,500-acre estate at Point Breeze. Along Farnsworth Avenue, Colonial, Georgian, Federal, and Victorian architectural styles offer a fantastic sweeping glance at changing American tastes in the 18th and 19th centuries. The Bordentown historic district includes the **Clara Barton School** (she moved on to other pastures to found the Red Cross after the town fathers insisted she have a male superintendent), **Bonaparte Park Garden House,** the **Friends Meeting House** (headquarters of the Bordentown Historic Society, **Hoagland's Tavern,** the **Thomas Paine House,** and many others.

Mount Holly, on Route 541 (exit 5 from the New Jersey Turnpike—also off Routes 38, 206, and 537) is a classic example of an early American settlement with charming pre-Revolutionary houses and buildings. You can tour the houses or even the **Burlington County Prison Museum** at 128 High Street, (609) 265-5476, which is an old stone prison used between 1810 and 1965, containing memorabilia from prison life, a haunted dungeon, Indian artifacts, and a lovely prison garden. Two miles west of Mount Holly is the Greek-revival **Smithville Mansion** (1830), and **Smithville Village,** a ruined early industrial complex with workers' homes on the site of the factory where the high-wheeled Star bicycles were manufactured. This Smithville should not be confused with the Smithville on the Jersey shore. Call (609) 265-5068 for further information.

Mount Holly is a beautiful area, and **Rancocas State Park,** nearby in Mount Laurel Township (off Route 537, just north of Masonville), is an ideal place for nature study with excellent boating on Rancocas Creek. Even though it is not a designated historic town and has no notable historic structures or sites, it is recommended that you visit the small town of Timbuctoo also, just so you can tell your friends that's where you went over the weekend; it's two miles east of Mount Holly.

Clementon Amusement Park is located on the scenic Clementon Lake, 15 miles southeast of Camden near Berlin on Route 534 in Clementon, and is open from noon to 10 P.M. from Memorial Day through Labor Day; the water park closes at 8 P.M. One of New Jersey's oldest amusement parks, it features 25 adult rides, 8 children's rides, and the biggest "log swim" in the country, called "King Neptune's Revenge," which carries riders in loglike boats over a section of the lake and down a water-filled chute, splashing them as they go. The Tsunami is the new wooden roller-coaster, and there is also a fine old carousel with hand-carved wooden horses. Call (856) 783-0263 for current admission charges. For dining in Clementon try **Baron's Steak House** on the White Horse Pike, (856) 783-3300, a huge restaurant with a 1950s atmosphere and special Wednesday night buffets that include lobster Newburgh and turkey mousse. They're open until midnight.

Swedesboro, a historic town south of Camden (take exit 2 off the New Jersey Turnpike onto 322 West, left on Route 551) is the center of what was to have been New Sweden back in 1703. Settled by Swedish colonists around 1620, New Sweden never came to pass because the attractive Swedish girls intermarried quickly with English gentlemen. There are still many Swedish reminders here, however, and King Olaf of Sweden visited the region in 1976 during Bicentennial festivities to pay homage to his ancestors. The **Community Episcopal Trinity Church,** "Old Swedes Church," was built in 1784 and is located on King's Highway. It is open every Sunday morning or by appointment. Call (856) 467-1227. The Gloucester County Historical Society maintains the old **Moravian Church** in Swedesboro, also on King's Highway, which was built by members of the Moravian sect in 1786.

Mullica Hill (about eight miles east of Swedesboro and eight miles west of Glassboro) on Route 45 is the center of antiques country for southwestern New Jersey. Antique hunters from all over the state, Pennsylvania, Delaware, and Maryland converge on the dozens of specialty shops lining both sides of the main street on Route 45. The shops are situated in the town's historic old grist mill, an abandoned produce warehouse and other historic stone buildings, and offer 18th- and 19th-century furniture, dolls, books, glass, Victorian lace, Persian rugs, Christmas specialty antiques, arts, crafts, reproductions, and other Colonial-type antiques. At one end of town there is a brick Quaker meeting house built in 1808, and at the other end the **Raccoon** (the original name of Swedesboro until 1750) **Valley General Store,** where you can buy nostalgic penny candies.

Just east of Mullica Hill is the city of Glassboro and home of **Rowan University**. The second glassworks in America was established in 1775 and most "South Jersey-style" glassmaking techniques were developed here, including log-cabin-shaped bottles made for the 1840 presidential campaign, called "Booz bottles," named after the Philadelphia distiller who filled them. The glass-works in Glassboro are gone now, though Owens Illinois, the Kimble Glass Company, and Anchor Hocking continue to manu-facture glass in South Jersey, and many early bottles can be viewed at the **Rowan University Library.** The town achieved some noto-riety in 1967 when Premier Kosygin met President Lyndon John-son there for a meeting that was determined to be halfway between Washington and New York (where Kosygin was staying). It was widely reported that Kosygin and his automobile-limousine entourage drove 35 miles per hour down the New Jersey Turnpike in many places in order to view the "beautiful industrial develop-ment." Mrs. Kosygin went off with Lady Bird by helicopter to the Governor's House at Island Beach State Park for tea and sand-wiches. Back in Glassboro, Kosygin and Johnson had their meet-ing surrounded by vast tomato fields and peach orchards where the famous South Jersey peaches were ripening to succulent and juicy fruition.

Salem, 10 miles south of the Delaware Memorial Bridge on Route 49 (exit 1 off the New Jersey Turnpike) is a town directly related to Wilmington, Delaware. At the turn of the century E. I. DuPont bought vast acres of land in the area where they produced gun pow-der and later dyes and other chemicals. In the late 1700s the land around Salem, overcultivated by Swedish, Dutch, and English colonist-farmers, became barren, which spurred a great migration west where nostalgic settlers renamed towns in Ohio, Indiana, Iowa, and finally Oregon after the original Salem in New Jersey. Salem prospered, however, after the discovery of marl (a rich fer-tilizer) around 1820. There are 150 old pre-Revolutionary brick and stone houses in the area, and a good place for starting a tour is the **Salem County Historical Society** at 79, 81, and 83 Market Street (there are 60 historic buildings on Market Street alone), which maintains many restored houses and displays in period rooms, historic Indian relics, rare glass, china, furniture, and farm implements. Call (856) 935-5004 for information. Salem's famous landmark is the **Salem Oak** in the Friends Burial Ground on West Broadway, a tree estimated to be 500 years old and 30 feet in cir-cumference. Acorns from this tree are in demand all over the world. Seven miles from Salem and five miles from the New Jer-sey Turnpike on Route 49 is Finns Point, an area on the Delaware in which the 124-acre **Fort Mott State Park** is located. It is also home to **Finns Point National Cemetery,** where 2,436 Confed-erate and 300 Union soldiers are buried. These were prisoners who died during the Civil War at Fort Delaware. There was never a battle at Fort Mott—in fact, its armament was removed and the fort was decommissioned in 1947—when the State of New Jersey acquired it, without ever having fired a shot in anger. Here you can spend the day fishing, picnicking, and gazing up and down the wide expanse of the Delaware. The **Killcohook National Wildlife Refuge** is also located here. The historic **Hancock House,** a state historical museum south of Salem at Hancock's Bridge, was the scene of a massacre of 90 sleeping revolutionists by the vicious Tories.

Route 49 takes you farther southeast (16 miles) to Bridgeton, an old glass manufacturing town and home of the **Nail House Museum** on West Commerce Street, (856) 455-4100. The museum features an excellent collection of glass, early nails, iron banks, and antique toys. The **Woodruff Indian Museum** at 150 East Commerce Street, (856) 451-2620, has over 20,000 artifacts relating to the Lenni Lenape Indians. The old **Broad Street Church,** built by the Presbyterians in 1792, is a landmark; so is **Potter's Tavern,** on Broad Street opposite the courthouse, which is an authentically re-stored 200-year-old tavern. Eight miles toward the Delaware, on the Cohansey River, is historic Greenwich, Cumberland County's oldest community and the site of a famous incident in 1774 wherein a group of young men, disguised as Indians, stole the tea a British merchant was trying to smuggle into the country, and burned it in a public bonfire in the center of town as a gesture against unjust taxation. The town, beautifully laid out, has many old houses carefully restored and researched by the county histori-cal society. Call (856) 451-2310 for a Greenwich walking tour. **Ye Olde Centerton Inn,** (856) 358-3201, a Colonial stagecoach stop at the junction of Route 540 and Route 553 midway between Bridgeton and Greenwich, built in 1706, is still in operation and is a fine historic place for a traditional American "mixed entree" from seafood on up. The basic entree is $16.95 with salad and vegetable. Hours: closed Monday; Tuesday through Thursday 5 P.M. to 10 P.M.; Friday and Saturday 5 P.M. to 11 P.M., Sunday 2 P.M. to 9 P.M.

Vineland, the largest city in area in New Jersey (69 square miles, population 53,200) was created in 1861 by John K. Landis, who bought 32,000 acres of swamp and sandy pinelands. His town, in the heart of South Jersey's farmland, is a mile square, surrounded with agricultural acres. All the streets in the central area are at right angles; the principal streets 100 feet wide, the secondary streets 60 feet wide. John Landis sold land in 5- and 20-acre plots, and required that the new owners set their houses back 25 feet in the city center, and 75 feet in the country acres. He also required that property owners plant trees and grass on the streets in front of their own property. The **Vineland Historical Society** at 108 South Seventh Street has exhibits about Landis and his fascinating town, including furnished period rooms, local memorabilia, and Indian relics. Vineland was the town where a dentist named T. B. Welch, a fierce teetotaler, developed a means whereby grapes could be made into juice without fermentation, thereby establishing the famous Welch Grape Juice empire. Another man from Vineland, John L. Mason, invented the famous Mason jar. Vineland is the poultry center of the East and is known as "the egg basket of the nation," with the largest egg cooperative in the world. Just west of Vineland is **Seabrook Farms,** which is one of the largest agricultural farms in the world, with over 60,000 acres.

◆

"Take Me Back To My Boots and Saddle"
at Cowtown, New Jersey

Cowtown Rodeo is a professional "ride 'em cowboy" authentic rodeo in the true tradition of the Old West. You don't have to travel as far as Oklahoma, Montana, or Colorado to see exciting bareback bronc riding, calf roping, saddle bronc riding, steer wrestling, Brahma bull riding, team roping, or enjoy the thrill of seeing hearty cowgirls barrel riding against the clock in the breathless barrel race. It is all happening here in beautiful Salem County at Woodstown—about 15 miles west of Vineland in the southwestern area of New Jersey called "the cow capital of the first frontier," referred to by regulars simply as "Cowtown." This arena features the best performing cowboys and cowgirls from across the country each Saturday night at 7:30 P.M. from Memorial Day to Labor Day. Tickets to the show are $12 for adults, $6 for children, kids under two free. There are special group rates for parties over 25. There is room for 4,000 in the stadium. This rodeo has been run by the Harris family since 1929, only interrupting its rodeo activities during the World War II period. The current owner-producer

Robert Heide (left) and John Gilman (right) in cowboy attire at Woodstown's famous Cowtown Rodeo, with a rodeo champion from Dodge City whose actual name is "Bronc Buster."

is Grant Harris, who himself is a champion rodeo cowboy performer with national prizes in the saddle bronc category. Cowtown raises its bucking horses and most of its bulls as well. At Cowtown on Tuesday and Saturdays from 8 A.M. to 4 P.M. there is a farmer's/flea market with over 500 merchants selling everything from prize Jersey tomatoes to sweet white "silver queen" Jersey corn. On Tuesdays a livestock market is included. The word at Cowtown is "you name it, we sell it." Put on your cowboy boots, jeans, snapbutton western shirt, and ten-gallon hat; join in the fun. Bring along the whole family or a gang of friends. Parking is free, and there are refreshment stands. Call (856) 769-3200 for information. Cowtown is affiliated with the Professional Rodeo Cowboys Association and the Cowgirls Rodeo Association. Write: Cowtown Rodeo, 780 Route 40, Pilesgrove, NJ 08098, to receive a rodeo brochure with pictures of real cowboys in action—in color.

To get to Cowtown Rodeo the New Jersey Turnpike to exit 2 to Swedesboro. The rodeo is located on Route 40, eight miles east of the Delaware Memorial Bridge and two miles west of the township of Woodstown itself. Take Route 40 West if you are coming from Vineland. If traveling south on Route 295 take exit 4 (the Woodstown exit) and follow the road signs pointing to Woodstown. The rodeo is about six miles down the road on the right side of the highway. If traveling from Delaware, cross the Delaware Bridge and follow signs for Route 40 East to Atlantic City. From this point the Cowtown Rodeo is eight miles down the road on Route 40 on the right side.

1. Clinton Historical Museum
2. Auto Graveyard
3. Hot Dog Johnny's
4. Delaware Water Gap National Park

The **Delaware Water Gap National Recreation Area** is a 70,000-acre region located on both sides of the Delaware River in northwest New Jersey and Pennsylvania. It is connected on the Jersey side to Worthington State Forest and Stokes State Forest by a section of the **Appalachian Trail.** The famous trail runs through Worthington and Stokes to High Point at the very top of the state and traverses over to Wawayanda State Park. There are designated areas permitted on this trail for overnight stops, but it is not recommended as a hike for the uninitiated. A day trip to the region to investigate might be a good idea; and having someone pick you up, if you *do* come back one day to make the hike, is another good idea. Then you won't wear out your hiking shoes and you won't have to retrace your steps. There is much to see and do in northwestern New Jersey. One way to get there, directly on Interstate 78, would be to start with a visit to the historic town of Clinton. The entire town has been designated a bird and wildlife sanctuary owing to its location on the migratory route of many rare bird species. At the center of town is a 200-foot-wide waterfall at the junction of Spruce Run and the Raritan River, flanked on either side by two historic mills. On the west bank is an old red-frame mill, housing the **Red Mill Museum Village,** its four floors exhibiting a variety of rural daily life artifacts from the 18th, 19th, and 20th centuries. Additional buildings connected to the museum include a blacksmith shop, general store, post office, an 1860 schoolhouse, and a log cabin. On the east bank stands a carefully restored stone grist mill dating back to Colonial times. This mill, on the National Register of Historic Places and now operating as an art gallery, is a fine space to see, with its beautifully restored wood floors, original ceiling beams and interior supports, and white plastered walls. The art gallery is open all year round; the museum is open from April through October from 1 to 5 P.M. and Saturday and Sunday from noon to 6 P.M. Red Mill Museum Village, at 56 Main Street. The phone number is (908) 735-4101. Special events and concerts are regular occurrences and the Clinton antique show, usually held on the weekend before Memorial Day, features the early American country look in antiques. The town of Clinton is charmingly Colonial and well worth a visit for its preserved architecture. Try the **Clinton House,** 2 West Main St., for fine country dining: (908) 730-9300. Two state parks are nearby, **Spruce Run State Park** and **Round Valley State Park,** located in the crater of Cushetunk Mountain with 4,000 acres of woods and water, encompassing the second-largest lake in the state.

For an overnight stay in Clinton, try the **Holiday Inn** ($100–$125 double occupancy, [908] 735-5111). The **Stewart Inn** is a fine bed-and-breakfast easily accessible from Clinton (take Route 78 West to exit 4, about 12 miles). The Stewart Inn has modern conveniences, private baths, cable television, all set in a bucolic country landscape. Rates are reasonable, around $75 to $85 per night with breakfast. Stewart Inn, R.D. 1, Box 708, South Main Street, Stewartsville, NJ 08886. Call (908) 479-6060 for reservations. The inn is equally convenient for visitors to the Delaware River, Flemington, and Lambertville.

The city of Phillipsburg, just minutes west of Stewartsville, is like a miniature Pittsburgh, an industrial town set on a series of hills that steeply drop down to the Delaware. This is a city with a rich history, attested to by the neighborhood on the hill above the river filled with Victorian mansions built to order for the business executives who ran the iron mills at the turn of the century. The view west from Phillipsburg is of the larger, more prosperous city of Easton, Pennsylvania, just across the river.

Take Route 57 East to Route 31 North to the intersection of Route 46 at Buttzville. Here is where you'll find the unique Buttzville

Hot Dog Johnny's, famous throughout New Jersey and Pennsylvania. This highway spot is run by original founder John Kovalsky's daughter Pat, who has been working there since she was eight years old. Established in 1935 and still going strong, Hot Dog Johnny's specializes in farm-fresh buttermilk supplied by a local farmer, birch beer served in frosted mugs, and hot dogs. These hot dogs are really *hot,* not in the sense of a burning taste, but the sense of warmth; roll and dog are served to you steaming and wrapped in old-fashioned wax paper. These are truly mouth watering and afterward you may never want to eat a Nathan's Coney Island dog again. According to John and Pat, Hot Dog Johnny's was originally located at the stoplight in Buttzville, and business was booming when the Atlantic Gas Station across the highway provided the funds for a complete move down Route 46 to Buttzville center. It seems they were interfering with Atlantic Gas's own food concessions and causing congestion in the busy traffic flow in this little crossroads hamlet, which traditionally attracted the far-flung citizens from the Scranton coal region area. The customers always demand and get the best at Hot Dog Johnny's, and there is no trouble parking the car. There are picnic-style tables here and in nearby **Island Park** on the **Pequest River,** a spot shaded by tall trees and long favored by trout fishermen. The hours at Hot Dog Johnny's are loose, but usually open from 9 A.M. until quite late. Call (908) 453-2882.

After fueling up at Buttzville, drive west on 46 to the Delaware River, to Manunkachunk, to the Kittatinny Mountains and the **Worthington State Forest.** Explore!

Northern Mountains and Lakes

Bergen, Passaic, and Sussex Counties

The northern hill and lake country of New Jersey was thought of by the Germans who settled there at the turn of the century as reminiscent of old Bavaria and the green mountainous areas of the Old Country. Some of these early immigrants fondly referred to New Jersey as "New Germany." Today a variety of ethnic groups live in this verdant region; much of it continues to remain intact and unspoiled, only miles away from modern civilization. Travelers in the region should explore some of the exciting back roads like scenic Route 515, which has many steep curves and turns that take the driver up and around and into the forest valley that possesses great majestic beauty. We have all traveled over hill and dale in search of this and that, but here you will discover the same serenity of mountainous and mysterious woodlands so often associated with the Berkshires, Bear Mountain, Vermont, or New Hampshire. A fairy-tale Hansel and Gretel forest is all to be found here, in what is called the "Highlands" of New Jersey.

To get there: Take Interstate 78, a beautiful east-west highway, which connects Phillipsburg to Newark and New York, or Route 80 (also east-west), which connects the Delaware River at the Delaware Water Gap to the Hudson River at the George Washington Bridge. Route 206 is a viable north-south route off I-78 or I-80, and Routes 15 or 23 are good alternate roads for traveling into the regions of New Jersey north of Interstate 80. Forty-three percent of New Jersey is still forest, and the Division of Parks and Forestry maintains a great deal of it in state forests and parks, natural areas, and historic sites. Fish and wildlife management areas administered by the Division of Fish, Game and Wildlife comprise 154,000 acres, which are open for hiking, but without official swimming or camping facilities.

There are many parks, state forests, and specialty "good time" spots to hike, canoe, swim, ski, and play in New Jersey's "skylands." One particular vantage point with a wondrous view of the surrounding area is **High Point State Park** that is in the extreme northwest corner on the crest of the Kittatinny Mountains. The park, which has a camping area called **Sawmill Lake**, is connected at its southern tip to the 15,319-acre **Stokes State Forest**, which extends 12 miles southwest. Elevations here range from 420 to 1,653 feet (Sunrise Mountain). Highway 206 crosses the forest at Culvers Gap. There is daily bathing at the **Stony Lake** bathing area and camping is permitted here also.

Jenny Jump Forest has 1,118 acres with beautiful panoramas of the surrounding country and the Delaware Water Gap (between Interstate 80 and Route 46 off Route 519 near Hope). **Swartswood State Park,** located on the shores of both **Big** and **Little Swartswood Lakes** near the village of Swartswood in Sussex County (off Route 206), offers bathing in a sheltered cove with lifeguard protection and bathhouses. Picnicking and camping are allowed and in the winter cross-country skiing is the main outdoor activity.

Hopatcong State Park contains 107 acres including a section of the old Morris Canal. The clear water of Lake Hopatcong may be enjoyed by bathers at a safe sand-filled beach under lifeguard protection. A well-graded lawn, sloping toward the lake, encourages sunbathing. This park may be reached from I-80 (exit 28) by way of Landing or from Route 206 at Netcong. Amusement park aficionados like to remember and associate Lake Hopatcong with Bertrand Island Amusement Park, which, alas, was torn down. Period locations for Woody Allen's film *The Purple Rose of Cairo* were filmed at Bertrand Island. **Waterloo Village,** near Stanhope (off I-80 at exit 25 to Route 206 to Route 604—Waterloo Road) in the undeveloped **Allamuchy State Park,** is a beautifully preserved and restored 18th-century town. The **Waterloo Festival for the Arts** (May through October) offers a complete program of chamber music, a Saturday orchestra series, and afternoon concerts of jazz, folk, classical, and pop music on Sundays. There are 23 authentically restored homes and buildings with period furniture, rare antiques, and objects of art on display. Crafts can be bought at the well-stocked general store, including such novelties as period pottery, hand-dipped candles, brooms, wrought iron pieces, pine incense, and hand-loomed scarfs. Waterloo Village (973) 347-0900, is a National Historic Site situated on the winding towpaths of the old Morris Canal and there are dense forests, dark lakes, and rushing rivers to explore in the region.

Wild West City, (973) 349-8900 or www.wildwestcity.com, located in Byram, near Stanhope (exit 25 off I-80 to Route 206 north) is the place where the old Wild West comes back to life in northwestern New Jersey. You can watch the reenactment of the fight at the O.K. Corral, ride a stagecoach, ponies or an old iron horse railcar. Stop off at the **Golden Nugget Saloon** and enjoy food and a real Western stage show.

The Land of Make Believe (on Route 611 in Hope, 2 miles off exit 12 off I-80) is a real treat for children under 12. Here they can watch a Punch and Judy show, investigate Old McDonald's Farm, talk to a scarecrow that talks back, ride on the Indian River ride or a Civil War train. They can visit the Haunted House and receive a gift from Santa Claus at the North Pole. There are plenty

of amusement rides here for kids from 3 to 12 and a large picnic grove. For more information, call (908) 459-900 or visit www.
landofmakebelieve.com.

Space Farms (Route 519 in Beemerville, open from May to November) is also fun for kids who enjoy the petting and feeding zoo
and the large collection of wild animals and birds. For parents
there are classic automobiles, farm tool displays, carriages, Indian
artifacts and a display of antique dolls to ogle. Call (973) 875-5800
for information.

Vernon Valley Action Park (Route 23 to Route 94) is the largest
"self-participation" theme park in the world, with rides that include the Avalanche Water Ride, Alpine slides, Lola formula race
cars, speedboats, four water slides, super go-carts, the Kamikaze
Rapids Ride, and the Tidal Wave Pool. A bathing suit is a must
here. For smaller kids there's Water World and play park. Call
(973) 827-2000 for information.

Vernon Valley/Great Gorge Ski Area (Route 23 to Route 94 or I-80
to Route 15 to Route 94) is an ideal spot for a winter vacation. With
over 50 trails and slopes, 14 chairlifts and 3 rope tows, everyone from
expert to novice can join in the winter wonderland fun. Great
Gorge also has ski rentals, lessons, and the world's largest snowmak-
ing facility (in case Mother Nature doesn't provide!). There is also
night skiing for the truly adventurous. For further information about
resort hotels and dining in this area call (973) 827-2222.

Hidden Valley (Breakneck Road, Vernon, on Route 94 off Route
23) has ski slopes that range from beginner to expert. Hidden Valley Ski Lodge, in the pines at the base of the mountain, has a lim-
ited lift-ticket policy that ensures short lines and uncrowded
slopes. During the summer, visitors can hike, boat, play tennis,
and platform tennis. Banquet and party facilities are also available.
Call (973) 764-6161.

Wawayanda and **Greenwood Lake State Parks** and the undeveloped **A. S. Hewitt State Forest** form a vast green belt at the New
York–New Jersey border. There is swimming, boating, and hiking
a-plenty here—the **Appalachian Trail** runs through Wawayanda.
Northern Passaic and Sussex Counties are dotted with lakes including **Pompton Lakes** (off Route 23) in the Ramapo Mountains
and **Franklin Lakes**.

The Franklin Mineral Museum (on Evans Street in Franklin off
Routes 23 and 517) has beautiful displays of minerals from the
zinc mines of New Jersey including the unique franklinite. There
are fluorescent rock shows here, and family rock hunts between

April 15 and November 15. Monday to Friday, 10 A.M. to 4 P.M. Saturday 10 A.M. to 5 P.M., Sunday 11 A.M. to 5 P.M.; call (973) 827-3481 for information.

The Lorrimer Sanctuary (790 Ewing Avenue, Franklin Lakes) is a charming area maintained by the New Jersey Audubon Society offering self-guiding trails, outdoor classrooms, natural history programs, and courses for children and adults. Take Route 208 and follow the green-and-white Audubon Nature Center signs.

The Ramapo Valley County Reservation provides excellent hiking and camping facilities beside the Ramapo River on Route 202, Mahwah. There is a lake for canoeing and rafting, a fishing pond, and a waterfall. Write the ranger for sketch maps of the trails (610 Ramapo Valley Road, Mahwah, NJ 07430).

Darlington County Park in Mahwah has three lakes, two for swimming, one for fishing. There are snack bars, comfort stations, and playgrounds provided for summer residents and visitors.

Ringwood State Park (from Route 23 to 511) is located on the New Jersey–New York state line and offers fishing and boating in Shepherd Lake with facilities for bathing in the summer and ice skating and skimobiling in the winter. There are hiking trails and picnic areas, a small pond, a blacksmith shop, formal gardens, and the beautiful **Ringwood Manor House.** Built during the Victorian period, it is a beautiful 51-room mansion, and is now a museum with American furniture, firearms, implements, and artifacts. Also located here is a 44-room Jacobean mansion with a 300-acre botanical garden called **Skylands.** There is a lodge with a cafeteria, snack bar, and boat and canoe renting facilities. Call (973) 962-7031 for further information regarding the many special activities held year-round at this lovely spot. At the park's south end is the **Ramapo Mountain Forest,** an undeveloped but beautiful area encompassing another 3,500 acres with many hiking trails and good fishing.

A particularly charming spot is **Lake Girard,** a small intimate place with hillside picnic areas with tables and fireplaces and swimming and canoeing, located at Hardyston on Route 23, halfway between Stockholm and Hamburg, situated next to the **Hamburg Mountain Wildlife Management Area.** Also near Hardyston on Route 23 is a legendary country restaurant, in business for over 50 years. **Victoria's Mountain Inn** (formerly **Jorgensen's Inn**) serves American fare in an old-fashioned style. Open year-round, call (973) 697-6000. For an exceptional drive before dinner at Victoria's, take Route 515 off Route 23 at Stockholm. This is a scenic road you will surely enjoy.

Another scenic region, in a different sense, is Boonton, which was the largest iron center in the country in the 1800s. It's an industrial town from the past, built into a ledge overlooking Rockaway Gorge. Route 202 goes through the center of town (take 202 from Route 46 or I-80, five miles away) and you won't believe the precipitous mine-stripped view of the Gorge and the train embankments beyond offered from the pavilion next to the bank. The antique shops on the steeply twisting streets of the old city offer rewards to collectors of hard-to-find records and early recording machines. Pop-culture enthusiasts will find shops carrying early industrial antiques including porcelain enamel advertising signs. Automobilia is also a craze in Boonton—stop in at the **Kanter Auto Products** showroom at 76 Monroe Street and prepare to ogle the Packards—Fred Kanter supplies mechanical, trim, and restoration parts for collector cars, with a full line of engines, suspension, brakes, and water and fuel pumps as well as convertible tops, carpets, car covers, leather, and seat covers. He ships worldwide, and sells and repairs all kinds of vintage cars, and his specialty is America's best—"Ask the man who owns one." Call (973) 334-9575.

High Point Day Trip

1. Newton Fire Museum
2. Walpack Inn
3. Deckertown Turnpike
4. High Point
5. Gingerbread Castle

This is a day trip to the highest point in New Jersey, located in the northwest corner at **High Point State Park.** The quickest way to get into the region of Sussex County is to take Interstate 80 to exit 25 to North 206. **Lake Musconetcong** and **Lake Hopatcong State Parks** are on your right, the undeveloped **Allamuchy State Park** on your left as you drive northwest to Newton, the Sussex County seat. Newton is a 19th-century town filled with historic brick buildings set on a public green. The most impressive building is the 1847 County Courthouse, a Greek Revival structure on a steep hillside. The **Town Hall** at 39 Trinity Street distributes free pamphlets for sightseeing highlights and the **Newton Fire Museum** (150 Spring Street), built 150 years ago, has a museum with antique firefighting equipment and memorabilia, open Friday 5 to 8 P.M. and Saturday 10 A.M. to 3 P.M. Call (973) 383-0396. The **Sussex County Historical Society** headquarters and **Museum** is located in the Hill Memorial Building at Church and Main, (973) 383-6010. The museum has local handmade furniture, old household utensils and clothing, photographs and postcards; but the really exciting thing here is the mastodon found outside town in the 1960s, which is on display also. If you're hungry, try the **County Seat** restaurant on Route 206 and Clinton Street on the north side of town. **Swartswood State Park** for swimming and boating and **Whittingham Wildlife Management Area** (with 1,500 acres apiece) are to the west and south of Newton on Route 619.

If it's staple food at a classic diner you're after, stop at the **Five Star Diner,** Route 206 North, Branchville. The other place you might want to stop at is the **Yellow Cottage,** between Branchville and Culver Lake. The Yellow Cottage, on the lefthand side of the road, has been there for decades. They make sandwiches, sell their own pies and breads, and feature out-of-this-world brown Bettys. Get them with coffee and fill the thermos. Drive past Culver Lake through **Culver Gap** and you'll find yourself in **Stokes State Forest,** deep in the Kittatinny Mountains. Pass the entrance to Stokes Forest, watch carefully (there should be a state 4-H camp signpost here) and take your next left onto Strubble Road. Drive down scenic Strubble, which turns into Dimon Road to **Tillman Ravine.** This is a designated natural area, undisturbed by man, a virtual laboratory where natural forests, rocks, and soil at the mercy of climatic conditions and natural processes may be observed. It is spectacularly beautiful, canopied over with tall, graceful hemlocks and other kinds of old growth trees. There are masses of native rhododendron on the steep banks of Tillman Brook, which slides down long waterworn channels over huge boulders in fine cascades. There are parking areas here; but no picnic tables, camping grounds, or other recreational facilities exist to mar the natural beauty. After hiking the forest paths and crossing the quaint wooden bridges, drive on down the mountain on Brink Road to Main in **Walpack Center.** This is a preserved ghost town (complete with ancient cemetery) maintained as part of the **Delaware Water Gap National Recreation Area.** If you thought the forest was something, the great natural beauty and the vistas across the beautifully maintained fields in **Walpack Valley** will take your breath away. Take a swim, if you like, in Flat Brook and drive up north on Route 615 (Walpack–Flatbrook Road) to the **Walpack Inn.** This is a no-reservation place with a lovely outdoor eating terrace where you can eat while watching the deer eat. Specialties run from steak and fresh fish served with salad bar and baked potato or rice with entrees ranging from $21 to $40. They are open on Friday and Saturday from 5 P.M. to 9:30 P.M., Sunday 11 A.M. to 2:30 P.M. brunch, and 4 P.M. to 8 P.M. dinner. There is a wonderful piano player named Jim Woolsey who will play anything you want on his grand piano. Call (973) 948-3890 for more information. To get back onto Route 206, drive north on 615, take a left on 521 to 206. The Walpack Inn is about seven miles south of Route 206.

The summer months are the most beautiful to catch the sunset from High Point. To get there after dinner or after a picnic in Stokes State Forest take Route 206 North to Route 653 (Clove Road) to Route 650 (Deckertown Turnpike). Turn right and drive east on Deckertown Road into Stokes Forest to Sawmill Road. Take a left on Sawmill Road and drive north along the crest of the Kittatinny Mountains. You can't miss **High Point Monument,** (973) 875-4800. Dominating the summit of the mountain and astride the greatest elevation in New Jersey (1,803 feet), this 220-foot-high granite-faced landmark, built in 1930, has views westward across the valley of the Delaware to the ridges of the Pocono Mountains in Pennsylvania. Nestled in the valley 1,300 feet below lies Port Jervis, New York, with Tri-State Rock marking the common boundary of three states at the juncture of the Neversink and the Delaware Rivers. The Port Jervis line (Metro North commuter railroad operated in conjunction with NJ Transit) out of Hoboken travels up in New York through Orange County and terminates in the bustling railroad town of Port Jervis. Northeast in the distance one can see the Catskill Mountains. To the southeast lies the valley of the Wallkill River, checkerboarded with the farms and woodlands of Sussex County. Sunrise Mountain in Stokes State Forest may be seen in the middle distance. This 13,398-acre park was a gift of the late Colonel and Mrs. Anthony R. Kuser of Bernardsville to the people of New Jersey in 1922. Mrs. Kuser's money came from the Prudential Insurance Company.

Route 23 is the best way to get back to civilization from High Point. Take it east about 18 miles all the way to Hamburg in the Pochuck Mountains where you will have to screech on the brakes when you see the **Gingerbread Castle.** This unbelievable place was built in 1930 by Florenz Ziegfeld's famed stage designer Joseph Urban, at the behest of a successful businessman named F. H. Bennet, who loved the immortal stories of "Hansel and Gretel," "Snow White and the Seven Dwarfs," "Little Red Riding Hood," "The Three Little Pigs," "Little Miss Muffet," and "The Old Lady Who Lived in a Shoe." This was the place to recapture the spirit of childhood; conducted tours of the castle and its adjacent grounds were led by expertly trained local school children dressed quaintly in period costumes. The boys were transformed into "Hansel" and the girls became "Gretel," all of them reciting in awed tones the fairy tales connected with each display in the castle. They pointed out Humpty Dumpty perched atop his famous wall and Prince Charming astride his prancing charger. Then they would show you the spitting black cat that stands guard over the castle up in a turret, and the wise old owl who watches every move through unblinking yellow eyes. Children were warned not to touch the walls of the castle lest they turn into stones. There was a dungeon, a witch's trophy room, and in the

Left to right: Humpty Dumpty statue at the Gingerbread Castle in Hamburg; the mysterious and wonderful Gingerbread Castle itself.

main hall your Hansel and Gretel guides would point out the gingerbread cookies and peppermint sticks studding the walls. Later they would show you the evil witch astride her broom ready to flee from reproachful eyes, and the witch's evil kitchen where a big black cauldron contained the bones of the hapless children trapped in her lair and cooked alive. The tour over, you would be led through a narrow door onto a landing high up in the battlements and down a brick stairway past animal-cracker balustrades formed by elephants. Because it has fallen into disrepair, this Humperdinck German-style castle has been closed until further notice, but the current owner, Frank Hinger, is trying to raise funds to renovate the castle and bring it back for the enjoyment of the public. Yes, Humpty Dumpty is looking to be put back together again! Call (973) 827-1617 for more information. Route 23 will take you to Route 46 or I-80 near Paterson, where you can connect up with the Garden State Parkway.

"Hello from the Jersey Shore"

Notes on Road, Ferry, and Train Travel

The old route to fun and sunny good times at the Jersey shore out of Manhattan Island from the Lincoln or Holland Tunnels is New Jersey State Highway 1-9. Route 1-9 becomes simply 9 at Woodbridge (US Route 1 goes straight on down to Trenton). Some drivers at this point followed 9 through the Cheesequake State Park area, Freehold, Lakewood, Toms River, and farther on down all the way to Cape May. US Route 9 originally was an old Lenape Indian trail, and later became Kings Highway before being designated an official state highway. Other drivers preferred to swing into South 34 at Cheesequake, which is actually closer to the shoreline, taking the road through the beautiful farm regions of Holmdel and Colts Neck. During the summer months fresh white-and-yellow Jersey sweet corn and every variety of Jersey tomato is sold at farm roadstands on Route 34. Highway 35 will also take you to the shore through the antique-center town of Red Bank, which has many historic buildings, Shrewsbury, Eatontown, and eventually into Asbury Park and Spring Lake all the way south to Seaside Heights. Much of Route 35 is now mostly commercial with immense shopping malls.

The route to the North Jersey shore—Keyport, Keansburg, Atlantic Highlands, Sea Bright, Monmouth Beach, and Long Branch—is the old Route 36 (north coastal highway). Route 36 is a beautiful drive along the Atlantic Highlands with many views of Sandy Hook Bay, the Navesink and Shrewsbury Rivers, and the Atlantic Ocean. Often you drive almost alongside the crashing waves. At Long Branch "the shore drive" changes into Route 71 through Deal, with its splendid ocean-front mansions, and into Asbury Park, Ocean Grove, Bradley Beach, Avon-by-the-Sea, Belmar, Spring Lake, Sea Girt, and Manasquan. Most New Yorkers prefer the relatively fast-lane travel along the New Jersey Turnpike to the Garden State Parkway at Woodbridge. North Jerseyites will simply get onto the Parkway at an earlier point from the Meadowlands Arena, the Oranges, Union, or other points north. Philadelphians can travel to the southern Jersey shore on any number of interesting old highways like Route 70 to Lakehurst and to Point Pleasant Beach, or from 70 onto Route 72 to Barnegat or Ship Bottom on Long Beach Island. The old Route 30 to Pleasantville and into Egg Harbor City, Absecon, and finally Atlantic City is a wonderful and rewarding ride in and of itself. Routes 40 and 49 are also well-traveled South Jersey highways that connect the shore region with the Delaware Memorial Bridge. Of course, speedsters in a hurry to gamble must take the Atlantic City Expressway; but the

Seashore resorts booklet (back cover) showing New Jersey coastal towns from the Pennsylvania Railroad system, 1923, printed by Edward Stern & Company.

old roads out of Philadelphia and Camden are a great deal of fun if you can enjoy just the sense of motor touring as people did in the old days, when there was no cause to be in such a big hurry. It was one of these old roads that Thornton Wilder refers to in his play *The Happy Journey to Camden and Trenton*. No one today thinks of the Turnpike as a "happy" road, though the southern part of the Garden State Parkway is quite beautiful, particularly through the Pine Barrens. Even so, old Route 9, which almost exactly parallels the Parkway, is far more leisurely, beautiful, and interesting. The added benefit is that you may stop at roadside points of interest, farm stands, antique shops, old taverns, and eateries along the way. Old-style motels, cabins, and trailer parks can be found on these routes for a night's rest that can be more fun and intimate than one of the bigger chains. However, there are hotels, inns, motor lodges, and many motels offering clean and reasonable lodging. Recommended, therefore, is a sane and happier return to a slower, more enjoyable pace on a back road or an old highway.

To get to the shore area via water from New York, take the ferry to Pete's Pier and the Conyers Hotel in Atlantic Highlands—

call Seastreak at (800) BOATRIDE or visit www.seastreakusa.com for ferry schedules leaving Pier 11 on Wall Street. Also running service are New York Fast Ferry at (800) 693-6933, and New York Waterway at (800) 533-3779. By car begin your coastal adventure just South of the Edison Bridge in Sayreville with a visit to the **Peterpank Diner,** run by the original owner's son Alex Panko Jr. The Peterpank is at 967 Route 9 North, so if you are heading south, which you will be if you're going down to the Jersey shore, you'll have to go under the underpass at the gigantic shopping

Lighthouse tile on bathing pavilion in Spring Lake.

mall in Sayreville, just down the road, and come back up. Open 24 hours a day, it's easier to get that last hot cup of Jersey java on the way home as well. Chow down on good diner food and home-baked goodies at this popular spot for truckers and shore trekkers from New York and New Jersey.

You can also get to the New Jersey shore by train from New York's Penn Station or Newark's Penn Station (NJ Transit's North Jersey coast line). The train stops at 10 seaside towns from Long Branch to Bay Head the end of the line and most beaches are only a 5- to 15-minute walk from the station. During the summer NJ Transit runs a Shore Express with bargain excursion and round-trip ticket offerings. From New Jersey call (800) 772-2222; from out of state call (973) 762-5100 or log on to www.njtransit.com. Buses, of course, travel to all points. In May 1989 Amtrak began direct-rail service to Atlantic City from points along the northeast rail corridor. Round-trip fares from Philadelphia to Atlantic City are low and encourage train trippers with special deals to specified casinos. Call Amtrak for rail connections from New York, Newark, and other points at (800) USA-RAIL or visit www.amtrak.com. A Cape May ferry to Lewes, Delaware, makes the southern Jersey shore points and the Delaware Bay (New Jersey side) easily accessible to Delaware and Maryland. The Chesapeake Bay Bridge Tunnel from the Delmarva Peninsula to Norfolk make points from Cape May a distance from Virginia not much further than from New York City. The Cape May–Lewes Ferry has been in operation since 1964. They are 5 immaculate vessels 320 feet long, 68 feet wide, and 17 feet deep. Each ferry holds 800 passengers and 100 cars. Call 1 (800) 64-FERRY for information or visit www.capemaylewesferry.com.

Sandy Hook Day Trip

· ·

Via Keyport and Keansburg

Sandy Hook, part of the **Gateway National Recreation Area,** is a narrow barrier beach that curves out off the mainland at Atlantic Highlands. Sand beaches along the oceanfront are on one side of this seven-mile-long peninsula, once an island, at the tip of New Jersey's north shore. On the other side are the shifting marshland ecosystems of the Sandy Hook Bay. The road leads down the middle to the visitor's center, a ranger station, and the dunes and ocean. **Seagull's Nest** is a popular spot noted for its two-story cement concession stand, and entertainment is scheduled throughout the summer. You have to take a hike of half a mile to get to Gunnison's Beach, which is the only "bathing attire optional" beach in the National Park system. **Spermaceti Cove** (named after a whale), **Horseshoe Cove,** and historic **Fort Hancock** are on the bayside. At the tip is the **Sandy Hook Lighthouse,** the oldest in the United States (1764), a US Coast Guard station and weather station. A trip to Sandy Hook may be made at any time of year; spring and fall are preferable to the strong bitter winds of winter, though some fishermen, birdwatchers, a few lone hikers, and other appropriately dressed hearty souls enjoy the bracing elements off-season. Year-round the area is home to hawks, peregrine falcons, seagulls, ducks, osprey, great horned owls, whippoorwill, and 270 more types of birds, 50 of which are considered rare. Pack a lunch, bring the family, don't forget plenty of liquids and coffee, and get there early. Sunrises and sunsets at Sandy Hook are remarkable. For information call the Gateway National Recreation Area at (732) 872-5790.

Two waterfront towns, less than 40 minutes from the Holland Tunnel, between the Raritan River crossing at the Edison Bridge and Atlantic Highlands on the coast, are good beginnings or ends for a day trip to the shore. Just over the Edison Bridge or the Garden State Parkway bridges turn onto Route 36 to Keyport. The Matawan Creek enters Raritan Bay here and the estuary makes for a beautifully green and natural spot with a sweeping water-level view of Staten Island, New York City, and Long Island. Keyport is a quiet, turn-of-the-century town and at 149 West Front Street, right on the water is a landmark 1920s lunch and dinner restaurant called **Ye Cottage Inn,** (732) 264-1263, serving seafood specials and steak platters at comfortable tables and affordable prices. There is ample parking and you can stroll along the waterfront dock out to the municipal pier to catch a sea breeze and a closer view. Just across the road from Ye Cottage Inn is the **Keyport Fishery** at 150 West Front Street, (732) 264-9723, which sells fresh seafood and probably the best deep-fried seafood sandwiches and platters to go anywhere. Try a shrimp or flounder sandwich and go sit on a bench on the dock and enjoy a little bit of gourmet heaven out in the open air. Prices here are cheap. They're closed on Monday, open the rest of the week from 9 A.M. to 8 P.M., Fridays until 9 P.M. Ye Cottage Inn is open from noon to 10 P.M., Fridays and Saturdays until 11 P.M., closed Monday. Don't forget to take a walk into the town of Keyport, which is close to the dock; it has the small-town charm of long ago. It is also a frequent visiting place for vintage car folks, who regularly have meets wharfside and cruise the neighboring bayshore towns in their nifty '50s vehicles. A good garage in Keyport with good mechanics with experience will give you a fair price on a brake job or a fine-tuning on your timeless treasure. Mike and the guys at **F. J. & Sons,** 49 Highway 36, (732) 264-0040, love the old cars they keep on the road and refer to them as "oldies but goodies."

Just as unique a town, but in a different and funky way, is Keansburg, a few miles east of Keyport, also on Route 36, situated on the banks of the lower Raritan Bay. Signs along the road will direct you into Keansburg. In the old days a steamship took passengers from Manhattan to Keansburg for a night of fun. The 1930s movie actress Ruby Keeler, who was married to Al Jolson, vividly recalled her days as a chorine in Texas Guinan's club in the 1920s. "We all piled into a boat after the New York speakeasies closed—and sailed across moonlit waters to party away the rest of the night in Keansburg." Sometime after World War II Keansburg became a wild shanty town filled with raucous bars like **Nickerson's** or the **Club Miami.** Barflies, factory workers, and ex-cons who wear rose tattoos, accompanied by their Sadie Thompson–type broads, all intertwine here in search of a crazy wild night or honky-tonk fun on the boardwalk. Motorcyclists and their leather gals eat what may be the best french fries on the East Coast. They have been dousing them with white vinegar and salt for years from the same boardwalk vendor. The **Old Heidelberg Inn** has been on the midway for almost 90 years; it serves an authentic red hot (a hot dog with hot red relish) with a mug of beer or root beer, both on tap. At another concession try a cinnamon cruller with a cup of Maxwell House coffee. There are amusement park rides, games of chance with numbered spinning wheels, penny arcades, and an old-time merry-go-round. Keansburg has a beach on the bay for those who like a dip, and there is a large outdoor pool, as well as a state-of-the-art waterpark and a 2,500 foot fishing pier. Call (800) 805-4FUN.

Continuing on Route 36 five miles you reach the Highlands; watch for signs that point to a road that says "scenic drive" (near **Stewart's Root Beer Drive-in**). Drive up for a scenic overlook from the highest point on the East Coast, **Mount Mitchell** on

Ocean Boulevard. This will give you a very good view of Sandy Hook; and (on a clear day) Coney Island, New York's answer to Keansburg.

Following this viewpoint, head back down the road to Sandy Hook for a day of sun and fun. Sandy Hook, site of the strategic **Fort Hancock,** was a gift from the United States Army to the public in 1962.

North Shore

J ust opposite Sandy Hook's entranceway at the top of Jersey's north shore are the historic **Navesink Twin Lights,** which once signaled the entrance to ocean ships as they sailed into New York Bay and harbor. The view out to sea, across the harbor and down the Jersey coast, is breathtaking from this high point where the bay converges with the ocean. Visit the Twin Lights museum and climb the steps of the north tower for an even higher view. The north tower has a small blinking beacon, though it's nothing like it used to be when sailors could see its glow 70 miles out to sea. Decommissioned as a light station in 1949, Twin Lights is now maintained as a state park. Call (732) 872-1814 for more info.

Restaurants notable for seafood right in Atlantic Highlands (just next to Sandy Hook) include **Bahrs** at 2 Bay Avenue, (732) 872-1245, and the **Clam Hut** at the foot of Atlantic Street. Both places serve moderately priced seafood dinners and lunches, and have lobster specials. Gourmet seafood preparations at a higher price are superb at **Doris and Ed's** at 36 Shore Drive, (732) 872-1565. If you are looking for something other than seafood try the **Hofbrauhaus** at 301 Ocean Boulevard, (732) 291-0224, for German food. Ocean Boulevard is also called "scenic drive" and just across the road from this restaurant is a spectacular view of the ocean, bay, and surrounding areas. Specials here are the best of German meats and sausages, including *kloster Weissbeir*, jaeger schnitzel, Wiener schnitzel, Kassler rippchen (smoked pork chops), sauerbraten with potato dumpling, and German pot roast with potato pancakes. A Hofbrau special including pork chop, knockwurst, bratwurst, sauerkraut, and German potato salad is also offered. On Friday and Saturday nights and Sunday afternoons during Oktoberfest (the end of September running into the middle of November every year) there are authentic German bands and Bavarian dancers. Highway 36 continues south from the Highlands right alongside the Atlantic Ocean. On a stormy night in days gone by you could hear the pounding of the waves against the rock-solid seawall. This was before the army corps of engineers enlarged and widened the beach with white sand. There are points at which you may want to stop and climb up the wooden stairways to the top of the rocks to look at the ocean and breathe the fresh salt air. The town of Sea Bright has a small public beach, restaurants, and shops.

Turn inland at this point for a side trip (take the Sea Bright–Rumson Bridge, Route 520) through swanky Rumson to Red Bank, a town long frequented by antique dealers and enthusiasts. Red Bank is easily accessible on Route 35 (exit 109 off the Parkway).

The town was established in 1870 and is set on the Navesink River, bordered by the towns of Shrewsbury and Little Silver. There are lovely parks, like Marine Park at the foot of Wharf Avenue on the Navesink River, old Victorian homes, and a first-rate hotel-restaurant, the **Molly Pitcher Inn**, 88 Riverside Ave., (732) 747-2500, which is right on the river. You can find anything in antiques at the **Red Bank Antiques Centers** at 195 and 226 West Front Street. There are four buildings housing over 200 permanent dealers in indoor booths. Call (732) 842-4336 or 842-3393 for further antique center information. Back at the shore, Monmouth Beach, just below Sea Bright, with its big rock formations and yellow sand is a good "stop point" for a refreshing dip in the ocean. You should have your swimsuits on underneath your casual summer attire, however, as facilities for changing are not provided.

Long Branch is the point on the North Jersey shore that opens up to the vast expanse of the sea (exit 105 on the Garden State Parkway or continue to follow Route 36 south). The seaside town of Long Branch, once famous for its fishing pier and amusement area, which collapsed in a fire a few years ago, is still known far and wide for great Italian food. One of the best spots for pizza in New Jersey is **Freddie's Pizza** at 563 Broadway, (732) 222-0931, featuring a small personal pizza for $4 up to $9 for the 16-inch plain. This is an attractive restaurant with a beautiful Pizzaman neon sign in the front. Johnny Scialla is the host. Another charming small restaurant for ziti and ravioli, served piping hot and freshly made, is **Nunzio's** at 230 Westwood Avenue, (732) 222-9798, located in a glass brick-and-neonized building near the railroad station. The pizza pies here are also first rate. The prices at Nunzio's are not the only attraction; the food is very tasty and is prepared by the Nunzio family with care and in an authentic old-world style. Don't let the plain decor fool you, this is no-nonsense Italian food at its best. They're open from 4 to 8 P.M. and closed Tuesday. Say hello to Snuffy. Right next door to Nunzio's is **Tuzzio's,** a fancier restaurant with a full bar at 224 Westwood Avenue, (732) 222-9614. Prices here are more than reasonable, and well worth the price. Meat entrees (all served with salad and pasta) are the specialty and they have veal and peppers, calamari, and shrimp marinara served hot and sweet. Since everything is cooked to order you must allow about a half hour over a drink. All the Long Branch restaurants are family owned and operated. The food is served with love and care; and a trip to Long Branch at anytime—even just for dinner—is highly recommended.

A site to see in West Long Branch is the **Monmouth College** campus clustered around the graceful old French-style 130-room mansion, which was the setting for the movie *Annie*. It originally contained a theater, a chapel, and gold-plated fixtures. The mansion is now named **Woodrow Wilson Hall** to commemorate the

California Mission-style mansion on Ocean Drive in Deal, which has some of the most beautiful homes to be found in New Jersey.

period in which it served as a summer White House. The **Guggenheim Memorial Library** at Westwood and Norwood Avenues was the Guggenheims' 35-room mansion. This manse, with its high ornate iron fences and luxurious gardens, was later given as a gift to the college.

The five-mile Ocean Avenue drive along the shore from Long Branch through Deal and Allenhurst is a wonderfully scenic car tour of the old Georgian and Mission-style mansions of these two classy resort towns. There is minimal access to the beach in this area since most of the homes are right on the ocean.

Other things to see and do in the Monmouth County area include the **Monmouth Battleground State Park** at Route 33 and Wemrock Road in Manalapan Township. This is where Molly Pitcher struck a blow for freedom and ultimately for the cause of women's liberation in a pivotal 1778 Revolutionary battle. The 1500-acre park has walking trails, two picnic areas, and a playground. Hours are 8 A.M. to 8 P.M. **Owl Haven** at Route 522 in Manalapan Township is a park maintained by the New Jersey Audubon Society, where you can hold a live owl on your arm. Other than these big-eyed birds that eat live mice and other rodents, there are snakes, turtles, and other special wildlife-related exhibits to be seen. Open Tuesday through Sunday from 1:30 to 4:30 P.M. **Longstreet Farm** in Holmdel Park is a working New Jersey farm near the shore area that still uses farm equipment of the 1800s. It is maintained by the Monmouth County Park System. The farm's hours are 9 A.M. to 3:30 P.M. daily. The **PNC Bank Arts Center** at Holmdel, located right on the Garden State Parkway (exit 116) just one hour away from New York and one hour away from Philadelphia, is a futuristically designed 9,000-seat outdoor amphitheater in which you can buy a ticket to see classical or pop concerts, musicals, operas, dance events, and ethnic folk festivals. The likes of Bob Dylan, Bon Jovi, and Jack Johnson attract packed houses. The **Monmouth Park Racetrack** is at Oceanport Avenue in Oceanport just off Route 36 (Parkway exit 16). For more information call (732) 222-5100.

A favorite outdoor antique flea market in Monmouth County in the Tinton Falls area on Route 34 and Route 33 (exit 100A, Parkway) and just beyond the US Naval Weapons Station Earle (often itself the scene of weapons protestors) is the **Collingwood Park Auction and Flea Market,** (732) 938-7941. Here you will find old and new mixed together at outdoor stalls. A large indoor market features bargains galore in clothing, homemade pickles, homemade Polish bologna, bread counters, a spice shop, a pet store (with puppies and kittens for sale), hardware shops, a bookshop, a vintage magazine and comic book dealer, canned goods, vacuum cleaner attachments, a vinyl upholsterer, plaster statuettes, *junque,* endless whatnot stalls, and several small restaurants specializing in good home cooking. One outdoor area is devoted to local farm produce. Jersey tomatoes, red or yellow, and Jersey sweet corn, white or yellow, are the order of the day in the summer months. Peaches, apples, and the Jersey eggs sold here are the freshest and best. The indoor market is open Friday from noon until 8 P.M. and all day

Saturday, 10 A.M. to 8 P.M. and Sunday from 10 A.M. to 5 P.M. Bidding for the auction begins at 5 P.M. on Saturday.

The **Delicious Apple Orchards** store on Route 34 in Colts Neck sells its own sweet apple cider by the cup, half gallon, and gallon. The homegrown apples are also used in fresh doughnuts, homestyle pies, and cakes. Delicious Orchards sells farm produce (New Jersey summer produce, autumn squash, and select winter shipments), fancy cheeses, hickory-smoked bacon, home-baked breads, specially packaged homemade cookies (buttercrunch, chocolate chip, and oatmeal raisin), Vermont maple syrup, sugar candy, and other fine culinary items. It is certainly worth a stop along the road; and picnic tables are provided for your doughnut-and-cider repast or to eat the lunch you packed at home. If not, you can pick up whatever you need at Delicious Orchards, and you can be sure it is better quality than what you will buy at a highway supermarket.

The granddaddy flea market of them all is **Englishtown Auction Market** on Route 527 (Old Bridge Road) five miles south of Route 18, a tradition since 1929. Englishtown is one of the first flea markets that originated out of the country farm market in the early 1950s. There are buildings housing produce, dealers in canned and dry goods and butchers, bakers, and candlestick makers. You can buy fresh fish, cheese and dairy products, and goats and live chickens, turkeys, and rabbits. In recent years the merchandise at the outdoor market has tended toward the new, and it is harder than ever to find a treasure there now, prompting most people to bring out their flashlights and get there before dawn. It is an important market, attracting up to 10,000 people at the height of the season, and worth the long trudge from the parking lot to the dealer sections, that are spread out over vast acres of land.

Freehold is horse country and the **Freehold Raceway** offers the best in harness racing—trotters and pacers. There is dining in the track's clubhouse, located at Route 9 and Route 33 in Freehold; (732) 577-1144.

Open April through Thanksgiving is the renowned **Wall Township Speedway,** which has stock car racing every Saturday on Route 34 (Garden State Parkway exit 98, or exit 35B off I-95) and also hosts sporting events and concerts. Call (732) 681-6400. Also in this area is the **Allaire State Park,** boasting a restored Revolutionary bog iron community, the **Pine Creek Railroad** (for a short steam ride), picnicking, campsites, riding trails, walking, bicycling, a nature center, and playgrounds. Allaire also hosts many fine antique and crafts markets throughout the spring, summer, and fall. Route 547 at Farmingdale; (732) 938-2371. Call for special events and a seasonal schedule.

Ocean Grove Day Trip

1. Jersey Shore Arts Center
2. Gifts by Tina
3. The Kitch and Kaboodle
4. Nagles Apothecary
5. The Great Auditorium
6. House by the Sea
7. Ocean Grove/Asbury Park Railroad Station

Ocean Grove is a very easy day trip to take in spring, summer, and fall, and up through the Christmas season when there are special events and pageants. It is no more than an hour from Manhattan by car and NJ Transit's North Jersey Coast Line leaves Penn Station at reasonable intervals; there are late-night train returns as well. Exit 100A off the Garden State Parkway onto Route 33 East through Neptune and onto Route 71 leads you to the majestic town gates of Ocean Grove, and the moment you enter Main Avenue, the main thoroughfare, you are transported to yesteryear.

This is a truly old-fashioned magical place that almost feels out of another century. Founded by the Methodists as a camp meeting resort in 1869, Ocean Grove is an architectural treasure of Victorian and American Picturesque-style seaside hotels, homes, cottages, gazebos, open bandstands, and other turn-of-the-century buildings, which are still standing intact as a testimony to the function and beauty of things past that continue to serve us well in the present. The boardwalk and ocean are at the end of all east–west streets, and the bathing beaches are immaculate. The huge **Great Auditorium** is used for various religious services and meetings, and used to attract special pulpit speakers such as Dale Evans and Bishop Fulton Sheen. Summer entertainment appearing at the auditorium might include gospel singing groups, the Lettermen, the Ferko String Band, Pat Boone, Lou Christie, Lesley Gore, Doo Wop concerts, Peter Paul and Mary, Neil Sedaka, Michael Feinstein, K. T. Sullivan, the Glenn Miller Orchestra, and Little Anthony. In the summer of 2005 Peter and Paul gave a heartwarming concert, without Mary, who was ill. Joining them was the Chad Mitchell Trio and Tom Paxton in a great folkfest. In previous years the Fred Waring Orchestra and Glee Club were a popular attraction. Call (732) 775-0035 for program schedules.

"The Grove," as old-time residents called it (and still do), was thought of as a tonic for those in need of both physical and spiritual recovery, and even today attracts many who retire there to live out their last years near the ocean, breathing in the salt air. Of late many more cosmopolitan people have come to Ocean Grove in search of a relaxing time. The Great Auditorium is a Victorian wooden structure that was 100 years old in 1994. It has an 18-foot neon cross on the outside, a huge electric-lightbulb American flag inside, 7,000 seats, plus one of the largest pipe organs on the eastern seaboard. Surrounding this auditorium are 114 summer tent houses. This is not a typical tent community, with outside latrines, kerosene lamps, and outdoor campfires. Instead, the tents fit onto permanent wooden structures that give the occupants 336 square feet with open porches and flower gardens filled with zinnia, black-eyed Susan, and petunia. When lit by electric light at night these big-sized canvas house tents with striped canvas porch awnings are a restful sight to behold. Tent houses have been in existence in Ocean Grove for over 115 years. The many Victorian hotels on Pilgrim's Pathway and Lake Avenue, with their ginger-

Ocean Grove tent houses.

Vintage cars abound on the streets of Victorian Ocean Grove.

bread finials, fretwork, cupola, transoms, turrets, and tracery have spring and autumn rooms for rent at off-season rates. The town center on Main Avenue is filled with quaint Victorian-style shops. At **Kitch & Kaboodle,** 76 Main Avenue, (732) 869-0950, chenille bedspreads, floral and geographic-print tablecloths, linens and doilies, kitchen chatchkas, dinnerware from the forties and fifties, and other homey oddball usables abound in this fun-filled kitschy store. Across from "The Kitch" stop at **Gifts by Tina,** 73 Main Avenue, (732) 774-0457 owned by Tina Skokos, who specializes in jewelry. A new attraction to Ocean Grove is the **Jersey Shore Arts Center,** which occupies a beautifully restored historic building that was once Neptune High School. Saved by the Ocean Grove Historic Preservation Society, the Arts Center (Main Avenue and Main Street in Ocean Grove) is a place where concerts and plays are performed and is an arena where Jersey artists can develop, perform, and display their work. For information on what is going on, call (732) 502-0050. The complex includes the Shoreline Dance Academy and a music studio.

One of the finest restorations in town is **Nagles Apothecary Café,** 43 Main Avenue, (732) 776-9797. From a turn-of-the-century drugstore which contained an old fashioned soda/ice-cream counter, Nagles has utilized old medicine bottles, advertising signs, and vintage products found in the store's cellar to create just the right nostalgic atmosphere that suits Ocean Grove. Nostalgic music is piped in over speakers, and hamburgers, ice-cream sodas, and egg platters are served all day long, as well as American-style suppertime meals such as meatloaf with mashed potatoes and string beans. This is the kind of atmosphere and food that America has always been about.

Called "God's square mile of health and happiness," Ocean Grove's hotels and white-sand ocean beaches welcome anyone of any denomination to its healthful, old-fashioned, and serene environment. Ocean Grove was designated landmark status by the New Jersey Register of Historic Places, and is also a National Historic Monument. It is in Neptune Township, and it can be seen as the setting for Woody Allen's film *Stardust Memories*. In fact, Woody Allen repaired the neon cross on the auditorium, which had not been working, as a gift to the town.

A great place to stay for a weekend or week in the summer is **The House by the Sea,** 14 Ocean Avenue, a bed and breakfast which stands on a corner lot directly facing the Atlantic Ocean and the boardwalk. A cozy old-fashioned atmosphere pervades this hotel, and its interior is decorated with original Victoriana treasures. It is owned and run by Sally and Alyn Heim, a charming couple who live here year round and enjoy having guests during the summer months. Three open porches provide ocean breezes, rest, and wicker rocking-chair relaxation and a splendid view of the sea and the surrounding great Victorian houses of "The Grove." There are two large sitting rooms at this bed and breakfast gem and the quaint, sparkling bedrooms are the home-away-from home for happy visitors to the extraordinary historic town that maintains the style of a seashore resort from the 19th century. Call (732) 774-4771; e-mail housebysea@monmouth.com; or visit www.travel guides.com/bb/house_by_the_sea. Another exquisite Victorian B&B is **The Melrose** at 34 Seaview Avenue. Nearby is a walkway along Wesley Lake, a small park with tall shady trees; and it is just a short walk to the ocean and boardwalk. Hosts Dan Margo and Randy Bishop stay open all year round, and allow guests to bring small dogs, and enjoy baking their own muffins for breakfast. The men have been known to leave tins of their homemade

The House By The Sea, an oceanfront B&B on 14 Ocean Avenue in historic Ocean Grove.

cookies at the door of your room. All rooms have private baths and air-conditioning, and luxury suites provide a jacuzzi or a steam sauna. Call (800) 378-9004 for more information. The following is a list of other recommended hotels to call for reservations. The Ocean Grove Chamber of Commerce, (732) 774-1391, will send you a list of others with brochures.

The Cordova Inn, 26 Webb Ave, (732) 774-3084.

Ocean Plaza Hotel, 18 Ocean Pathway, (732) 774-6552.

Quaker Inn, 39 Main Ave, (732) 775-7525.

Lillagaard B&B, 5 Abbott Ave, (732) 988-1216.

Shawmont Hotel, 17 Ocean Ave, (732) 776-6895.

The famous resort town of Asbury Park, just north of Ocean Grove across Wesley Lake, is now in the process of development and revitalization. Though many things are changing, the beautiful parks that gave the town its name are still there. The restored **Convention Hall** and **Paramount Theater** on the boardwalk are active. The **Stone Pony** (on Ocean Avenue and 2nd Street) is featuring rock groups that promote the Asbury Sound, like Bruce Springsteen, a Jersey boy who began his illustrious career here. Bruce's album *Greetings from Asbury Park* and his follow-up albums were inspired by the tough, gritty, leatherjacket lifestyle that has been so much a part of this honky-tonk seaside town. Springsteen occasionally drops in to sing and play guitar at the Stone Pony and at **Rum Runners** in Sea Bright. Na-

Antique saltwater taffy box from the Criterion Tea Shoppe and Restaurant. Criterion Candies are gone, but the spectacular 1950s Howard Johnson still serves up good grub on the boardwalk in Asbury Park.

Greetings from Asbury Park, picture postcard.

169

Palace Amusements in Asbury Park (demolished in 2004).

tional label bands play at the Stone Pony and Rum Runners and at the **Brighton Bar** in Long Branch. Live rock and new alternative music and dance music—including some punk—is heard all over New Jersey. Recent bills at the Stone Pony have included "Hurdy-Gurdy Man" Donovan, Gary U.S. Bonds, the Graham Colton Band, La Bamba's Big Band, Borialis Phantom Planet, Amfibian, Critters Buggin', and Juggling Suns. Call (732) 502-0600 for programs or visit www.stoneponyonline.com. Two other places in Asbury: **T-Birds Cafe,** 707 Main Street, which has an acoustic unplugged venue, and **Fast Lane II Asbury Baronet Theatre,** (732) 775-5535, at 4th and Kingsley, a rock concert bar and theater. The place to stay in Asbury Park is the attractive and recently renovated Art Deco **Berkeley Carteret Hotel,** a landmark built in 1925, at 1401 Ocean Avenue, (732) 776-6700. Danny DeVito likes to eat at the **Adriatic,** and Nat Lane's **Fishermen's Pier** draws seafood lovers in. Nightlife in Asbury can often be raucus and rip-roaring—the place to be on Friday and Saturday nights is **Club**

Though Bruce Springsteen sang in other Asbury Park clubs, it is the Stone Pony where the great New Jersey rock-and-roll singer first gained recognition and a following of fans that remain faithful to "the Boss" to this day.

A *fantasy seahorse detail from Convention Hall on the boardwalk in Asbury Park* (top). *The bottom photo shows the old carousel building in Asbury Park.*

Paradise/Empress Hotel, (732) 775-6663, 101 Asbury Avenue, with its four bars, disco dance floor, outdoor terraces, clubhouse, and Miami Beach–type pool. Compared to Ocean Grove, which is a dry town, Asbury Park is filled with bars. If you take one of the old pedestrian bridges across the Wesley Lake from Ocean Grove, it's as if you entered into some kind of pleasure island. If you are looking for characters, you will see them in Asbury Park, which, in its more elegant days, was seen as a smaller version of Atlantic City. The best store at the Jersey Shore for antiquarian books, memorabilia, postcards, Jerseyana, and more is **Antic Hay Books,** 721 Cookman Avenue, (732) 774-4590, www.antichay.com. Asbury Park Web sites of interest: asburypark.net, asburymusic.com, and homestead.com/savetillie for (Asbury's mascot) Tillie's history and preservation.

The Rising of Asbury Park

"Tonight I'm gonna take that ride across the river to the Jersey side
Take my baby to the carnival and I'll take her on all the rides
'Cause down the shore everything's all right
You and your baby on a Saturday night."

—From the song "Jersey Girl" by Tom Waits, sung by Bruce Springsteen.

Born in New Jersey, USA, in Freehold, Bruce Springsteen found fame singing in Asbury Park. Many of the songs he sings are ballads about the ordinary life of workers and bikers in Bruce's home state.

The rockin' hero of Asbury Park, Bruce Springsteen, continues to perform at the Jersey shore at the Asbury Park Paramount Theater and at the Stone Pony whenever he is not touring the land or crashing in his country house in nearby Colt's Neck. His 2002 concert in Asbury Park was broadcast on gigantic loudspeakers and was heard all the way down the Asbury boardwalk and into the next town of Ocean Grove. It was part of his tour to promote his album *The Rising*. A good part of the "rising" of the new Asbury Park may be due to Springsteen's effort to restore the old resort town to its glory days. With Bruce singing "Come On Up For The Rising," that night the dream was on its way to becoming a reality.

Springsteen's 2005 album of spirituality and redemption, *Devils & Dust*, also has its roots in the town where the Boss had his start. In those early days, it was a forgotten Jersey town on the skids, while today it is experiencing a renaissance in terms of real-estate development, art centers, antique emporiums and shops, restaurants, and hotels. The rebuilding of Springsteen's "City of Ruins" is attracting tourists to Asbury as in the days when it was referred to as a mini-Atlantic City.

For the 2005 Christmas season, Bruce Springsteen released a new package set that includes a rare two-hour 1975 concert DVD with interviews, choice outtakes, and never-before-seen materials including a re-digitized CD of *Born to Run*. In an editorial by Helene Cooper in *The New York Times* on Friday November 18, 2005, itself entitled "Born to Run," the writer calls the album, which was originally released in 1975, "the world's best driving album." She particularly cites the opening song "Thunder Road" as one of the best to listen to while driving down the highways and byways. "Everybody on *Born to Run* is out, or trying to get out" Springsteen says on the DVD. So next time you hit the road in Jersey with your copy of *O' New Jersey* in the glove compartment, slip the *Born to Run* CD into the slot, turn up the volume, put your foot on the accelerator, and get out and go!

Gay Asbury Park

New Jersey Gay Pride Day is an annual festive celebration that takes place on the first weekend in June one week after Memorial Day. When May turns into June, the "summer at the shore" officially begins. While the Friday and Saturday of New Jersey Gay Pride weekend have many fun events to attend in Asbury Park, the big day—the day of the Jersey Pride Day Parade—now referred to as a gay, lesbian, transgender, and intersexed celebration—takes place on Sunday. Jersey Pride, Inc., the event organizer, says over 15,000 people attend each year. Saturday morning that same weekend is the day of a spectacular flea market held in the next town south, Ocean Grove, on the Pilgrim Pathway from the Great Auditorium to the boardwalk. This is a gay shopping paradise. Information about specific Asbury Park Gay Pride events may be obtained by calling (732) 214-2965 or by visiting www.jerseypride.org.

Sunset Park, across from the Berkeley-Carteret Hotel and the Paramount Theater/Convention Hall complex on the boardwalk, is the spot where the main event takes place. The daytime rally includes many tents and booths with free pamphlets, fliers, booklets, pinback buttons, bumper stickers, caps, hats, and T-shirts, which advertise a variety of organizations and affiliations. Rainbow-colored flags, kerchiefs, pins, and even rainbow collars for gay dogs are offered up for sale. A stage setup offers gay and lesbian comedians, singers, and gay politicians the chance to rally up support and promote equal opportunities and same-sex marriage for Jersey gays. There is plenty of Lambda legal advice available, not to mention AIDS health and safe-sex issues, and booths devoted to real-estate interests in the "new" gay mecca, expensive Asbury Park.

A fully formed gay community in Asbury Park is turning the town around with real-estate and property improvement. Cookman Avenue, Asbury's main street, has a flurry of fanciful antique, furniture, clothing, and boutique shops. The **Asbury Gay Center,** P.O. Box 832, 704 Mattison Ave, Asbury Park 07712, can be contacted at (732) 774-3416.

There is plenty of fun, parties, festivals, and nightlife during Gay Pride Weekend and all summer long, for that matter. One of the main hot spots is the **Paradise,** at 101 Asbury Avenue, (732) 988-6663, www.paradisenj.com, where there is a great disco (two dance floors), six bars, including an attractive and cozy backroom lesbian lounge barroom, lounging areas, a heated pool with deck chairs for sunning in the nude, and other attractions. Overnight rooms are available at the adjoining luxury motel called **The Empress,** (732) 774-0100 or www.asburyempress.com. The Empress was Judy Garland's motel of choice in her later years when she stayed in Asbury Park with her entourage when she was performing at the Garden State Art Center (now the PNC Bank Art Center). Rumor had it that Judy Garland and her bunch even checked out on the run, skipping the bill. Garland, always broke and plagued by financial woes in those days, probably had no dough to spare. The Paradise/Empress has a large parking lot available for those who drive in from all over the state.

A new gay-friendly place to stay in Asbury is the **Hotel Tides & Restaurant Spa,** 408 7th Avenue, established by Marty Santomenno, Douglas Wentz, and Joseph Ruffino. It has 20 rooms, private baths, a pool, dining facilities, a wraparound porch, continuous breakfast, and it's only 2½ blocks to the beach. Call the guys at (732) 897-7744; toll free at (866) 897-7744.

If making the rounds of gay bars in Asbury Park is your thing there is a lot happening at **Anybody's,** 108 St. James Place (www.anybodysnj.com) and **Georgies,** 812 5th Avenue, (732) 988-1220. A fine place for cocktails on porches overlooking Wesley Lake and the Victorian Ocean Grove skyline is **Moonstruck Restaurant and Cocktail Lounge,** which is known throughout New Jersey as a premier restaurant. It is located at 517 Lake Avenue; call (732) 988-0123 for reservations or visit www.moonstrucknj.com.

◆

The following restaurants are a short drive from Ocean Grove and Asbury Park, and are good places to eat after a day of sun and fun. **Mom's Kitchen** is the place for dinner in Neptune, 1129 5th Avenue, (732) 775-4823, and is one of local son Jack Nicholson's favorite hangouts. There are pictures of the actor, who grew up in Neptune, with John and Anjelica Huston on the wall. Mom's pasta dishes are out of this world, the saltimbocca and calamari are delicious, the pizzas excellent, and the atmosphere friendly and upbeat. Booths and tables are in a spacious pine-walled dining room and there is a comfortable bar. They're open every day except Tuesday from noon to 10 P.M., 11 P.M. on weekends. **Pete and Elda's Tavern and Carmen's Pizzeria** is another *must* in this area. Operating together as one establishment, it is located on Highway 35 in Neptune City; (732) 774-6010. The hours are 11:30 A.M. until 2 A.M. for drinks; with dinner served until 1:15 A.M. Here the pizza is cracker-thin and melts in your mouth and the pasta dishes are very good. Also on Route 35, farther south in Wall Township, is **The Circus,** a roadside drive-in restaurant that is built to resemble a circus tent. The carnival atmosphere here is as much fun as a barrelful of monkeys, and it's a great place for families and children. There are specials for kids under 12, like a hamburger, an ice cream cone, and a soda for $3.59. Other than tasty hamburgers and charcoal hot dogs there are shrimp dishes, soft-shell crabs, and barbecue meats, some with names like "wild animal special" (½ pound of ground beef on a hard roll) or "the juggler" (a grilled cheese and tomato sandwich), and "the fire-eater" (hot chili). There are sundaes, malts, and combos of all kinds for kids and adults. This sideshow of a drive-in is a perfect place for a birthday party or special cele-bration—call (732) 449-2650—or just drive in. The Circus has been here since the mid-1950s.

Due West out of Asbury Park on the "Circle" at Routes 33 and 34 in Wall Township is the **Roadside Diner,** which will transport you to yet another twilight zone. The '50s jukebox plays only 1950s 45s of Buddy Holly, Elvis, or the Big Bopper. The waitresses wear 1950s "new look" outfits with poodles and rhinestones ap-pliquéd onto their skirts, and wear their hair in ponytails. The bright clean walls are covered with nostalgic icons of that decade, including Coke signs and photos of vintage cars and James Dean. You don't need a reservation here and the food runs from deluxe sandwiches to blue plate specials such as meat loaf and mashed potatoes. The "in" colors to wear on a date are pink-and-black—and if you drive a pink convertible (circa 1955) park it right in front. If you want to stick close to shore, head on over to **Klein's Waterside Cafe,** 708 River Road in Belmar, (732) 681-1177, for grilled fish, steamed lobsters, clambakes, and fried shrimp out-doors on the shore of the Shark River, between the highway and train bridges. For affordable outfits for diner visits stop at Pat Tecza's **Nostalgic Nonsense,** 903 Main Street, (732) 681-8810 in Belmar. Pat, Rosalita, or Ken will help you look like Sandra Dee, Connie Francis, Fabian, or Elvis with dressy and casual dresses, separates, "unisex" men's jackets, and a full line of accessories. Pat also specializes in '60s and '70s fashion originals—all to be had at fair prices.

As you drive south on Highway 71 from Ocean Grove to Bradley Beach to Avon-by-the-Sea to Belmar, you will note that each town is separated by lakes, rivers, and parklands. A major inlet to the ocean is at Belmar on the Shark River. A good geographic point for boat watching, it attracts fishermen year-round. Driving along the oceanfront south from the youthquake Fort Lauderdale-style playground beach town of Belmar you pass through a gateway structure just over Lake Como that serves as the entranceway to the resort town of luxurious and very upper-crust Irish Spring Lake. The **Boardwalk Pavilion** and **Municipal Pool,** decorated with 1920s art deco tiles depicting fish and wading birds, is one of the architectural high points here, as well as the lovely two miles of beaches, with their white sand and black rocks, and the gracious boardwalk that proudly contains no amusements or rides in favor of spatial elegance.

1920s advertising fan for early real estate development of Shark River Hills near Belmar on the Shark River Inlet.

Spring Lake has a beautiful lake next to its small but charming old-style downtown shopping center. The park and the lake are surrounded by tall, beautiful shade trees, shrubbery, pine groves, winding gravel paths, rustic wooden bridges, and contain indoor tennis courts. By the lake you can feed the many ducks and swans. Spring Lake is a wonderful blend of country, town, and shore, which make it a truly special place in which the traveler can escape the hurly-burly of congested city living. In fact, in the film *The Subject Was Roses* (1968), starring Jack Albertson, Martin Sheen, and Patricia Neal, it is Spring Lake that Patricia Neal goes to by bus to escape her dingy New York flat, her loudmouth drinking, unfaithful husband, and her unfeeling son, who has just returned from World War II. In Spring Lake, the sad and tragic woman finds a sense of peace and serenity, if only for a few hours, walking along the beach and dining in an elegant hotel restaurant. There are many fine places to stay in and around Spring Lake, from the grand to the humble. A good time can be had at Annette Bergins's bed-and-breakfast **Down the Shore** at 201 Seventh Avenue in Belmar, (732) 681-9023. Write for a list to: The Greater Spring Lake Chamber of Commerce, 1315 Third Avenue, Spring Lake, NJ 07762, or call (732) 449-0577. There are also summer rentals of individual houses in the area. Try contacting the MacGowan Agency (732) 449-9400—a local realtor—in March or April to see what kind of listings they have. You could start in December at the **Spring Lake Christmas Bed and Breakfast Tour.** This is an annual event featuring a tour of gaily decorated and beautifully appointed Victorian inns, usually followed by a festive holiday tea. Call the Chamber of Commerce for the exact date. Other places in the area for dining, dancing, drinking, and having fun galore include the **Columns** in Avon, as well as the **Breakers,** the **Hewitt Wellington Hotel** in Spring Lake, and the **Parker House** in Sea Girt.

From Spring Lake driving south you will pass through the small seashore communities of Sea Girt, Manasquan, and Brielle, which is known as a commercial fisherman's town. Brielle is at the mouth of the Manasquan Inlet, and you can buy bluefish, striped bass, tuna, fluke, kingfish, big bull stripers, snappers, and other fish at well below market cost directly from the fishermen at the Brielle landing just off Route 34 (under the bridge).

The grand Essex and Sussex, once one of New Jersey's finest seashore hotels, in Spring Lake.

In Manasquan try the **Carriage House Antique Center** at 140 Main street, (732) 528-6772. Residents of Manasquan and the surrounding towns all know about the gourmet food at **Squan Tavern,** 15 Broad Street, (732) 223-3324; it is served up every night but Monday. Dominic and Marguerite Bossone started the restaurant in 1964, and with the help of Dom III, Joe, Ro, Trish, and Michael, all members of the family, have turned the place into a legend. The pizza is good, salads and antipastos are carefully prepared, pastas and entrees are superb, and the wine list includes everything from a glass of Cabernet for $6 to a $65 Brunello di Montalcino Riserva from Italy. The pinewood paneling on the walls and the neon lighting create an intimate setting for dining and bar drinking here.

Crossing the Manasquan River over a drawbridge south of Brielle you will enter Point Pleasant Beach and the township of Point Pleasant. This is where Agnes Boulton and playwright Eugene O'Neill had a house together, and the place where Sean O'Neill and Oona O'Neill Chaplin played as children. Agnes Boulton continued to reside year-round in the old house in old Point

The Beach House Restaurant and the Tudor-style Warren Hotel once resided on Ocean Avenue in Spring Lake before being demolished in 2004 to make way for new housing.

Pleasant until her death. Point Pleasant is an inviting summer resort lying along the coast on the peninsula between Manasquan Inlet and the Metedeconk River at the head of Barnegat Bay. The road along the inlet toward the beach (first turn over the bridge onto Broadway) is lined with motels and eateries.

Recommended for seafood is **Spike's Fish Market and Restaurant** at 415 Broadway, (732) 295-9400. The **Broadway Bar and Grill,** down the road, is good for a quick beer and a submarine before boarding a fisherman's boat at **Ken's Landing** for a day of sea fishing or a night of moonlight cruising. In season call (732) 528-6620 or 892-3377 to reserve a spot on the *River Belle,* a 140-passenger replica of a Mississippi River paddleboat, which cruises the Manasquan River and Barnegat Bay on a variety of daylight and evening cruises. There is a two-hour Sunday brunch cruise with an all-you-can-eat brunch as well as hour-and-a-half and two-hour-and-a-half cruises with lunch, Monday through Friday. The *River Belle* is moored at the inlet on Broadway in Point Pleasant Beach where you can book yourself for ocean voyages as well. Point Pleasant has wide white-sand beaches and an ocean-front boardwalk that attracts singles to its rowdy nighttime bar scene at **Jenkinson's Pavilion** and **Martel's,** both with loud and sometimes rockin' entertainment. The northern Jenkinson's area on the boardwalk leads to the Manasquan Inlet where people fish on the rock jetty, and fishing boats embark continuously in winter or summer looking for that big catch. An indoor aquarium is the place to get a good look at those scary sharks, and there is a new "state-of-the-art" miniature golf course. For Point Pleasant weekly summer rentals check with Linda at Ward Associates at 106 Ocean Avenue, (732) 892-2700.

Point Pleasant has a number of very good, unpretentious Italian restaurants—one of the best is **Tesauro's** at 401 Broadway. Carmelo Marafioti offers pizza appetizers—their specialty the classic Trenton "tomato pie" for $8 for two. Famous seafood specialties include "flounder formaggio," which is a fresh filet baked in a Dijon cheese sauce with mozzarella, $17.95, and "Tesauro's 'famous' scampi," $17.95. Their telephone number is (732) 892-2090.

Point Pleasant Beach is the point that separates the northern shore from the beginnings of the southern shore. The ocean seems to change here, the water is clearer and it is also more turbulent. In

The Ocean Bay Diner on Route 35 and Route 88 on the circle in Point Pleasant, as it used to be.

fact, New Jersey historian John Cunningham writes about what is called among experienced men of the sea "the treacherous shoals of Barnegat," which pounded ships to pieces, flinging their cargos and the dead and dying sailors and passengers onto the sands. He described how ships destroyed by the moody ocean littered the beaches in the old days. The coast he referred to stretched from Point Pleasant to Little Egg Harbor, an ocean area that merited the reputation as the most dreaded and feared shoals north of Hatteras.

The small downtown area of Point Pleasant is now noted for its many interesting antique shops. The **Point Pleasant Antique Emporium,** which is housed in what used to be a furniture showroom, has three floors and 100 dealers under its roof. Many fine antiques from yesteryear are to be discovered here from among the individual little shops that create an antique "department-store" ambience. Open seven days a week, the emporium is at Bay and Trenton Avenues, and the hours are 11 A.M. to 5 P.M. Call (732) 892-2222. Check out shops like **Fond Memories,** the variety antique store just across the street, and the former Woolworth's five-and ten-cent store on Arnold Avenue, now a full antique center with multiple dealers and a changing stock.

After you pass through Point Pleasant, keep to the shoreline on Highway 35. The road narrows down to two lanes when you hit Bay Head, the end of the line of the NJ Transit North Jersey Coast Line. The beach is only a few blocks from the tiny railroad depot. Bay Head is the beginning point of Barnegat Bay and the first seashore town on the peninsula that eventually ends at Island Beach State park. From Bay Head on the Metedeconk River all the way south to Beach Haven where Little Egg Harbor joins the Great Bay and opens onto the Atlantic, the expansive stretch of

Point Pleasant Beach souvenir postcard folder.

water that comprises Barnegat Bay, filled with blue crabs, turtles, mollusks, horseshoe crabs, clams, and fish, varies in width from 3 to 6 miles and extends itself alongside almost 50 miles of barrier beach with the ocean on one side and the swampy, marshy borders of the mainland on the other. Extending for almost one third of the entire Jersey coast, it resembles in many ways the protected bays along the eastern coast of Florida. The big Barnegat Bay offers many unexcelled facilities for motorboating, sailing, rowing, swimming, fishing, and crabbing. Many varieties of wildfowl and bay birds are to be found in the salt marshes along the fresh streams of the mainland. It is at Bay Head that vacationers may begin to enjoy the advantage of the attractions of the Atlantic Ocean and the delights of the wide waters, tides, and bay breezes.

The beach at Bay Head is one of the best on the coast with black-rock jetties creating interesting deep-water pockets for swimming. The beautiful old oceanfront homes are right on the beach. Initially the 1.25-mile stretch of beach was open only to residents and their guests and those visitors who stayed at the old hotels or rooming houses. Now nonresidents can buy day beach privileges although you must already be dressed for the beach since there is no bathhouse in which to change clothes. Bay Head was a resort as early as the 16th century, when it was used as such by the Lenape Indians, who were later referred to as the Delawares by early white settlers. Seashore land and improvement companies began here in 1879; and Bay Head truly opened up to visitors in 1882 when the railroad arrived. The town of Bay Head is architecturally pure New England–Cape Cod with a bit of Victorian Rococo thrown in for good measure. Bridge Avenue at Bay Avenue is the main shopping area that contains the Victorian-style **Dorcas Ice Cream Parlor and Restaurant,** a cheese shop, an antique emporium set on a wharf, a German bakery, a bookshop, a liquor store, a delicatessen, and a few smart clothing shops.

Lodgings in Bay Head include: The **Bay Head Sands** bed-and-breakfast, open from April through November at Main Avenue (Rte 35) and Twilight Road, (732) 899-7016; **Conover's Bay Head Inn** bed-and-breakfast at 646 Main Avenue, (732) 892-4664; and the lovely old **Hotel Grenville,** 345 Main Avenue, which offers a complimentary continental breakfast, (732) 892-3100.

How to get there: Take the pleasant drive down the peninsula between Barnegat Bay and the Atlantic Ocean to Seaside Heights. Starting at Bay Head, Highway 35 is a two-lane road until it widens south of Mantoloking, the latter sometimes called "millionaire's row" because of the huge summer mansions along the beachfront and bayside. Katharine Hepburn, Mary Roebling (Roebling Steel), and Richard Nixon all summered here. Continue driving south from Mantoloking, passing through many small beach communities like Normandy Beach, Lavallette, and Ocean Beach until you hit Seaside Heights. If you use the Garden State Parkway, exit at 82 onto Route 37, which takes you directly into Seaside. If you are coming from Philadelphia or western New Jersey, hook up with Highway 70 East that will lead you into Route 37 West at the US Naval Air Station at Lakehurst.

For a great day trip, a day at the beach, good food, and an exciting time, bring your date or the whole family to Seaside Heights, definitely Funtown USA, New Jersey-style. Its expansive mile-long boardwalk and a lengthy pier that stretches out over the ocean are jam-packed with the latest fantastic rides like the Himalaya, Bobsled, the Wild Mouse, or the Zipper. There is a beautiful Dentzel/Looff carousel at the north end of the boardwalk of the classic variety, and it is the best to be seen and ridden anywhere. Dr. Floyd Moreland, a classics professor and dean at City University in New York, was instrumental in saving the carousel from destruction, and now devotes much of his time operating and

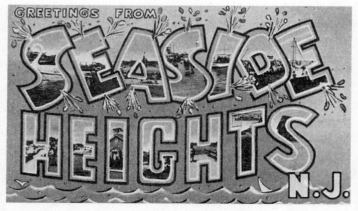

Seaside Heights Greetings, published by Parlin Photo Service.

The Casino merry-go-round with its beautifully carved horses at Seaside Heights.

restoring it. The music is provided by the only continuously operating Wurlitzer Military Band Organ, built in 1923. It plays with a
pneumatic system generated by leather bellows, and the notes are
activated by perforated music rolls, like a player piano. The horses
and other animals, many dating from the 1880s, and the snare and
bass drums, the cymbals, the handmade wooden organ pipes, and
the 16 bell bars on the glockenspiel combine to transport you to
another less-stressful century. Dr. Moreland also owns the **Magical Carousel Shoppe**, featuring the Jersey Shore's most extensive
line of carousel, amusement park, whimsical, and nautical-
themed gifts and collectibles "inspired by the atmosphere con-
jured up by an old-fashioned amusement park by the sea," he says.
Call (800) 830-8374 or visit www.magicalcarousel.com. The
carousel operates daily during the summer from 10 A.M. to midnight. Weekends and holidays it's open all year round from noon
to early evening. Games of chance with their spinning wheels
continue to be a main attraction on this wooden walkway right
next to the Atlantic. Here you can win stuffed panda bears, tigers,
even sharks and snakes; and you could go home with a basket
filled with canned groceries and boxed products, a turkey, a television set, or a carton of factory-fresh cigarettes. From sweaters to
the latest in T-shirts to Popeye the Sailor and Mickey Mouse, you
will find it all on the Seaside Heights boardwalk. It's a veritable
feast of Italian sausage or meatball sandwiches, corn on the cob,
clams on the half-shell, and pizza. In fact, the pizza pies (or
tomato pies as some of these establishments still like to call them)
are in themselves a reason for stopping by this glittering amusement area. Actually, the very best pizza to be found in New Jersey,
or anywhere for that matter, is right here at **Maruca's Pizza.**
Maruca's on the boardwalk will not reveal the treasured secret of
their family recipe, but it is guaranteed to literally melt in your

The Maruca twins, Dom (left) and Joe (right), showing off the best pizza pies on the Jersey coast, at Maruca's Pizza on the Seaside Heights boardwalk.

mouth and delight your taste buds. Connoisseurs of good pizza, take heed—you will not want to miss one of these hot-out-of-the-oven pies served up by the Maruca twins, Joseph P. and Domenic A., or their sister Maria. Maria Maruca is also the Executive Director of the Seaside Park Business Improvement District and suggests you call Summer in the Park at (732) 914-0100 for more information about the goings on in "The Park." Maruca's emanated out of Trenton in 1947 where the family had a pizza parlor restaurant for many years, but since 1950 they have only operated on the boardwalk. There are booths provided, and very friendly waitresses, to accommodate larger groups and families. Pennsylvania Dutch root beer, coffee, or other drinks accompany your mouth-watering slice or whole pie (with or without extras). In 2005 Maruca's began a franchise business—who knows, a Maruca's may be coming to your neighborhood soon. Maruca's is actually in Seaside Park right on the borderline with the Heights at 1927 Promenade, (732) 793-0707; www.marucaspizza.com. is where you will find other locations in Jersey, like New Brunswick, Cherry Hill, Warren Township, Hoboken, and more.

One old-time bar that is a really good-time hangout (and has been for years) is **Klee's Bar** on Dupont Avenue and the Boulevard. A mix of singles, regulars, and local characters, it is worth the trip to come there whether in summer or winter for the entertainment, which is a hodgepodge of country-western and true-blue American. The atmosphere is old-fashioned and the knotty pine walls and neon beer signs give this place a special warm glow. The thin-crusted pizza is very good and the tap beer is ice cold. Mussels, deli sandwiches, and basket foods (chicken, fried mushrooms, etc.) are served until 1:30 A.M., when the kitchen closes. The bar stays open late and you will have a helluva lot of fun. Tropical

Klee's Bar beer coaster (left).
Klee's Bar on Boulevard and Dupont serves excellent pizza and New Jersey's favorite beers.

Early animated Madame Zita machine at the Central Arcade, that picked out a card that told the future for a dime in days gone by.

drinks are a specialty, but Rolling Rock beer seems to be the most popular brew. Ireland-brand coffee is served up on the fishing pier (same as the amusement pier) in a little shack perched right on the edge and looking out over the breaking waves of the ocean. Accompanied by a bag of Oreo cookies or caramel popcorn from Johnson's on the boardwalk, the coffee often hits the spot after playing the pinball games at the **Central Arcade** on the boardwalk at Hamilton Avenue.

The **Berkeley Sweet and Taffy Shop** is a place from times gone by that continues to exist on the great boardwalk. At the Berkeley, located at the enclosed merry-go-round to the south, you can send anyone a box of saltwater taffy, eat a caramel or candied apple, or a particularly good chocolate, strawberry, or vanilla-coconut candy patty. Other homemade candies are available in bags or in

A game of chance in which you can take home a prized Popeye the sailor doll, boardwalk, Seaside Heights (top). A spectacular pop culture sign display at Kohr's famous custard and orangeade stand on the boardwalk at Seaside Heights, one of several such outstanding concessions up and down this boardwalk and in other places along the Jersey shore (bottom).

colorful boxes. A second Berkeley Taffy branch is several blocks down the way on the boardwalk, in case you passed it up the first time. **Johnson's Popcorn** has served its own particular brand of delicious caramel popcorn or salted buttered popcorn in simple cardboard boxes on the boardwalk for decades. A primitive hand-painted mural at Johnson's shows Goofy and his pal Mickey Mouse downing the sweet gooey caramel concoction. **Kohr's** soft custard stands (there are at least three on this boardwalk) serve blueberry ripple, fresh banana and peach, orange-and-raspberry sherbet, and chocolate peanut-butter custard creme as well as their trademark fresh-squeezed refreshingly iced orange drink. The design concept of the Kohr's stands is pop art in a combination of blue, orange, and white colors. The sanitary and efficient manner of Kohr's and the clean and immaculate porcelain interiors make these stands a nice place to patronize.

Seaside Heights seems to really sparkle at nighttime when the boardwalk lights glitter and the bars and discos, like the **Bamboo**

Bar, or the other night clubs on "Boulevard," which is the main strip, are in full swing. The lights from the amusement rides on the pier as they reflect into the ocean and the night sky are a sight to behold. After a day in the sun, a walk on the boardwalk at night seems just right, seeing the sights and the people, some in outlandish offbeat attire, and feeling those cool evening breezes from the sea. The beach at Seaside Heights has soft white sand and the ocean waves here are often powerful, attracting large numbers of surfers. You can swim on the beach at Seaside Heights and in-season there are some bathhouses along the boardwalk for changing your clothes. For an overnight, weekly, or longer stay in Seaside and the area, check out oceanfronts, bayfronts, single-families, multi-families, and condos at Seaside Realty, 1220 Boulevard, Seaside Heights, NJ 08751. Call (732) 793-5200 and ask for Mike Loundy or send an e-mail to mikeloundy@aol.com. The **Hershey Motel** at 1415 Boulevard in Seaside Heights—(732) 793-5000; www.hersheymotel.com—is open year-round and is a big place with lots of rooms. Here you'll find a 50-foot pool, a kiddie pool, sundecks, and an on-premises restaurant serving breakfast, lunch and dinner. Motels that allow pets are few and far between; two that do are **Lazy River by the Sea** and **Lazy River by the Bay** (whichever your dog or iguana prefers)—call 866-SHOREHOUSE. One of the most interesting spots to stay in Seaside Heights, right at the northern tip of the boardwalk, is the **Aztec Ocean Front Resort Lounge and Motel,** 901 Boardwalk, (732) 793-3000. This is a funky people-who-like-people place with a bar/lounge that plays live music, a swimming pool, and small shops. In one of these shops you can have your name written on a grain of rice that is then put in a globe and attached to a necklace. This is a place to have a really crazy-fun weekend or an entire week for that matter. The summer season at **The Aztec** begins in March.

Island Beach is a state park divided into a botanical zone, wildlife sanctuary, and recreation area for beachgoing and swimming. This is the best place to swim on your Seaside Heights day trip. It is a 10-mile-long natural barrier beach going to the tip of the peninsula. One side of this land is Barnegat Bay while the other is the Atlantic Ocean in its wildest and purest state. This is a truly wondrous environmental showcase for the state of New Jersey. To visit Island Beach with its snow white sand, its natural grassy dunes, its thick shrubbery, its holly trees, and its swamp grass and many varieties of wild plant life, is to confront the elements at the shore as they have been since the very beginnings. Wild rabbits, red fox, and other creatures inhabit the thick brush, and there are many varieties of birds that make this spot a bird-watcher's delight. Recently the hawklike ospreys returned to their nests of twigs and branches perched on top of telephone poles. There are two public beach areas located halfway down the park with modern bathhouses with showers, refreshment stands, as well as beach lifeguards. The "aeolium" has a display of plant and wild animal and bird life. There is a pathway here into the dunes with signs naming the various outdoor pine bushes, plants and trees, including cacti and beach plum shrubs. There is an oceanfront Cape Cod–style summer mansion on Island Beach, used by the incumbent governor of New Jersey, and the estate has a smaller house on the bay for visiting dignitaries and guests. South of the public beach area there are numbered parking lots for fishermen who consider Island Beach a paradise, winter or summer. For 30 years the State of New Jersey pondered whether to buy this strip, which was privately owned; they finally decided to go ahead when real estate developers were beginning to make propositions. In 1952 the state acquired it for $2.75 million, and the park was opened in 1959. Eight miles south of the entrance the two-lane road ends at parking area A-23. Here is a good opportunity to park the car and take a hike down the beach at the water's edge. A mile and a half down you will reach the tip of Island Beach, the Atlantic Ocean surging into Barnegat Bay through Barnegat Inlet. Barnegat Lighthouse—"Old Barney"—is across the inlet at the northern tip of Long Beach Island, and to your right, on the bay side of Island Beach, are the dunes and marshes of a protected bird nesting area. Bathe your feet and linger in the changing pools of the inlet before returning to your car. Note: When the parking lots at Island Beach are filled (mostly on hot weekends during the summer) traffic into the park is halted at the entrance, and you must either wait for a certain number of exiting cars or bathe elsewhere.

Bordering Seaside Heights to the south is Seaside Park, which claims a small portion of the Heights boardwalk but in the main is a quiet, sedate beach resort town that stands in sharp contrast to the Heights's frenetic activity, in the same way that Ocean Grove separates itself from the crazy nightclub activity in Asbury Park. Seaside Park's boardwalk is built over the wide, powdery-white sand beaches and has no amusements; it does have a number of summer house gazebo-like structures with green rooftops that are more like open porches, jutting over the sand. These have benches for a respite from the sun or a sudden lightning storm or summer shower. Seaside Park has many large barnlike houses that are almost like summer mansions as well as a few rental houses, and two or three places of the roominghouse variety; but for the most part it is very private. There are day beaches and bathhouses in the northern part of Seaside Park. For weekly or monthly rentals in the Park, with its spacious big homes all within an easy walk to the ocean or the bay, call the "Broker of Record," Judy Appleby at Appleby Realty, 1208 S.E. Central Avenue, Seaside Park, NJ 08752; (732) 793-6074. You can dine on "the best of land and sea" seven days and seven nights a week year-round at the **Top Of the Mast Restaurant,** (732) 793-1110 at 23rd Avenue at the ocean in Seaside Park, abutting Island Beach State Park. With its 65-foot surf bar, a happy hour from 4 to 6 P.M. with half-price drinks, and its excellent food the Top Of the Mast is attracting nature lovers and travelers all year round. Right alongside the restaurant, stretching west from the ocean, is a two-story, double-sided motel called **Island Beach Motor Lodge,** (732) 793-5400. Call them to reserve one of their 76 units from single-bed motel rooms to a swanky penthouse facing the ocean, as well as efficiencies (kitchen, separate bedroom, Castro convertible couch in the living room) that can accommodate 4 to 5 people. During the season (July and August) these efficiencies have a two-night minimum; a one-and-a-half 2-bed efficiency is $130 daily, $150 Friday and Saturday, or $900 per week. Apartments with a separate bedroom are $155–170, $1100 per week. Single units are $90–$105 per night. Doubles with two beds are $125 during the week and $145 on weekends. Special rates apply in September, October, May, and June, as well as November through April. This is definitely the place to go during the cooler months, or anytime, so be sure to call and make a reservation for rates in all seasons. Joe Leon, your gracious host at Island Beach Motor Lodge also runs the **Atlantic Bar & Grill** for cozy beach rendezvous. **Ebby's Deli** in South Seaside Park (open 7 days from 7 A.M. to midnight) features famous giant submarine sandwiches and excellent homemade crumbcakes, cannollis, fresh breads, fine meats, and other take-out goodies. **Ebby's Cafe Alfresco** serves sit-down dinners from 4 to 11 P.M., featuring premier Italian dishes like pasta frasioli, spiedini, mozzarella in carozza, and chicken Rossini. Call (732) 830-4775 for specials and delivery. To while away the evenings in Seaside Park, go to **Phoenix Rising** for new and used books and a whole lot more, including a café; live music Thursday, Friday, and Saturday; open mike; psychic fairs; a vinyasa- and sivananda-style yoga studio; unique gifts and cards; and internet access. The shop is located at 212 S. E. Central Avenue; call (732) 793-6967 or visit www.phoenixrising4u.com.

Bum Rogers, named after a local pirate of yore, on Central Avenue at 23rd Avenue (just outside the entrance to Island Beach State Park) in South Seaside Park is a bar and restaurant that stays open late (until midnight) and cooks up the very best hardshell crabs, softshell crabs, blackened fish (Creole style), lobster, and good seafood combo platters. There is the sense that this is an "in" restaurant. The lively casual ambience makes it a fun place to go, and prices are moderate. If you need to take a walk after eating you are just a block from the ocean and two blocks to the great Barnegat Bay. Seafood, beer, and ice-cold bone-dry martinis are also served up at the lively, happy-go-lucky, horseshoe shaped bar.

The **Pier House** on Central and 22nd Avenue, (732) 830-2250, serves breakfast from 7 A.M., lunch and dinners of steak, seafood, whole stuffed lobster with imperial crabmeat stuffing, with linguine or potato and bouillabaisse. The **Berkeley Fish Market, and Restaurant** is at 24th Avenue and Central. On the upper floor of this family restaurant you can view the expanse of Island Beach. Here you can enjoy fresh seafood specials and fish combinations deep fried or broiled at very reasonable prices. The homemade clam chowder is excellent; and at the fish market you can take a container home with you as well as fresh and prepared fried seafood. Breakfast (7:30 to 11:30 A.M.) here includes two eggs, toast, home fries, and coffee. Lunch (noon to 4 P.M.) of a hamburger or fish sandwich with french fries, coleslaw and chowder is a bargain and economical family dinners are served from noon to 10 P.M. The restaurant and fish market are open Mother's Day to the week after Labor Day. The family opened a new restaurant at 1747 Hooper Avenue (inland to Toms River on Route 37) in Silverton (in the Anchorage Square Plaza) that is open year round. At Central Avenue and First (still in Seaside Park) the **Windjammer Motor Inn,** (732) 830-2555, has an amiable cocktail lounge, good to visit to listen to the live organ music and eat the complimentary hot and cold hors d'oeuvres served at poolside. The Windjammer is open year round. If happy hour is not your thing, rent an outboard motorboat or a rowboat at the **Wheelhouse Marina** (24th Avenue and Barnegat Avenue in South Seaside Park) on the bay. Gary J. Grob and Don Matthews, who run this place right at the northern tip of Island Beach (a kind of end-of-the-line location), also have a no-nonsense coffee shop with home-cooked breakfasts

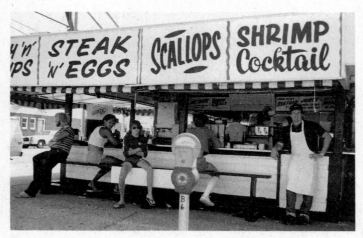

Barney's in Seaside Park with Barney's grandson Mike Loundy (right, in apron) with seated customers.

and American-style sandwiches on the premises, open from 6 A.M. to 8 P.M.

The weekend after Labor Day Seaside Heights has its annual Mardi Gras. (In Seaside Mardi Gras comes after Labor Day, not before Lent—a mercantile maneuver cooked up by local bars to cash in on the lingering summer mood.) It features incredible low, low price sidewalk sales, parades, floats, and merrymaking of every kind. Outlandish costumes, men in full drag as prom queens or street hustlers, are everywhere, camping it up at Klee's and the other hot spots for two whole days and nights. For some it is all innocent fun, laughs, and a happy time. For others it is a bargain hunt. Still others are on the proverbial "lost weekend," raising hell well before All Hallows' Eve when things are very quiet indeed in these parts. However, it should be mentioned that the Seaside Heights boardwalk concessions are open for business, chiefly on weekends, with many places open until Christmas and again, certainly, well before Easter (as soon as it warms up even a bit). The skilo and bingo parlors never close and keep the locals fascinated and away from their homes and the television set for many hours. Usually these are the places grandma can win a Butterball turkey for the holidays. And the historic carousel on the boardwalk is open weekends all year round. In Lavallette (north of Seaside on Route 35) at 601 Grand Central is the **Crab's Claw Inn,** (732) 793-4447, in the town center. It's noted for its fresh seafood dinners and its choice steaks. The Crab's Claw also has a 100-bottle wine list and serves up 135 different brands of domestic and imported beers. There is nightly entertainment with happy hour

A Victorian summer house in Seaside Park.

(half-price drinks) serving exotic and regular cocktails from 4 to 6 P.M. Lunch on the porch is a pleasant experience here. Lavallette has a charming, old-fashioned boardwalk laid right out on the sand. From here you can see the glittering lights of the Seaside Heights boardwalk just south.

West over the bridge from Seaside Heights and a few miles inland on Route 37 there is a turnoff before you reach Toms River. This is the beautiful, secluded community of Island Heights, which began as a Methodist camp meeting ground in 1878. Situated on Toms River proper, where it enters Barnegat Bay, this Victorian town, with its tall trees and spacious front lawns and gardens, its small yellow sand beaches, its quaint wooden boardwalk along the bayfront, is a varied area of hills, valleys, and lowlands, and a fine place to take in the bay breezes commingling with the sweet smell of the river, the pines, and the ocean. The **Ocean County Artists Guild** is located in a fine old home at 22 Chestnut Avenue, and often has art shows and related events. There is an art school, a dance school, several churches, and a few small shops, adding to the rustic flavor of this town. There is little that is gaudy or commercial and everything is pastoral, spacious, and green. The great Victorian homes by the bay, and the wide-paved streets, dimly lit at night to retain the old-time flavor of the past, make this geographic spot on the inland-waterway an ideal place to take a moonlight walk if you are staying out on the strip in Seaside Heights, and want to experience something very different and very pleasant. Highway 37 is filled with motel after motel for overnight accommodations and there are fish markets, farmers' produce markets, gas stations, automobile dealerships, a junk hubcap shop, plant and garden supplies, shopping malls, movie houses, diners, and fast-food spots galore. When you make the turnoff to Island Heights the changeover is remarkable and that is what is fun about New Jersey—its many "round the bend" surprises.

The Legend of the Jersey Devil

The great area known as the Pine Barrens, and other sections of southern New Jersey, are said to be menaced by the Jersey Devil, a demon reported to have a horselike face, red eyes, bat wings, cloven hoofs, and a forked tail. This demon beast, as legend has it, likes to play mischievous tricks on innocent tourists and children, sometimes half-scaring them to death from fright. The "Pineys," the local folk who live in the Pine Barrens, are said to be dominated by this devil and will themselves "give a scare" to outsiders for no apparent reason. Many Pineys are descendants of Hessian troops (German soldiers hired by the British) who hid out in the barrens after the American Revolution to avoid being captured. The Pineys call the Jersey Devil the "Leeds Devil," referring to the original legend that it was originally born to a Mrs. Leeds in 1735 at what is now known as Leeds Point near Smithville. One of the myths has it that the Devil's first meal was several sleeping children and another handed-down tale has him devouring the entire Leeds family. The monster so menaced this area that a clergyman in 1740 was called in to perform an exorcism that was said would last for 100 years. Unfortunately, the Jersey Devil did not completely disappear during this time; he came back in 1840 with a

Two postcards, left: The most famous New Jersey folklore character, known as the "Jersey Devil" or the "Leeds Devil," was said to be a monster born of a woman named Leeds in the early 1700s. The 1975 postcard is by Ed Sheetz. Right: "Atlantic City by Moonlight," a 1908 postcard with what appears to be a Jersey Devil creature emerging out of the sea to confront one vacationer who has had one too many highballs.

Jersey Devil by Earl Tyler, 1970.

vengeance and has not left since. Sometimes, throughout the 1,700 square miles of the Pine Barren wilderness region, blood-curdling screams and agonizing moans are heard at night that are attributed to this weird beast. The Jersey Devil is said to hide out in swamps and near dark ponds and lakes, and has been spotted often in the Atlantic City meadows as well as in the depths of the forests around Batsto.

In the Pine Barrens near Weekstown, not far from the winding Mullica River, there is a tiny coffee shop-restaurant called **Pat's Stand** with a screened-in porch, a whirring overhead fan, and rusty old 1940s Coca-Cola signs. One of the proprietors, a woman named Gladys A. Wilson, talks about the Jersey Devil. She tells the tale told to her by her grandfather, who knew of a family that lived deep in the woods. Traveling by horse-and-buggy these folk had to ride through a large cedar swamp and cross a rail bridge. One night on one of these journeys they had to fight their way across the bridge when a big hairy monster came out of the swamp and menaced them. The man grabbed a rail off the bridge and hit the beast, knocking it into the water. Then he jumped in his buggy and took off faster than lightning. Gladys's great-uncle William Bozarth used to be the caretaker at Batsto Village. At midnight he would go with his lantern to the barn to check the livestock. Walking down the path to the barn late one night he suddenly saw a strange-looking animal with a horse face, walking on two feet just in front of him. "Uncle Willy," she recounted, "was sure it was the Jersey Devil on his way into the barn to make a killin' for a midnight snack." Gladys also tells tales about recent occurrences of dogs, cats, geese, chickens, and ducks disappearing without a trace. When a group went into the woods with shotguns, the posse discovered deer bones, hides, dog bones, feathers, and the like all in one single spot. All suspected the Devil's work was at hand.

There were other stories of children being whacked so hard on the back of their necks by some kind of creature in the pinelands that their collar bones were broken. Gladys looks thoughtfully out at the horizon and says, "Things have been quiet of late. It's about time for that rascal to come galloping out of the swamps. I do hope he comes out and scares the hell out of the developers for messing in our Pinelands. They'll be sorry they destroyed the forest if their paths cross that of the Jersey Devil. Oh, by the way," Piney Gladys Wilson pauses, "the Jersey Devil is most certainly in Atlantic City!" Other Pineys now joke about the notion that the Jersey Devil took over the body of the person who originally sold out Atlantic City to gambling interests. Could she be referring to Reese Palley? In any case we know the Devil is alive and well in A.C.!

More recently, on May 9, 2005, a high school teacher named Frances Shepherd from Tranquility, New Jersey, described in a *Sun* exclusive report the story of her encounter with the Jersey Devil. On a solo visit to Wharton State Forest, Frances set up camp on a chilly night, building a fire near a deep, dark lake. She noticed that something strange seemed to be moving in the water, creating ripples. Suddenly a hideously shaped wildebeest with a horse's head broke the surface of the water. The snarling creature roared and moaned as if it were in great pain. Its red eyes glowed like two round burning coals in the dark of night. Frances felt it must have been Satan himself. Emerging on the shore, this large beast had big stingray webbed wings and a long slithering forked tail. In a state of panic Frances reports that she ran through the woods toward her van, but the huge monster came crashing right after her. Coming across her campfire, she picked up a big burning stick and wielded it. With the lit torch in her hand, Frances realized that this hideous creature must be the very Jersey Devil that she had read about in books and heard about from the local "Piney" people when she was a small child. Screaming and yelling, Frances swung the torch at the red-eyed beast. Glaring at her intensely for a time, the great demon suddenly, and for no apparent reason, jumped back into the deep of the swampy lake and disappeared.

A stunned Frances, leaving her tent, sleeping bag, and food hamper behind, made a desperate run to her van. Driving as fast as she could, she emerged from the forest vowing never to camp out alone again in the Jersey Pine Barrens.

Lakewood to Lake Rova to Forked River

Devotees of the American road always have loved old Route 9, a two-lane highway that parallels the Garden State Parkway on the eastern shore of New Jersey. When the pace was slower, Route 9 was the main roadway to Atlantic City and other southern Jersey seashore resorts. Jersey jaunters, in search of something simple and different, still can appreciate the many roadside diners and funky motels like the '50s-style **Moon Motel,** just north of Lakewood, with its fanciful neon sign of animated rockets heading for the moon. If you enjoy waterbeds, overhead mirrors, mirror-ball lighting, and special video installations, stay at the Moon or at one of the dozens of other motels—most of them clean and respectable—that dot the old road.

Lakewood on Route 9 became famous on the East Coast as the place where you could breathe in the fresh pine air. In the late 19th century it was the fashionable spot to vacation in the winter. Right up to the 1950s you would see women sitting in the noonday sun with their dyed hair and full-face makeup, wearing furs, diamonds, and pointed rhinestoned sunglasses on the front porches of the old Lakewood resort hotels, on Highway 9. Of course, many come in the summer to be among the pines, and to swim and hike along the many pine-needle trails in and around Lakewood. Great estates and mansions were built here when this health resort was at its peak, including those of John D. Rockefeller and George Jay Gould. You can still see **Georgian Court,** built along Lake Carasaljo's northern shore as the home of George Jay Gould in 1898–1900, with its Georgian and Renaissance architecture and elaborate gardens and fountains. The site is now a Catholic college for women. The former estate of John D. Rockefeller Sr. was acquired by Ocean County in 1940, and though the mansion has been torn down, the remaining trees from around the world and planted by Rockefeller himself form a public park with picnic grounds and a lake for swimming. To experience the great pines of Lakewood and to swim in its mineral-rich lakes you should turn right on Route 88 off Route 9 to **Ocean County Park** where you can picnic at tables with fireplaces and swim in the lake. Here are over 300 acres of white pine and hemlock trees towering high.

On the Manasquan River, boaters ply east and west, but their favorite tie-up place is **Peterson's Marina Grill,** 1600 Highway 70, Brick Township, (732) 840-1110, replete with docking facilities. Dock and dine on the à la carte menu and daily specials in the $21 to $25 price range. Hours are 11:30 A.M. to 10 P.M. Sunday through Thursday. Friday and Saturday they're open with a late-nite menu until 11 P.M. Also on the premises at Peterson's on the Manasaquan River there is an extravagant Liquor Centre with everything imaginable available.

Out of Lakewood there are many chicken farms where you can purchase candlelit eggs from free-running hens, organic eggs, or just plain Jersey eggs, which are delicious any way you like them. Some places also will sell fresh-killed chickens. Farm produce stands in this area always sell the best of the summer harvest from New Jersey farms. In the summer, silver queen white corn, every variety of Jersey tomato, including yellow acid-free tomatoes, eggplant, squash, peaches, and beach plums flood old Route 9.

◆

Six Flags Great Adventure

Heading west on 526 from Lakewood off Highway 9 toward Jackson and Trenton is **Six Flags Great Adventure** on Route 537 (about six minutes from Exit 91 off the Garden State Parkway). In the theme park is a 3-lane, 4.5-mile drive-through safari (about 350 acres) with 1,500 wild animals from all over the world, some of which will jump on your car; so convertibles or vinyl-top hardtops are not permitted in this area of the park unless you want a hairy orangutan or mandrill on your lap. This family-type planned environment has a kiddie kingdom with merry-go-rounds and other rides. There are over 100 rides, shows, and attractions here. You will find restaurants and five hours of specialty shows daily, concerts, dolphin acts, aquatic acts, and more.

The 2,200-acre park has a daily season that runs from May to September and a weekend-only season (Saturday and Sunday) from March to May and September through November, including a special Columbus Day celebration and hayrides, a Halloween party, and costume events on October 31. At the end of October there are also Oktoberfest Bavarian festivals with German entertainment, food, and strolling oompah-pah brass bands. One of the main attractions for this family-oriented park is a 15-acre water ride called Adventure Rivers, a collection of water slides, tubes, and streams that will leave you wringing wet—so dress accordingly— bring a change of clothing or wear a rubber suit. There are also hair-raising rollercoasters, including the highest in the world (with a 465-foot drop) and the speediest in the world (with speeds up to 120 miles per hour), which are a-thrill-a-minute with loops, dives, and curves that create a rush of terror, fear, and excitement for those young and brave souls who enjoy a good scare and a good scream.

If twists and turns don't excite you, you might want to try the parachute jump. Bring plenty of extra dollars for souvenirs, food, and parking. The safari trip, in which car windows must remain closed, can be stifling in summer if your auto does not have air-conditioning. The drive-through takes an hour with giraffes and wild elk sometimes standing in front of the car looking for a treat to eat.

Great Adventure is very much a shlock pop-culture experience, but it can be an entertainment and distraction for a family looking for a good time. Some return again and again, and it is the closest you can get to the controlled environment of a Disney park in the northeast. It is just one hour either from Manhattan or Philadelphia. In summer put on insect repellent as you will find yourself at the top of the Pine Barrens region and mosquitoes are legendary. Theme Park and Safari ticket prices can be purchased separately or as a package; there are special discount prices for seniors and kids under 54 inches—infants three and under free. Call (732) 928-1821 for further information.

There are lakes farther west on Route 526 for swimming and picnic grounds to enjoy, as well. Route 528 West out of Lakewood is a lovely drive to Cassville, where you will turn right at the sign to Rova Farms, an old White Russian resort. At one point Routes 528 and 527 are joined, but at the Van Hiseville Juncture stay west on 528. On the 527-528 neck of the journey **Butterfly Pond Fish and Wildlife Management Area** (which features a quail farm) is an interesting stop.

At **Rova Farms** in the Pines is **Lake Rova.** The **Rova Farm Bar and Restaurant** serves excellent Russian peasant-style dishes, sauerkraut and homemade kielbasa, pelmini in butter and sour cream, roast duck with kasha, and delicious Russian borscht. The old White Russians—and their offspring—sing Russian songs and drink Russian vodka without ice. The large simple restaurant room has pictures of Anton Chekhov and other Russian greats on the wall. Throughout the year there are many festivities such as folk festivals, Russian picnics and concerts, and all are always welcome here. A great open porch winds around the restaurant, and a little store sells folk items imported from Russia. There is an enclosed dance pavilion on the lake where these folk will dance wildly into the night. The grounds, including the formal **Pushkin Gardens,** dominated by an imposing statue of the famous Russian writer Pushkin, has the feeling of old Russia: the pine trees, the shrubbery, the holly trees, the thick grass and wildflowers, and the broad graveled walks evoking the novels of Turgenev and Tolstoy. Even the dark Lake Rova seems more like a great pond than a lake. **St. Vladimir's Church** at Rova Farms is a copy of a 16th-century Russian chapel with a great ornate gold dome, and with many broad stairs climbing up the hill to its prominent site. It is painted cream white and has colorful tile mosaics of the saints. There is also a gazebo and a small graveyard where many of Tolstoy's kin—including his daughter—are buried. The Russian priest wears long white robes and has long hair and a beard. Russian Christmas and Russian Easter are celebrated here, and the restaurant is open all year long with very reasonable prices. This is a wonderful Sunday drive and you should call (732) 928-0928 for the restaurant hours and a calendar of the special festivities. The area is surrounded by small farms where you can buy honey, corn, tomatoes, summer squash, and other products.

"Old Peg-Leg John" drained a swamp near Cassville in 1845 to grow cultivated cranberries in the pines. He was so successful in selling them in Philadelphia that soon a cranberry industry flourished throughout the Pine Barrens. There are still cranberry bogs in the Pines as well as blueberry farms, but not to the degree that there were in earlier years. (See "Southwestern Farm Country" for cranberry and blueberry statistics.) Sailing vessels used to take supplies of cranberry on board for a long voyage, believing these tart red berries prevented scurvy. The Lake Rova–Cassville area is also approached out of Toms River on Route 571 that crosses Route 528 at Cassville. Check your map.

Take Highway 547 one mile out of the Borough of Lakehurst to the **Lakehurst Naval Historical Society,** (732) 323-2620, for a self-guided tour past Blimp Hangar #1, which contains a memorial at the site where the famous *Hindenburg* burst into flames on May 6, 1937 after its third transatlantic crossing, 36 passengers perishing in the flames. The folk of the Pines, the "Pineys," are not lovers of progress—in fact, during Prohibition the men who made "white lightnin'" in the pineland stills thought the airships were "revenoors" and were always shooting them up with holes as they glided over the woods. The *Hindenburg* disaster, broadcast to the world from an on-the-site observer, spelled the end of airship travel in the 1930s. Call **Ocean County Parks and Recreation** (609) 971-3085 for special group tours of the area.

The **Ocean County Historical Society,** 26 Hadley Avenue, in Toms River, (732) 341-1880, is a must-not-miss museum visit. The ladies of the society have helped to create a house in which history lives. The schoolroom on the second floor, with all the original articles of its reading and writing work in place, the charming playroom, the roughhewn bedrooms of its former occupants as well as the kitchen and family rooms downstairs, create a startling effect. The ladies will point out such curiosities as the pot at the foot of the bed. "A spittoon?" you will ask. "No, it's for holding turpentine to kill the bedbugs." The Victorian mansion, which seems to be waiting for that family to return a century later, is connected to another exhibition area that features historical aspects of Ocean County, including impressive dirigible memorabilia and a research center.

The **Cowboy Saloon,** built to resemble an Old West cowtown, is below Toms River, in Bayville, on Route 9. In the past Willie Nelson and Mickey Gilley played here. Today live entertainment on weekends is supplied by groups like Dusty Saddlebags. This rip roaring Wild West saloon is open late. Call (732) 269-5545 to find out what's going on, pardner.

Farther south on Route 9 there is a state game farm at Forked River where you can see thousands of penned-in peacock, golden pheasant, quail, and other wild game, including deer, all in a beautiful setting, just drive in off Highway 9.

Gigantic two-gun painted-metal road sign, 45 feet high and vividly red neon at night, beckons travelers to the Cowboy Steakhouse and Saloon on old Route 9 in Bayville.

Four miles out to sea, 19 miles from its northern tip at the **Old Barnegat Lighthouse** to its southern tip at Beach Haven Inlet on Little Egg Harbor, Long Beach Island has long been a favorite vacation resort for New Jerseyans, New Yorkers, and Philadelphians. "Old Barney," the main attraction on the island, is over 100 years old, but ceased being used as a lighthouse in 1927. It was saved from destruction by concerned citizens in the 1920s who rallied to save the lighthouse beacon that once guided ships into the narrow and fast-moving Barnegat Inlet, and helped to rescue those that were in distress or sinking. It is still an experience to see this red-and-white tower, designed by George Gordon Meade, from a distant approach or at close range. A gift shop, a museum, a restaurant, and a bait and tackle shop now surround Old Barney, which was built of thick strong brick and is a great symbol and monument to the sea and of times past; if it could speak like some of the old fishermen who like to spin tall tales of the ocean, it would have many adventurous sea stories to tell.

◆

Sinbad, the Legendary Four-Legged Sailor

A legend has developed around a 24-pound brown, black-and-white mongrel named Sinbad who came aboard the Coast Guard cutter *Campbell* in 1937 and served as a "sailor-mascot" aboard this vessel throughout World War II. Sinbad was buried in 1951 at the ripe old age of 14, at Barnegat lifeboat station. Many stories about the heroic dog have been chronicled in *Life* magazine and in newspapers. A book about his life, *Sinbad of the Coast Guard* was published, and there was a film called *Dog of the Seven Seas* that was released by Universal Pictures in 1947. The "salty sea dog" ate and slept with the crew, and was also known as a "bar hound" who, when on shore leave, frequented the bars with his buddies, jumping up and sitting on a barstool, lapping up his boilermakers just like any sailor. First he would lap up a mug of beer, followed by a shot glass of bourbon, which he favored over Canadian whiskey blends. His pals always paid for these drinking jaunts. Staggering back to the boat with the others he would be given aspirin the next morning to help bring him back to a "ship-shape" condition. Sometimes Sinbad would remain on board but would always be sitting on deck when the ship was in port to help escort a drunken sailor to his bunk. Sinbad was regarded by his crew not just as a mere mascot but as a good-luck charm, having seen the gobs through many World War II battles, such as the one

when the *Campbell* had a 12-
hour duel with a wolfpack of
German submarines. When the
ship rammed a German sub,
sinking it into the icy waters of
the North Atlantic, the Coast
Guard vessel itself was badly
damaged, and the crew, including Sinbad, had to be transferred
onto a convoy escort. The many
fighting battles that Sinbad was
an active part of brought him a
good deal of attention in state-
side newspapers; following the
war this sailor-dog went on a pub-
licity tour all over America for the
benefit of the US Coast Guard. It
is fitting that this outstanding and

*Sinbad the Sailor, United States
Coast Guard dog.*

unusual canine, who served honorably for 14 years in the Guard,
should come to a final resting place near his beloved beacon of
light—Old Barney—New Jersey's world-famous lighthouse.

At Beach Haven you can visit **Lucy Evelyn,** the site of a three-
masted schooner that was destroyed by fire in 1972, and the wharf
has several shops as well as **Schooner's Wharf** at the corner of Bay
Street and 9th. Since 1985 Beach Haven has **Fantasy Island
Amusement Park,** owned and operated by Gary Phillips, who for
many years owned the Central Arcade in Seaside Heights. Fantasy
Island was designed with a Victorian air and features an elegant
Family Casino Arcade open year round, free entertainment, a
food court, old-fashioned ice-cream parlor, and great rides like the
Sea Dragon and the Giant Wheel. The handsome, enterprising
Mr. Phillips bears a striking resemblance to the movie actor
George Montgomery when he played a carney barker who tames
a honky-tonk singer played by Betty Grable in the 20th Century
Fox 1940s technicolor film *Coney Island.* Gary loves the amusement park business and collects antique amusement park games,
fortune machines, pinball machines, and early Wurlitzer jukeboxes that he lovingly restores. Some of these are on display for all
to see and enjoy, and you can still drop a coin and play a few of the
oldies, like a baseball game with miniature players (such as Jimmy
Foxx and Hank Greenberg) in painted lead from the early 20th
century. Fantasy Island is at 320 West Seventh Street, Beach
Haven; call (609) 492-4000 or visit www.fantasyislandpark.com.

On Route 22, just a few miles west of the Parkway, you'll encounter dozens of carved tiki gods alongside the road. These be-
long to **Tiki Murph,** who creates and sells tiki bars and tiki heads
in the Jersey Pinelands.

Gary Phillips, the handsome George Montgomery look-alike, with his prize 1930s bakelite, wood-and-chromium jukebox, and 1932 baseball game.

Many people came to Long Beach Island to seek relief from pollen and hay fever in the old days. Surf City established itself as a resort in 1873, and Barnegat City, at the north end where the lighthouse stands, began in 1881. North Beach Haven developed in 1887, and Ship Bottom in 1898. The ride from Highway 72 (off Route 9) from Manahawkin becomes a series of high bridges that give one the scope of the bay and the marshes that surround it. New Yorkers like to think the island itself resembles Long Island and its many beaches. Long Beach Island is very accessible from Philadelphia and Camden on Route 70, which switches into Route 72 at Lebanon State Forest. From New York, of course, it is the Garden State Parkway (exit 63) or old Highway 9 to Manahawkin.

Old Route 9 Day Trip

From Barnegat to Oyster Creek

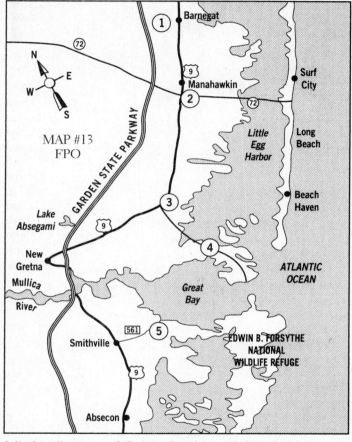

MAP #13
FPO

1. Hurricane House
2. Bay Avenue Diner
3. Tuckerton Emporium
4. Great Bay Boulevard
5. Oyster Creek Inn

The old New Jersey road south to Atlantic City and Cape May, for those who lived and toiled in the industrial northern towns like Newark, Perth Amboy, Rahway, Elizabeth, Paterson, or Passaic and the suburbs that surround them, was the always-wonderful two-lane Highway 9. In times past when life seemed easier and the pace was slower with no superthroughways, turnpikes, and parkways, you could enjoy the towns and places Route 9 passed through. Often your destination might not be the ocean resorts but one of the towns on Route 9 that were on Barnegat Bay, Man-

Abandoned fishing shack on an island in Barnegat Bay in Barnegat.

ahawkin Bay, or the series of smaller bays and inlets down the eastern seaboard to the very tip of the state. Cabins and overnight lodgings were always to be found along this highway and still are. This is quite a surprise when you consider that most of these places from the twenties, thirties, and forties were replaced in the 1950s with the newer, cleaner, more efficient motel equivalent. The giant Holiday Inns of later decades were unimaginable back then and are still scarce in this laidback southern region. As you drive south into the Pine Barrens, you will notice that tall shrub pines, open meadows, yellow sandy soil, and great pine groves predominate, giving the feeling of being in Georgia rather than Jersey. Barnegat is a quaint bay town with a boat dock and small boardwalk on the bay, practically inside **Barnegat National Wildlife Refuge.** Barnegat has several antique shops in the town center, some interesting Victorian architecture, and an old ice cream parlor called the **Hurricane House,** which serves Arctic Ice Cream and sandwiches in a pleasant atmosphere with whirring overhead fans and an old screen door.

Old Highway 9 is still noted for its many antique shops, and things do mysteriously turn up in this Jersey Devil country out of the attics and into some of the stores and flea markets. Usually, prices are very fair along this highway now, because most vacationers are speeding along the Garden State Parkway, which parallels Highway 9 all the way down to Cape May—but the old route is for the adventurous and back roads are always where the good times are.

The next point south on Route 9 following Barnegat is Manahawkin, which is an old Lenape Indian expression meaning "good corn land." Right at the crossroads of 9 and 72 there is a small cranberry bog lake, and a pine grove for picnics or just to park and relax (no charge).

In Tuckerton, situated on **Lake Pohatcong** (another good spot for a picnic) there is a very nice drive-in: **Stewart's Root Beer,** situated on the highway just opposite the lake. The town proper has a diner as well as small shops. One of the most interesting spots is the **Tuckerton Emporium,** with a dozen different shops at 2 East Main Street (Highway 9), (609) 296-2424, open from 10:30 A.M. until 6 P.M. every day, offering new stained glass, custom framing, pine furniture, local art, imported fashion sweaters, Victoriana, and flower arrangements, as well as a shop that sells unique things like handmade black dolls, and "exquisite curiosities" in addition to exotic Chinese kites and garlic jellies.

Just beyond Tuckerton and off Route 9 the road signs will direct you to Little Egg Harbor and Mystic Island, which leads you into the **Great Bay Fish and Wildlife Area** on Beach Haven Inlet, Little Egg Inlet, and the Great Bay. This is a particularly beautiful southern New Jersey wildlife area. The drive along the Great Bay Boulevard, a sandy dirt road, is breathtakingly beautiful. Following Route 9 again south you will pass through the **Bass River State Forest** (9,400 acres), and **Lake Absegami.**

The next town, New Gretna, has some good seafood restaurants; and one of the best is **Allen's Clam Bar,** (609) 296-4106, a plain affair run by Win Allen, who is a New Jersey state oyster shucking champ. The oysters and scallops here come from the Great Bay, just a few miles away, and for $6.50 you can truly enjoy a platter full of clam fritters with french fried potatoes, coleslaw, and Jersey tomatoes, or deviled clams, crabs, flounder, or lobster (from $7 to $20). The clam chowder is filled with vegetables, potatoes, onions and tomatoes, and the oyster stews (when in season) are rich and creamy. Be warned: the horseradish will clear out your city pollution sinus condition. During the summer Allen's is open from 11 A.M. until 9 P.M., winter from 11 A.M. to 8 P.M., closed on Monday.

Just beyond New Gretna, Highway 9 merges with the Garden State Parkway to cross the vast marshes at the mouth of the broad Mullica River, which enters the Great Bay here at **Brigantine National Wildlife Refuge.** This is a 20,000-acre area of bays, marshes, and tidal inlets that serves as a vital system in the ecology of the entire Pine Barrens region, home to such rare birds as snow geese, brant, blue-winged teal, black ducks, gadwall, shorebirds, egrets, herons, ibises, and warblers. After crossing the river take the very first exit (48) over the bridge and get back onto Highway 9.

This will bring you right into **Smithville**, which was a stagecoach stop in the late 1700s on Kings Highway (eventually called New York Road, now US Highway 9). Today Smithville is a restored town, which also has many quaint shops in rebuilt and restruc-

Bonny Wyckoff, in Early American garb, at the Smithville Antiques Center on Route 9.

tured small buildings, each with its own history: a general store, a tobacco store, a bakery, a bookshop, a Jersey Devil souvenir shop with the infamous devil imprinted on T-shirts, postcards, posters, and other Pine Barren souvenirs, a cheese shop, a Christmas shop, a toy shop, and a candy shop, as well as several antique shops and an indoor antique center.

Smithville might have remained just a forgotten little hamlet had it not been for Fred and Ethel Noyes, who were antique dealers from down the road in Absecon. The Noyeses bought a deteriorating inn for $3,500 and restored it into a 42-seat restaurant in 1952. The inn, built in 1787 by James Baremore, originally served travelers on a stagecoach route between Leeds Point and Camden. The Noyeses had a vision of surrounding their restaurant with restored 18th- and 19th-century buildings, which typified those found in this area of southern New Jersey. Old houses and stores were literally "collected" and brought onto the land in the 1950s. In 1975 Fred and Ethel severed their association with Smithville when they sold the entire village to a subsidiary of the American Broadcasting Company. When the tourist spot did not live up to ABC's expectations of profitability, it was sold again to the Cadillac-Fairview Corporation, which then included two subsidiaries called Inns and Shoppes Inc., and Historic Smithville Development Company. Smithville is thriving now with infused business from the people who live in nearby developments, built to house the Atlantic City casino workers. The Noyeses, meanwhile, opened the **Noyes Museum** farther down the road in Oceanville (733 Lily Lake Road), which features selected works from Fred Noyes's collection of American art plus "working" decoy ducks, sculptures, and summer string quartets; call (609) 652-8848.

The **Smithville Inn**, (609) 652-7777, is a focal point here for tourist dining, serving South Jersey American fare for lunch, including bruschetta, chicken, Colonial meatloaf, and eggs Benedict. The "Pony Express" lunch in the tavern section offers sandwiches, quiche, and chef salads at reasonable prices. A buffet of over 50 hot and cold specialties draws a large daily crowd (mostly in buses from Atlantic City).

You will find a few other fancy "Ye Olde Tavern" type eateries in Smithville, but if you turn left on Route 9 near the old graveyard— at a sign that says LEEDS POINT, you can take a three-mile drive along Old Moss Mill Road (Alt. 561) through woods and marshes—to the very tip of Leeds Point on the Great Bay and smack in the middle of the Brigantine Wildlife Refuge. At Oyster Creek you will come upon the **Oyster Creek Inn** where boats dock up at the pier, some sailing and motoring in just for dinner.

Waterwheel mill is now an antique shop at Smithville historic village.

Rustic sea shanties and fishermen's shacks surround this old restaurant that serves excellent seafood dinners in a plain atmosphere—and you can come dressed as you like. An "old salt" serves cocktails at a friendly bar (in the shape of a boat) and the open-view picture windows look out onto the bay. On a clear night you can spot the glittering lights of not too distant Atlantic City to the south and Beach Haven on Long Beach Island to the northwest. Big fish are mounted on the knotty pine walls, and the lights are cheery and bright so that you get to see exactly what you are eating. The fisherman's combination platter is a real taste treat, and the crab cakes, soft-shell crabs, bluefish, shrimp, and oyster fries are all excellent. A clam stew is nicely creamy without being too thick, and the clam chowder is just right. Dinners include the typical choice of french fries or baked potato, coleslaw, with coffee or soda. The seafood combination at the Oyster Creek Inn includes flounder, scallops, a crab cake, a deviled clam, and shrimps—either fried or broiled. The Oyster Creek Inn, 40 Oyster Creek Rd. on Leeds Point, is open Tuesday to Saturday from 4 to 9 P.M. and Sunday from 1 to 9 P.M. Call (609) 652-8565 for reservations or just drive out. The inn is set practically on the spot where the Jersey Devil is said to have been born, so watch out for strange happenings in these parts. An after-dinner walk down the old dirt road among the tall marsh grass and along the bay is a very pleasant experience here.

Pine Barrens Day Trip

and the Carranza Memorial

1. Carranza Memorial   2. Lake Atsion   3. Batsto

Wedged in between the New Jersey Turnpike on the west side of the state and the Garden State Parkway and Route 9 on the eastern estuaries forming the Barnegat Bay, Little Egg Harbor, and the Great Bay, are the 337,000 acres of New Jersey's famed Pine Barrens. US Route 206, state Routes 70 and 72, and secondary highways like 532, 534, 541, 542, and 563 cut through the Barrens, but it's still a vast wilderness that includes over 50,000 acres of pine forest, a rare dwarf pine tree (sometimes called stunted pygmy pine) forest and 17 trillion gallons of pure glacial-ice-quality water (beneath the Pines' deep sand beds). The great wild beauty of this vast area, with its more than 400 varieties of wildflowers, its blueberry, gooseberry and huckleberry bushes, its cranberry bogs and varieties of pine trees, its wild orchids, waterlilies, and curly leaf ferns, is breathtaking and awe inspiring. Congress created the Pineland National Reserve in 1978 and it was later designated as a coastal plain reserve by UNESCO, the United Nations agency.

Chatsworth, at the junction of Route 523 and Route 563 in Woodland Township, is the central town in the Pine Barrens, with about 100 homes, a post office, a church, a firehouse, and a schoolhouse. Like a town of days gone by, the Pineys, the locals of the region, many of whom work in the cranberry bogs, gather in the general store to drink coffee and tell tales of the forest and the mysterious creature known to them as the "Leeds Devil."

Naturalists, canoeing enthusiasts, bird and wildlife watchers, poets, writers, and artists seek peace and solitude in this natural wilderness area, filled with deer, rabbit, opossum, and other creatures of the wild who are protected against the encroachment of suburbanization. The Pine Barrens fall primarily within Burlington County, which is New Jersey's largest, but they also extend into Ocean, Atlantic, and Camden Counties.

To experience it firsthand drive the back roads, walk, or if you like, paddle a canoe. Hikers can walk for hours in the Pines without seeing another soul—other than some deer, a hawk, and an occasional screech owl.

For an exciting day trip into the Pine Barrens turn right off Highway 9 at New Gretna onto Route 542 to **Batsto Village** and **Batsto Lake.** Batsto is located in the southern realm of the **Wharton State Forest,** which contains almost 108,000 acres and is the largest tract of land administered by the state park service in New Jersey. The word *baatstoo,* or *steambath,* was introduced by the Scandinavians and Dutch. The Indians borrowed the word, referring to it as *Batstow,* or *bathing place.* Here you will see an early industrial village where a glass factory and a lumber business in the 19th century replaced the 18th-century bog iron settlement, which flourished during the Revolutionary War. Complete with the gentleman's mansion on the hill, workers' homes, an iron furnace, a grist mill, a sawmill, glassworks, and a brickyard, this now "deserted village" once was a community of 1,000 people and was an important part of the industrial development of the United States. Batsto has a pig slaughterhouse, a general store, a blacksmith shop, a typical worker's home, a craft and pottery house, and other interesting buildings from days gone by. You can almost "feel" and "see" the retrogressive photographic images (the ghost presence) of those that had been here before as if you were in the twilight zone in another century. You also have the dark eerie feeling here of the Jersey Devil, but then—this is Jersey Devil country. Batsto is open Memorial Day to Labor Day from 10 A.M. to 6 P.M. and Labor Day to Memorial Day from 11 A.M. to 6 P.M., (609) 561-3262. Guided tours are conducted at 11 A.M., 1, and 3 P.M. through the Victorian **Batsto Mansion,** former home of Joseph Wharton, the Philadelphia industrialist who over a period of 30 years bought the many parcels of land that comprise the Wharton Forest. He planned on damming the streams to create reservoirs so he could

sell water to the city of Philadelphia, but his scheme was stopped
by the legislature of the state of New Jersey, which prohibited the
exporting of water. The state acquired the land in 1954 and 1955
and has left large areas undeveloped in order to preserve the natural habitat.

Primitive campsites are found throughout the forest and there
are two family camping areas with numbered sites, and seven
group campsites, including the **Batona campsite** (150 people),
the **Mullica River wilderness campsite** (100 people—no cars or
vehicles of any kind allowed), and **Goshen Pond** (200 people).
There are nine cabins situated along the north shore of **Atsion
Lake.** They can accommodate from four to eight people and have
indoor toilets and showers and hot and cold running water. Reservation information may be obtained from the Atsion ranger station or the Batsto visitors center. Atsion Lake also has a protected
bathing lake.

Located deep in the heart of the forest is the famous **Carranza
Memorial,** notating the spot where Emilio Carranza, a 23-year-
old Mexican pilot, challenging Lindbergh's solo flying record
across the Atlantic, met his end trying to fly solo from Mexico City
to New York. Tragically he crashed in the first hours of his return
flight to Mexico City, on July 13, 1928, and died deep in South
Jersey's Pine Barrens. To get to the Carranza Memorial (a trek un-
dertaken by not a few) take Route 563 south out of Chatsworth to
Speedwell. Turn right and drive to the **Batona Trail.** Here, after
walking through a long stretch of scrub pine, you will find the
stone and cement memorial to that brave pioneer of flight, Señor
Carranza.

Though rich in history and well stocked in ghosts, the Pine Barrens are sparsely populated, though most small settlements and
villages have grocery stores and places to eat and there are many
cut-out-of-the-woods-by-the-side-of-the-road taverns which serve
up hearty fare and good drink. When you're ready for "fancy dining," head to the shore regions. Remember that this is a vast area
and not to be explored in a day.

Atlantic City Day Trip

1. White House Sub Station
2. Tony's Baltimore Grill
3. Caesar's Atlantic City
4. The Taj Mahal
5. Garden Pier
6. Absecon Light House

It has been said in aggressive Jersey travel-tourist advertisements that "all roads lead to Atlantic City," and in a sense this is true. Atlantic City has been and still is at the center of things in New Jersey; and the geographic point at which it is located has always been ideal for sea breezes and a swim in the ocean.

Route 9 leads directly onto Absecon Highway (Route 30) into Atlantic City. This old causeway has a number of 1930s cabins and 1950s motels and interesting pop-culture architectural oddities, notably the **Santa Maria House,** built by J. Vaughan Mathis in 1926 as a landmark for his real estate development north of Atlantic City. The building, a two-story replica of Christopher Columbus's ship, has been a restaurant and is now an antique shop.

Route 322 out of Pleasantville (also off Route 9) is the southern road into Atlantic City and is known as the Black Horse Pike. Two pop oddities are the old **Studebaker Showroom** in the 1920s mission-architectural style (now an antique-boutique complex) and the **Sand Castle,** a charming fairy-tale building in the Spanish-adobe architectural style, facing an unbroken expanse of bay and sky. This building,

Sheet-music cover for the song "Atlantic City" from the Novelty Music Company.

now unoccupied, used to be one of Barbara Hutton's—the poor little rich girl Woolworth heiress—summer getaways. Plans are afoot to use this area for some other purpose, so don't be surprised if this architectural gem is gone with the wind before you know it.

The Atlantic City Expressway, a toll road, will get you there in a big hurry from Philadelphia; and, of course, for Philadelphians and others who connect at Philadelphia and Cherry Hill from all points, there is the Amtrak train into Atlantic City. Naturally people are now loaded onto daily and hourly express buses from local candy and cigar stores, and from points all over the Northeast for a big day of gambling at the casinos. But in the spirit of old times, it is still recommended that you take the old routes by car into the excitement of Atlantic City. Maps of Atlantic City are plentiful in the casinos.

One spot that still has the quality and boardwalk "flavor" of old-time Atlantic City, and is surely the best place to start a visit (or end one) is the **White House Sub Shop** at 2301 Arctic Avenue, at Mississippi. The White House, which claims to have originated the submarine sandwich, has been in business since the early 1940s, and still makes its own bread and uses U.S. grade #1 bolognas, salami, steak, hot sausage, and other meats with its own special green hot relish. The original hot or cold submarine sandwiches are meticulously made with the inside dough pulled out and the meat piled on thick. There is no stinting here; good Ireland-brand perked coffee and Pennsylvania potato chips (made with pure lard) are served, all at very reasonable prices. The gleaming white interior is set off with blue-and-orange neon advertising signs, bright lighting, comfortable sit-down booths, and friendly waitresses who serve with a smile. Some of the celebrities who loved their delicious

The Black Cat (outlined in green neon) Tavern in Absecon was just outside Atlantic City.

White House subs include the Beatles, Frank Sinatra, Eydie Gorme, Jerry Lewis, Liberace, Tiny Tim, and countless others. The walls are adorned with photographs of smiling, satisfied movie stars, radio and television personalities, sports figures, and nightclub entertainers, all holding their giant subs. The White House is open until midnight and some nights until 1 A.M., and should not be missed by food buffs who never have tasted a real sub sandwich. No soft, skimpy Blimpies here; call (609) 345-1564.

New Jersey resorts booklet showing a bathing beauty and a lady in a rolling wicker chair on the Boardwalk in Atlantic City during its golden era; from the Pennsylvania Railroad system, 1923.

Tony's Baltimore Grill, 2800 Atlantic Avenue, is one of the great mainstay establishments in Atlantic City. As you enter the restaurant, lit by red neon light, there is a horseshoe-shaped bar on one side and comfortable booths on the other. Another large room is filled with booths and tables throughout. The kitchen is in full view, and patrons can watch, for all practical purposes, their meals being cooked or the pizza dough thrown. There is a buzz in the place, and an atmosphere of warmth and good cheer. The food served here is good Italian-style seafood, spaghetti concoctions, and first-rate pizza (whole pies only). The prices fit the tourists' pocketbook, and the servings are ample. Try antipasto, fried shrimp, or crab cakes for starters. The Baltimore Grill seafood special, including fried shrimp, scallops, and crab cakes, or spaghetti with meatballs, sausage, clams, or anchovies are both good choices for entrees. Cheese pizza is served with sausage or other ingredients—the special is a cheese, mushroom, and sausage pizza. The Baltimore Grill pizza is mouth-wateringly delicious, and is big enough for a meal for two. The prices are low, and the service and food are just fine. Atlantic City regulars rave about this place and

Two Fralinger's Saltwater Taffy containers. Left: an original from the 1930s. Right: a 1990s tin-litho reproduction.

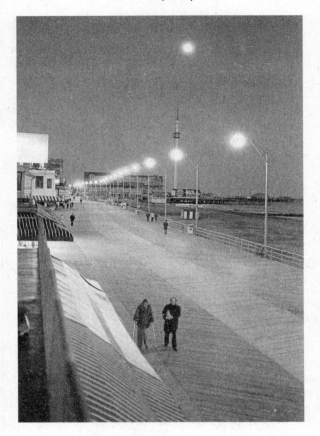

Atlantic City Boardwalk at night.

the proprietor—in the manner of Atlantic City—says he keeps the joint open around the clock; call (609) 345-5766 or 345-9461.

In its biggest boom since gambling started in 1978, Atlantic City expanded its airport and built a new **Convention Center** (1997). Near the Convention Center, in front of the Sheraton Hotel in Atlantic City, is a life-size statue of Bert Parks, Miss America's long-time master of ceremonies. And if you put your head underneath the crown he holds out, he'll even sing to you. It's one of the things that makes Atlantic City weird. The original **Convention Hall** is now used as a special events arena.

For more information on Atlantic City tourism, go to www.atlanticcitynj.com; contact the Atlantic City Convention and Visitors Authority, 2314 Pacific Avenue, Atlantic City, NJ 08401; or call (609) 449-7154. To go from the future back to the past, visit the preserved and restored Garden Pier on the Boardwalk at New Jersey Avenue, where you can visit the Atlantic City Art Center and the Atlantic City Historical Museum (609) 347-5839).

Fun and Games in Atlantic City

Charles Darrow, a Philadelphian who vacationed in Atlantic City, sat down in his living room one day in 1930 and created a game called *Monopoly* based on Atlantic City real estate. Like a good many others, Darrow needed money in the Great Depression to support a wife and child. This play-money property game contains a pertinent fantasy element that holds players' interest beyond the normal 45-minute attention span of most board games. However, initially the Parker Brothers were skeptical of the game's sales potential on the marketplace, and turned the proposed game down in 1934. They changed their thinking, however, when Darrow proceeded to have a few thousand sets made up that sold like hotcakes at Philadelphia department stores. Needless to say, Darrow made his own Atlantic City fortune out of this Monopoly game. Oddly enough, the success of the game in the Depression arrived on the scene at a time that the Big Bad Wolf nearly did in the biggest resort on the eastern seaboard. After the Wall Street stock market crash and bank closings, many Atlantic City hotels were empty and nightclubs and restaurants were forced to shut down. By 1933, the worst year of the Depression decade, the city could not meet its own payroll, and issued the equivalent of "play" money in scrip certificates, which were to be

Mickey Mouse pushes Minnie, who is sitting in a rolling chair, on the Boardwalk. The famous cartoon mice are shown on an Atlantic City tin sandpail, which originally was filled with saltwater taffy. Pail is marked Walter E. Disney Enterprises, circa 1934, and was purchased at the Atlantic City Antique Show for $1,200 in 2003.

redeemed when the American economy returned to normalcy. Today it is not play or scrip money, but the clinking of coins in paper cups and the clatter of rolling dice on the crap tables, the high rollers and the low rollers, all out to win big in the fun and games stakes of Atlantic City.

The casinos provide the excitement of gambling, shopping, fancy dining, and nightclubs with top performers, which have included Joan Rivers, Paul Anka, Boyz II Men, Cindy Lauper, Regis Philbin, Diana Ross, Dean Martin, Al Martino, and Frank Sinatra. Comfortable hotel rooms are not the least of Atlantic City's attractions. The casinos are:

Resorts Casino Hotel, (609) 344-6000, the first to open, May 26, 1978, located on the Boardwalk between North Carolina Avenue and Pennsylvania Avenue. Resorts features a 1,700-seat superstar theater where it presents top-name entertainment and championship boxing. The actual casino area of Resorts is almost the size of two football fields, with more than 1,700 slot machines and 120 gaming tables. There are over 700 guests rooms in the renovated Chalfonte-Haddon Hall and more than half-a-dozen restaurants from gourmet to moderate to economical. To top it all off, Resorts recently added the **Nikki Beach Nightclub** with a 50,000-square-foot outdoor performing venue.

Caesar Augustus of Prima Porta, an 18-foot replica of the original, dominates the corner of the Boardwalk and Arkansas Avenue. (Photo courtesy of Caesars Atlantic City)

Caesars Atlantic City extends from Pacific Avenue to the Boardwalk between Arkansas and Missouri Avenues. A prime attraction is the 18-foot-tall exact replica of Michelangelo's **David,** weighing nine tons and handcrafted in Italy from Carara marble. Caesars was the second casino to open in Atlantic City, on June 26, 1979. Entertainment at the **Circus Maximus;** lounges include the **Forum, Gladiator Sports Bar,** and the **Toga Bar;** restaurants are **Nero's Grille, Bacchanal,** and **Planet Hollywood.** Caesars' telephone number is (609) 348-4411.

Bally's Atlantic City Hotel Casino and Claridge Towers, (609) 340-2000, opened in December 1979 on the Boardwalk between Park Place and Michigan Avenue, on the site of the destroyed Marlborough-Blenheim Hotel. It also incorporates the completely gutted and refurbished Dennis Hotel, and a 37-story tower. The refurbished Claridge Hotel, also part of Bally's, which was built in 1930 and modeled after the Empire State Building, closed in 1973 after playing host to world celebrities like Princess Grace of Monaco, Bob Hope, and Alfred G. Vanderbilt. The present hotel casino, originally done all in English style, has been revamped to sport all-American décor in keeping with the fast-paced style of Atlantic City; it includes a theater, a cabaret, and 15 restaurants, among them the renowned **Johnny Rockets.**

The most obvious feature of Bally's is its size—60,000 square feet, accented by neon lighting and diagonal ceiling mirrors. (Photo courtesy Bally's)

Sands Hotel and Casino, (609) 441-4000, opened in August 1980 between Indiana Avenue and Illinois Avenue just off the Boardwalk at Brighton Park, and advertises itself as "the most precious jewel in the tiara of East Coast gaming!" The Sands has an aggressive entertainment program and has gained the reputation of being the boxing center of the East Coast. There are seven restaurants, including the excellent **Brighton Steakhouse.**

Harrah's Casino Hotel, (609) 441-5000, was the first casino to open away from the Boardwalk, in November of 1980 on a 14-acre site located adjacent to the Brigantine Bridge. This 15-story, brightly lit glass hotel casino can be seen for miles around. Special features here include the marina for nautically minded gamblers, and an 850-seat Broadway-by-the-Bay Theater, lounges galore, and eight restaurants.

Atlantic City Hilton (originally the Golden Nugget), (609) 340-7200, on the Boardwalk between Boston and Providence, opened in December 1980 and features a Victorian decorating theme, including a 120-foot-wide by 10-foot-high mural depicting the 1890 Atlantic City Easter parade. The place features more than 100,000 linear feet of brass railings and grills, has a theater, and nine restaurants from gourmet to economical, including the continental style **Peregrine's,** and **Caruso's.**

Tropicana Casino and Resort, (609) 340-4000, (formerly the Tropicana Hotel and Casino) opened in November 1981 at the Boardwalk between Iowa Avenue and Brighton Place, on the site of the former Ambassador Hotel. The Tropicana resembles a geometric work of art with its multilevel cubical design and 17-story tower with bands of black and white. The motto here is "where every second sizzles" and an interesting feature is the glass elevator ride to the **Top of the Trop,** a lounge with an observation corridor providing panoramic views of the entire Atlantic City area. There is the famed Comedy Stop Café and Cabaret, an IMAX Theater, and a three-story Havana-themed central arcade with shops, clubs, and 16 restaurants including **Cuba Libre, Corky's BBQ,** and **A Darn Good Crab Shack.**

Trump Plaza Hotel and Casino, (609) 441-6000, opened at Mississippi Avenue and the Boardwalk in May, 1984. It features a 37-story gleaming white-and-black obelisk, called Atlantic City's "centerpiece." Panoramic views can be had here also, and why not try **Harvey's Deli, Shangri-La Café,** the **New York,** and **Starbucks,** among the ten restaurants on the premises.

Trump Marina, (609) 441-2000, which opened in May 1985 (at the Farley Marina area) is on Brigantine Boulevard and is popular with boaters; Donald Trump's yacht was docked here for use by the high rollers in the first few months of the gala opening. It has theaters, lounges, and eight restaurants.

The comedy team Abbott and Costello share a hat—Lou Costello (left, with cigar) and Bud Abbott (right). Bud Abbott was born in a circus tent in 1895 and raised by his circus performer family in Asbury Park. Costello was born in Paterson in 1906 and died in 1959.

◆

Showboat, (609) 343-4000, at Delaware Avenue and the Board-walk, has entertainment at the **New Orleans Square and House of Blues, French Quarter Buffet, Mansion Cafe, Casa di Napoli, Canal Street Bread & Sandwich Co., Rib & Chop House, North Sea Village, Noodle Bar, Sanctuary Beach Bar, Starbucks,** and the **Showboat Bowling Center,** open from 10 A.M. to midnight for more active sportsmen and women. The New Orleans theme is carried in fifty exotic suites.

Trump Taj Mahal, (609) 449-1000, at Boardwalk and Virginia Avenue, was once the largest casino in the world. Its casino, the size of four football fields, is glittering with hundreds of crystal chandeliers, and its miles of public corridors are studded by rare works of sculpture and art. Here is the **Etess Arena** (for shows), the **Casbah** and **Oasis** lounges, the **Scheherazade Restaurant** and **Safari Steak House,** both gourmet, the **Bombay Cafe,** and **Sultan's Feast** (moderate). At the top of the escalator, hung with three of the world's largest crystal chandeliers, is a granite-faced branch of Tiffany's, the great New York jewelry store.

The Borgata, (609) 317-1000, on Huron Avenue in the northwest Marina area, opened in 2003 and was expanded in 2005 for more

Nancy Sinatra sings her popular songs, "These Boots Are Made For Walking," "You Only Live Twice," and "So Long Babe," when she appears at the Atlantic City casinos.

entertainment space and condo apartments. This $1.1 billion mega-resort has ten restaurants including the famed **Old Homestead Steak House** and **Noodles of the World,** comedy clubs, lounges, and theaters. This newest casino is known as a "full service destination resort," and its motto—"always turned on"—caused a ripple in the news when they instituted new rules for waitresses, demanding that they comply with weight specifications or they would be fired. The svelte ones who comply and get their weight down become members of the sexy cadre known as the "Bodacious Borgata Babes" at this upscale casino.

For a breath of air try a walk at the northern end of Atlantic City at the **Abesecon Light House.** Take a drive north across Absecon Bay to Brigantine Island with its other attractions and funtime bars.

Atlantic City itself features more restaurants in just the casinos alone than exist in the entire state of Rhode Island. Three good ones, outside the casinos, include the architecturally fascinating **Knife & Fork Inn** at Atlantic and Pacific Avenues, (609) 344-1133, presided over by the brothers Latz since 1927, serving fine seafood, of course, fresh vegetables, and an extensive wine list; **Dock's Oyster House** at 2405 Atlantic Avenue, (609) 345-0092, serving seafood since 1897, and specializing in poached salmon and live lobsters in the tank; and **Angelo's Fairmount Tavern** at Mississippi and Fairmount Avenues, (609) 344-2439, established in 1935 and featuring the best in Italian pasta.

Remember, this is an all-night town for bars, casinos, and some eateries. Something is always happening in A.C.!

Old Atlantic City

. . . .

In the 20th Century–Fox technicolor musical film *Three Little Girls in Blue* (1946), Vivian Blaine, June Haver, and Vera-Ellen, three beautiful blonde farmgirl sisters, go to one of the old Atlantic City hotels in 1905 in search of millionaires. The film, which also starred George Montgomery, Frank Latimore, and Celeste Holm (now a New Jersey resident herself and also an active conservationist), contains the well-known standard "On the Boardwalk in Atlantic City" written by Josef Myron, Harry Warren, and Mack Gordon, which extols the virtues of boardwalk rolling chairs, summer love, and saltwater air in a magical place. The popular rendition of this happy seashore tune was recorded by Dick Haymes in the 1940s. After renting a fabulous suite for $9.25 a day (quite a sum in 1905) one practical-minded sister complains about expenses while another more romantic one says breathlessly, "Atlantic City! Oh . . . come on . . . what's money? At last we're free!"

Such has always been, it seems, the reckless spirit of a city known as America's answer to the Riviera, built on sandy Absecon Island on the Atlantic Ocean. The first tavern inn to operate in Atlantic City was licensed to Aunt Millie Leed in 1839. Could this have been a relation of the same Leed family at nearby Leeds Point who

Three Little Girls in Blue, *a 1940s technicolor 20th–Century Fox musical set in Atlantic City at the turn of the century, introduced the song "On the Boardwalk in Atlantic City." 1946 lobby card.*

The beautiful Marlborough-Blenheim Hotel depicted on a 1908 postcard printed in Germany. Though this grand and sturdy structure had been declared an official landmark by the State, it was nevertheless demolished to make way for casino gambling.

let loose a Jersey Devil into the world? By 1854, with the advent of a steam-powered railroad line from Camden, more than half-a-dozen rooming houses appeared, and by 1860, 4,000 people could rent a room with breakfast and dinner at places such as the Surf House, Congress Hall, the Mansion, and Odd Fellows. People flocked here initially believing that salt air and the ocean could cure illness, particularly sinus, bronchitis, walking pneumonia, consumption, and other 19th-century ailments. Even the mentally infirm who suffered from various "nervous disorders" or "attacks" were brought to Atlantic City for a cure.

Atlantic City historian Vicki Gold Levi, who wrote the book *Atlantic City — 125 Years of Ocean Madness* with Lee Eisenberg, remembers an Atlantic City filled with deep blue, pink-and-purple hydrangea bushes. They surrounded the old hotels and were particularly lush at the Marlborough-Blenheim. Vicki herself was the "Hydrangea Queen" of Atlantic City, and her father was Al Gold, Atlantic City's chief photographer from 1939 to 1964. Vicki wanted to be the girl on the high-diving horse on the Steel Pier, but her dad discouraged that occupation when he showed her some of the dangers involved in such a feat. There was a lot going on in Atlantic City that Al Gold told his wide-eyed daughter; one story involved a high-level mobster convention held there on May 14, 1929, attended by Al Capone, Louis "Lepke" Buchalter, Meyer Lansky, Dutch Schultz, Frank Costello, and Lucky Luciano. Much of the changeover from old-world Atlantic City charm to the Las Vegas–style stretch pants pomp of casino Atlantic City can be seen in the brilliant film *Atlantic City*, directed by Louis Malle, written by John Guare, and starring Susan Sarandon and Burt Lancaster.

◆

In 1994, the **Atlantic City Art Center** and the **Atlantic City Historical Museum**, (609) 347-5839, celebrated the Gala Opening of
their permanent homes, both located on the Garden Pier on the
Boardwalk at New Jersey Avenue. Vicki made the initial gift to the
museum, seven cartons of memorabilia she had collected over the
years, including period postcards, change purses made from
seashells, porcelain mermaids, china bathing dolls manufactured
in West Germany, and plates and saucers made in Japan—all with
an Atlantic City overprint—mother-of-pearl pins, salt-and-pepper
shakers resembling lobster tails, kewpie dolls, snowflake glass balls
with Miss America inside—and hundreds of photos she assembled from her own collection of her father's photos of Atlantic
City, now designated as the Al Gold Memorial Collection. Vicki,
who was the founder of the museum with Florence Miller and
Tony Kutschera, was also the principal consultant for the Walt
Disney World "Atlantic City Boardwalk" Resort, which opened in
Florida in 1995.

*Bess Meyerson, after having been crowned Miss America in 1945, is ecstatic
while Atlantic City's own Vicki Gold Levi (author of* Atlantic City, 125 Years of
Ocean Madness) *carries the velvet train.*

Official program and souvenir album of the famous Miss America beauty pageant. Diving girl, Convention Hall, and the sunburst pattern make a striking cover for this 1933 event.

The first saltwater taffy sold in Atlantic City was produced at a James saltwater taffy stand in 1883 (six pieces for a nickel) with Joseph Fralinger following with his taffy shops in 1885. In 1985 **Fralinger's,** the most famous candy-taffy-maker in Atlantic City, celebrated its 100th anniversary. These gooey chewy concoctions in pastel colors and a variety of flavors (originally just chocolate, vanilla, and molasses), were just the thing to offer a beautiful lady in her rolling chair on the Boardwalk.

The great Boardwalk, as we have come to know it, is 40 feet wide and 4 miles long (some 1920s brochures described it as 7 to 8 miles long and 60 feet wide), and was completed in 1896 following in the footsteps of 5 smaller previous boardwalks. The Boardwalk flourished at the turn of the century and in the teens, with many commercial establishments, restaurants, and piers such as the Heinz (57 varieties) Pier, known as the Crystal Palace by the Sea, which offered real pickles, pickle pins, and other free samples until 1944, when the pier was swept away by a hurricane. The Steel Pier opened in 1898 and was known as the "showplace of the nation" and the Steeplechase "funny place" Pier opened in 1904. The Million Dollar Pier opened in 1906, offering entertainment through the years with Harry Houdini featured, as well as being the site of the crowning of the earliest Miss Americas.

Two great "sandcastle" style hotels that once stood on the Boardwalk were the Marlborough-Blenheim and the Hotel Traymore. The Blenheim was one of the first hotels to be made of reinforced concrete. Thomas Edison, who developed this method of construction, was on hand to supervise the raising of the building, which was completed in 1906. The ornamentation of imaginary sea creatures and devils, sea horses, bloated fish, sand crabs, and sea hawks were exquisite examples of Seaside Art Nouveau. Some of this original ornamentation used to be on display at the top of the waterfall escalator at Bally's, as if in homage to a better constructed, more imaginative Atlantic City. The luxurious old-world charm of the Marlborough-Blenheim, hot-and-cold seawater running in the bathtub tap in the great rooms, the formal dining rooms, lounges, sun porches, and library, was destroyed in 1979. The Dennis Hotel, now incorporated into Bally's complex and featuring the Dennis Lounge, is one of the few remaining public "rooms" where you can experience the grandeur of old Atlantic City hotel life.

The massive Egyptian Deco-style Traymore Hotel, designed by William L. Price, was destroyed in 1972 by massive dynamiting. The memory loss of these hotels is not just a case of nostalgia or sentiment for what was old and beautiful; but for what was serviceable, natural, grand, and functional. Now there is no openness to the ocean and its breezes, and everything seems shut off from its geographic location in order to focus in on the gambling tables. One new hotel mistakenly used mirrored gold plastic on the ocean facade that attracted hordes of gnats, flies, and other large bugs blown in from the Atlantic City meadows. Birds in flight

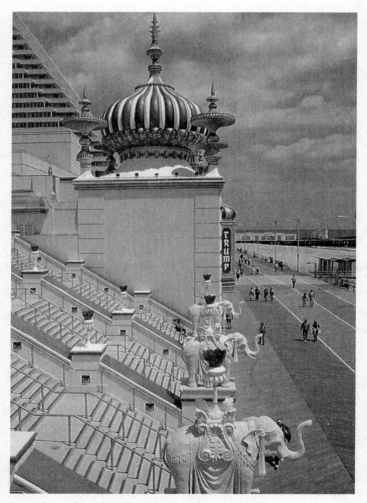

Postcard view of the Taj Mahal and Atlantic City Boardwalk.

also crashed into the yellow mirrored exterior in confusion. The Claridge (built in 1930) and Resorts Casino Hotel (the renovated Chalfonte-Haddon Hall Hotel) had the good common sense to incorporate the old into the new. All over Atlantic City today you will see a great deal of attention paid in photo murals and displays incorporating architectural details from old buildings to the memory-image of old Atlantic City.

Convention Hall, built in 1929, the year of the Wall Street crash, is another great monument to authentic old Atlantic City, and was the largest building of its kind to be built without posts or pillars. Political and corporate business conventions, gigantic antique shows and car shows, are still held in this vast architectural wonder. The famous Miss America Pageant was also held in the convention hall until 2006, when the event was released from its contract with Atlantic City and free to find other venues around the country. A built-in pipe organ—called the world's largest—has 32,913 pipes. The building's facade and the pillared porticos along the ocean side are beautifully decorated with cement friezes in the Art Deco style of dancing nymphs, sea maidens, and sea creatures.

When traveling from one end of the long Boardwalk to the other, the rolling wicker chairs were always favored. There were 2,500 of them in operation in 1925. Many of them have been salvaged and reinstituted, and are today pushed by college students. Jitney service (tiny little buses) still operates up and down Pacific Avenue and continues to give Atlantic City some of the flavor it once had as a "continental" city that attracted the great in show business, international society, and the business world. Today, with the focus on gambling, the atmosphere is filled with another kind of excitement.

Ocean City Day Trip

Driving south on Atlantic Avenue—the closest avenue to the ocean once you hit Ventnor (just south of Atlantic City)—is quite remarkable for its architectural beauty and simplicity. You will see single-family homes in large Georgian Colonials painted gleaming white as if they were the White House by the sea. Some have 1930s-style striped awnings, manicured lawns, and are surrounded by blue hydrangea bushes. Others are in the Hollywood Spanish Dolores del Rio hacienda-style and are painted sand color with iron gates and Mexican tiles incorporated into the design. On Ventnor Avenue, which is a main thoroughfare, there are some interesting shops, ice cream parlors, and seashore-antique shops as well as more homes and restaurants, each with their own unique atmosphere. Certainly, Ventnor is a posh suburb of Atlantic City.

Note: Atlantic Avenue, from the Atlantic City Lighthouse at Absecon Inlet (the northern tip of Atlantic City), south through Ventnor, Margate, and Longport, to the Great Egg Harbor Inlet, is part of **Ocean Drive** and is marked with signs featuring a flying seagull and the words FOLLOW THE FLIGHT OF THE GULL. Ocean Drive crosses Great Egg Harbor on the Ocean City–Longport Bridge, and continues on through Ocean City, Sea Isle City, Avalon, Stone Harbor, and Wildwood right on down to Cape May Point. It is a wonderfully scenic drive and is clearly marked; the distance from Absecon Inlet to Cape May Point is 44 miles.

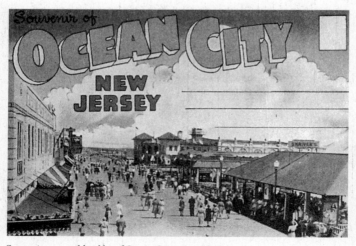

Souvenir postcard booklet of Ocean City, circa 1940.

South of Ventnor, in Margate (once called South Atlantic City) on Atlantic Avenue (Ocean Drive) and Decatur Street, you will see what must be the most remarkable of all seashore architectural oddities. This is the great **Lucy the Margate Elephant** building, 65 feet tall, made of wood and sheet metal. Her legs are 20 feet high and 10 feet in diameter. Her head is 58 feet around, her ears 17 feet long, her tusks 22 feet and her tail 26 feet. The trunk is 36 feet long. Her belly contains a 60-foot domed room and there are 18 windows. Built in 1881, this "elephant hotel" first attracted tourists in 1887 as a tavern, then became a rental cottage with a "rear view" window under the pachyderm's "rear end" tail. James Lafferty, the Philadelphia entrepreneur-developer who built Lucy to draw real estate investors to the Atlantic City area, built another elephant called the "Elephantine Colossus," a 37-room hotel in Coney Island. Built in 1884, it burned down in 1896; a sister pachyderm built in Cape May, the "Light of Asia," suffered the same fate in 1900. Today Lucy stands alone by the sea in Margate as a museum, thanks to concerned citizens who raised money and had her declared a historic site by the State of New Jersey. Fortunately, this treasure did not go the way of the old hotels in Atlantic City. Call (609) 823-6473 or visit www.lucytheelephant.org for information.

Lucy the Elephant. Two early postcard views of the only known elephant hotel in the world, now a major tourist attraction in Margate.

Longport, south of Margate, is a charming beach community at the tip of Absecon Beach, Sculls Bay to the west, and Great Egg Harbor Inlet to the south. From Longport you will be on Ocean Drive across the inlet on a series of bridges, passing through some beautiful marshland. It is a wonderful route to travel at dusk or dawn as you spot wild egret and other fowl flying across the harbor to and from the **Tuckahoe Corbin City Fish and Wildlife Management Area** nearby. There is a miminal toll on the last bridge as you enter Ocean City.

Ocean City is a gracious old seaside town that maintains much of the flavor and atmosphere of a turn-of-the-century resort. Its architecture is not Victorian in the way that Ocean Grove or Cape May are, but its fine old wood-frame houses are well maintained and intact. There are dozens of rooming houses, guest houses, and some fine genteel old-style hotels here. The **Ocean City Plaza Hotel** at 8th Street and Ocean Avenue, (609) 399-0110, is highly recommended. The sprawling boardwalk is high up off the surf and has some commanding scenic views of the oceanfront and the surrounding landscape. The air seems particularly fresh and clean, and the swimming and immaculate beaches are a delight. There is a sophisticated rather than a stuffy feeling here. The casual strollers on the boardwalk are Philadelphia-smart and well-dressed, many actually reading classic novels as they sun themselves on the beach. This is the place where Grace Kelly, as a young girl, came from Philadelphia with her parents each summer, and it is much like Spring Lake, another Jersey shore Irish-Catholic resort. This wholesome atmosphere is part of what will make you feel like you are in a resort town of yesteryear (no loud radios blasting here). The boardwalk has a number of inviting concessions, amusements, and rides. There is very good pizza at **Mack and Manco. Shriver's Saltwater Taffy Shop,** which has been on the boardwalk at 9th Street since 1898, is still here; and is now run as a division of the Dairy Maid Confectionery Company of Philadelphia. Their delicious taffy is made from sugar, corn syrup, molasses, peanut butter, cocoa butter, hydrogenated vegetable oils, nut meats, chocolate, natural and artificial flavors, and food colors. Ocean City has two boardwalk movie theaters (something to be missed in Atlantic City, which has none), the **Strand**—designed in the streamlined art moderne style of the 1930s complete with glass bricks and neon—and the **Moorlyn,** which is now twinned.

The wonderful Ocean City boardwalk music pier and auditorium was built out over the beach and ocean in 1928, and the folks still gather to hear live bands and singers perform light operetta-style music or Gay Nineties ballads in summer concerts next to the breaking waves. You will find a great deal of pleasure just taking a

Grace Kelly, movie star and the princess of Monaco, spent summers at the Kelly family home in Ocean City.

walk in Ocean City. The people are friendly and the entire place is set up for old-fashioned relaxation and enjoyment, the way Atlantic City had been in the beginning. A couple of restaurant tips are: the **Chatterbox** at 9th Street and Central Avenue, (609) 399-0113, serving burgers, super-thick shakes, sandwiches, and seafood—open daily from 7 A.M. to 9 P.M. and the **Dockside Cafe** at 10th Street and the bay, (609) 398-0451, which has been called by restaurant critics one of the Jersey shore's outstanding restaurants, serving seafood, coquille St. Jacques, and other specialties. Call for seasonal hours and reservations.

The **Flanders Hotel,** which opened in 1923, is a landmark in Ocean City at 11th Street and the boardwalk. Looking out on the ocean, the white stucco, red-tile-roofed hotel was newly developed and refurbished in 1997, featuring one-bedroom suites with queen-sized beds, sofabeds in the sitting room, kitchens, and private baths—recommended for 4 to 5 people. Rates for the ocean suites are $209; deluxe $179; 2-bedroom $229; junior penthouse $239. A 10 percent discount is offered to Triple A members. Check-in is at 4 P.M. and check-out is 11 A.M. Call (609) 399-1000 for reservations and low off-season rates. BYOB (remember, Ocean City is *dry*), try the miniature golf course, and of course the ocean is just steps away across the boardwalk. This may be the ideal place to spend a night or two if you are planning to go to Atlantic City casinos. Some of the feeling of Atlantic City's old Marlborough-Blenheim Hotel can be experienced at this fine hotel.

A very attractive 1950s-style place with a swimming pool right on the boardwalk is the **Beach Club Hotel** (formerly the Sting Ray). There are floor-to-ceiling windows with ocean views and balconies, and a restaurant called the **Café Beach Club,** (609) 398-7700. The stucco walls are painted white with turquoise trim and the name of the place is spelled out in vivid red neon. Summer rates for two in a room with double beds, television, and bathroom are $204 to $289 per night. An extra person is $10 more. These rates have to do with city view or ocean view. The Beach Club Hotel is at 13th Street and the boardwalk. Check-in time is 2:30 P.M.

and check-out is 11 A.M., but the Beach Club is thoughtful enough to offer their guests shower rooms with private lockers (for those who wish to stay and use the pool and other facilities after check-out time). Who wants to leave the beach at 11 A.M. on a hot summer day? Call (609) 399-8555 for reservations. Of course, off-season rates are lower, though the Beach Club Hotel closes in mid-October and doesn't reopen until the beginning of May.

An excellent bed-and-breakfast is the elegantly restored 1894 Victorian **Northwood Inn** at 401 Wesley Avenue, (609) 399-6071, which won a 1990 beautification award from the Ocean City Chamber of Commerce. There are spacious guest rooms with private baths, and a hearty gourmet breakfast is served. The rates are $110 up to $250, all with full baths and television. A fun place to stay here is the tower room ($250). Weekly rates are good, with the seventh day free; but the midweek rates (any day from Sunday through Thursday) are especially attractive—with more of a chance for pick of room. Northwood Inn is run by Marge and John Loeper and is open year-round and features low off-season rates as well.

While in Ocean City be sure to stop by the **Ocean City Historical Museum** at 1735 Simpson Avenue. Here you will see a Victorian dining room and bedroom as it was in Ocean City in the 19th century, as well as hundreds of pictures, maps, and books depicting life in this city more than 100 years ago. There is an excellent antique doll collection on view. The admission is $4, with summer hours Monday through Saturday from 10 A.M. to 4 P.M.; winter hours are 1 to 4 P.M., Tuesday to Saturday, (609) 399-1801.

The 35-mile section of Ocean Drive south of Ocean City, from Corson's Inlet Bridge at Strathmere toward Wildwood and Cape May, is always a very pleasant trip indeed. You will find many points of scenic interest along the way with a good number of antique shops for which this southern tip and cape is noted. The southern shore area includes many waterways, bays, and inlets, as well as the beautiful wide, white-sand seashore towns of Strathmere, Whale Beach, Sea Isle City, Townsend's Inlet, Avalon, and Stone Harbor, all noted vacation spots with motel units for an overnight, weekend, or week's lodging. Avalon has particularly high sand dunes, charming old homes, and is dedicated to a vacation style that is quiet and serene. The **Stone Harbor Bird Sanctuary,** a famous spot for heronry, is just south of Stone Harbor on Seven Mile Beach. Inland on Route 9 at Swainton, between Avalon and Sea Isle City Boulevards, is one of the most beautiful gardens in New Jersey, called the **Leamings Run Gardens.** You can relive the days of the earliest settlers here as you tour the intact settler houses surrounded by tall pines and flowers. Open June through October daily from 9:30 A.M. to 5 P.M., (609) 465-5871 for further information.

The real hot spot seaside resort in the southern tip is Wildwood-by-the-Sea. To the north is North Wildwood, and to the south Wildwood Crest. The Wildwoods offer five miles of wide, safe beaches, and a three-mile-long boardwalk packed with amusements, rides, and games. There are motels every few feet, nightclubs, bars, restaurants, movies, hotels, diners, and stores and concessions that

Greetings from Wildwood-by-the-Sea, linen postcard.

jump day and night with excitement and activity. There are several amusement piers with every conceivable ride jutting out over the beach, which, like Atlantic City's, is free. The many concessions and jumping joints on the boardwalk remind one of the good times going on in the Seaside Heights summer community. The city area proper has large five-and-dime stores and other merchants to accommodate all your vacation needs. If fun and pleasure or sun and surf is your goal—and you are single—Wildwood is the place to be wild and free. Though teenagers are probably not too keen about it, the **Wildwood Historical Museum** has exhibits that trace the history of Wildwood over the centuries. It is located at 4400 New Jersey Avenue, (609) 522-2444. The convention hall provides facilities for varied events and seats 4,000. Motels along Ocean and Atlantic Avenues feature lots of neon and exotic names, from the **Acropolis** and the **Aquarius** to the **Royal Hawaiian,** the **Singapore,** the **Tahiti,** and the **Waikiki Oceanfront Inn.**

The main attraction at Wildwood are the six piers featuring the latest rides, including the Zoom Phloom, a maze of waterfalls, rapids, caverns, and a watery roller coaster, a Sea Serpent, and the 150-foot giant wheel adorned with 16,000 light bulbs. The piers include **Morey's Pier, Mariner's Landing, Hunt's Pier** (which dates back to 1905) and features the extraordinary roaring rapids ride that imitates the sport of whitewater rafting, the **Nickel's Midway Pier** featuring the German ride "Katapault" (the Nickel's Pier started out with a humble "guess-your-weight" concession years ago), and the **Fun Pier,** which received a major overhauling and facelift not long ago.

◆

Wildwood Motels Moderne

In 1991 Jack Morey started the Doo-Wop Preservation League, enlisting the owners of the 1950s moderne-style motels in Wildwood to preserve these architectural wonders. His movement was inspired by the Art Deco hotel buildings of South Miami Beach, which constituted the first 20th-century modernist-style neighborhood in the National Register of Historic Places. This "populuxe" style was first introduced as a new architectural concept at the World's Fair held in Chicago in 1933–34.

The many streamlined glass-and-concrete, neon-outlined buildings in Wildwood have come to represent the town in the same way that Las Vegas is defined by its style. Neonized signs advertise places like The Starlux, The Pink Champagne, The Caribbean, The Lollipop, La Vita, The Sea Star, The Bel Aire, The Kona Kai, and the Waikiki, with the latter two featuring azure blue swimming pools surrounded by plastic palm trees. The '50s futuristic

A "Funhouse" breeze-hole pinup, on a penny arcade slot machine postcard painted by Lugren.

design was initially developed to appeal to the average workingman who liked taking his family to visit Wildwood's boardwalk attractions and white-sand beaches.

Today, Doo-Wop concerts and 1950s dream-machine automobiles are an important aspect of Wildwood's summer-long reverie. Men wear Hawaiian shirts and blue suede shoes, and bolero skirts and ballerina slippers are the order of the day for the gals. Motel prices are still reasonable here, with some at less than $80. Families with kids, teenagers, college students, and swinging singles all come for the same kind of "Fun! Fun! Fun!" experience the Beach Boys sang about; and serious scholars who study the architectural vernacular of Roadside America come to write treatises on the design concepts that contribute to making this place truly unique. In fact, some years ago a Harvard study of Wildwood's motel architecture drew national attention, and today it's part of the architectural curriculum at many colleges and universities.

Although many of these snazzy '50s motels have been demolished—some for luxury condos—Wildwood is still the proud home of the world's largest surviving collection of Doo-Wop architecture, and residents are seeking historic preservation for the district. A swingin' place to stay in North Wildwood is **Summer Nites Bed and Breakfast,** 2110 Atlantic Avenue, which is a '50s-themed spot with a Marilyn room and an Elvis suite. Call (609) 846-1955 for more information.

Cape May Day Trip

By contrast to Wildwood, Cape May, five miles south, at the southernmost tip of New Jersey, is a place relatively uncluttered by pizzeria stands, T-shirt emporiums, or hot dog-sausage concessions. This geographic point is also the only place in New Jersey where you can watch the sun both setting and rising over the ocean. The colors of the sky at various times of the day are magnificent, resembling those wonderful sky colors found at Provincetown, Massachusetts. Cape May is a historic landmark district where there are over 600 gingerbread Victorian homes, all within a 2-mile radius. Birdwatchers flock to **Cape May Point State Park,** as it is a temporary landing and rest spot for over 50 species of birds. The many old hotels, guest houses, and bed-and-breakfast inns offer turn-of-the-century-type accommodations to guests looking to get away from the flash of city living or from suburban shopping mall "tremors." Beachcombers enjoy finding semi-precious quartz stones called Cape May diamonds along Sunset Beach or near Cape May Point Lighthouse.

Just 150 miles south from New York City and readily accessible from Wilmington, Delaware, and Philadelphia, this enchanted seaside fantasy place has a town proper with a restored street filled with quaint shops, ice cream parlor–luncheonettes, restaurants, candy, clothing, and gift shops, many with a distinct feeling of old-time elegance. This restored Cape May street is now called the **Washington Street Mall** (open year-round) where you will also find Cape May "diamonds" for sale, and collectible dolls at the **Treasure Cove,** the "original" **Fudge Kitchen,** selling fudge, taffy, peanut brittle, almond crunch, cashew turtles, butterscotch, molasses sponge, macaroons, rock candy, and other seashore sweets (locations at 513 Washington Street Mall, 728 Beach Drive, and 2112 Boardwalk in North Wildwood), **McDowell's Gallery of**

Vacationers at Cape May at the turn of the century.

Gifts (a store set in an 1895 bank, selling craft gifts, jewelry, glass-ware, pottery items), and many antique emporiums. Look at the Cape May landmark, **Morrow's Nut House,** on the promenade and the Washington Street Mall, where they make taffy from recipes handed down from a family tradition. The owners, Bill and Eleanor Morrow, met at the Philadelphia Sequicentennial Expo-sition in 1926, where they developed and sold their own delicious homemade sea foam fudge with nuts and other special ingredi-ents. Call (609) 884-3300. An original Victorian bandstand in the town square offers summer concerts just as it has for more than 100 years. Cape May is one of those places where the old values integrate smoothly with the new. Bookshops in the area include **Atlantic Books,** in Cape May at 500 Washington Street Mall, (609) 898-9694, and 711 Beach Avenue, (609) 898-0357; and **Book Shoppe** at Bayshore Mall in North Cape May at Ferry Road and Bayshore Road, (609) 884-7878, and at **Court House Village** on Dennisville Road in Cape May County Courthouse, (609) 465-8464.

Cape May is named after Cornelius Jacobsen Mey, the Dutch nav-igator who first explored this choice spot on the ocean and Delaware Bay in 1614. Cape May is divided into Cape May City (the hub of hotel life and the ocean boardwalk, and five-mile long swimming beach), Cape May Point (Cape May Point State Park), Sunset Beach, and the Cape May Migratory Bird Refuge where you can watch the migration of hawks in September and October from a special hawk-watch platform. **Cape May Point Lighthouse,** built in 1859, stands 170 feet high, has walls 8 feet thick, and its beacon of light is visible 19 miles out to sea. West Cape May is a part of this latter area, and the town called North Cape May (on the Delaware Bay) is also an interesting and beautiful spot.

The oldest Victorian guest hotel is the **Chalfonte Hotel** at Howard and Sewell Streets. It was built in 1876 by Colonel Henry Sawyer, who became the first exchange prisoner when he was traded in 1863 by the Confederacy for W. H. Fitzhugh Lee, the son of General Robert Lee, by order of an agreement overseen by Abe Lincoln. Rates at the large, gracious old hotel are from $120 to $190, tax and gratuity included as well as breakfast and dinner. Single rooms with sinks-only share hallway bathrooms. Many dou-ble rooms have private baths. For reservations call (609) 884-8409. The southern-style cooking is excellent at the **King Edward Bar;** recommended are the deviled crabs and southern fried chicken with spoon bread and homemade biscuits.

Picturesque Cape May is not only renowned for being the oldest seashore resort in the United States, but as a place to view the largest collection of Victorian buildings in the country. Walking tours of these architectural treasures, that are well maintained by proud owners who see them as functional historical monuments, are frequent. What is most exciting to anyone with a sense of respect for their American heritage is to find such a town at this geographic point, a point that stretches 20 miles "out to sea." For an even further excursion out to sea take the Cape May–Lewes Ferry, which connects Cape May to Lewes, Delaware. The year-round service (call (800) 64FERRY for departure schedule) plying the broad ocean mouth of the Delaware Bay is performed by 5 vessels that hold 800 passengers and 100 cars each. Reservations can be made at least one day in advance.

Victorian guest houses and bed-and-breakfast accommodations include: **The Mainstay Breakfast and Tea,** operated by David and Susan Macrae at 635 Columbia Avenue, (609) 884-8690, is a lavish and faithfully restored guest house, circa 1872.

The Ashley Rose at 715 Columbia Avenue, (609) 884-2497, features a wide veranda to sit and rock on or to lie in a hammock. The innkeeper is Sally Hulbert.

The Brass Bed Inn, open all year at 719 Columbia Avenue, (609) 884-8075, has lots of wicker and rockers with original furniture. John and Donna Dunwoody provide a hearty breakfast.

The Abbey Bed & Breakfast, a Gothic revival villa at Columbia Avenue and Gurney Street, (609) 884-4506, features exceptional architecture and is also open to the public for tours. Call Jay and Marianne Schatz, innkeepers.

Two places, also open all year round, are the **Gingerbread House** at 28 Gurney Street, (609) 884-0211, a tastefully restored 1869 Victorian cottage run by Fred and Joan Echevarria, and the **Columbia House** at 26 Ocean Street, (609) 884-2789, which features spacious apartments and rooms with 19th-century antiques, run by Laura and Jim Zeitler.

Other year-round bed-and-breakfasts are: the **Queen Victoria,** the **Duke of Windsor Inn,** the **Dormer House,** and **Captain Mey's Inn.**

Oceanfront motels include **La Mer** at Beach and Pittsburgh Avenues, (609) 884-9000; **Colton Court,** 105 Beach Avenue, (609) 884-5384; **Colonial Hotel and Motor Lodge,** at Beach Drive and Ocean, (609) 884-3483; the **Montreal Inn,** 1028 Beach Avenue, (609) 884-7011; and the **Camelot Motel,** (609) 884-1500.

Dining out in Cape May is always a special experience, as there are a good number of fine restaurants in this wonderful old Victorian town.

Columbia House in Cape May.

The Merion Inn has been serving satisfied diners since 1885. Having celebrated its 117th year, this family-owned and -operated restaurant, with its candlelit tables with fresh flower centerpieces, has an antique bar serving cocktails; there is period artwork on the walls. In this relaxed atmosphere you can try some of their fresh seafood dishes like stuffed lobster tail. Hours are 4:30 to 10 P.M. daily; 106 Decatur Street, (609) 884-8363.

Maureen's at Beach Drive and Decatur Street has won national acclaim for its gourmet dinners, professional service, beautiful ocean views, and their charming cocktail lounge. Proper dress is required here, (609) 884-3774.

Casual seashore dining can be had at **Mangia Mangia**, family-owned and -operated, featuring seafood specialties like bluefish provençal, mussels fra diablo, homemade crab cakes, French fried lobster and a shrimp/crab "delight." Their specialties are pasta, pasta and chicken and veal dishes. Broadway and Sunset Boulevard, (609) 884-2429.

Rated "best in New Jersey" with four stars by *The New York Times* four years in a row is **The Mad Batter,** featuring international and nouvelle cuisine including crab margarita, duck à les amis, Chinese dim sum, pasta pesto Freddo, and other interesting dishes served in a European atmosphere on the oceanview veranda, in the skylighted Victorian dining room, or by the fountain on the garden terrace. 19 Jackson Street, (609) 884-5970.

The **Hotel Alcott,** with nightly room rates ranging from $140 to $300, has the gracious **La Veranda Restaurant,** serving continental seafood and grilled fish, with a French flair. Off Beach Drive on Grant Street, (609) 884-5868.

Special off-season events in Cape May include: The Tulip Festival, with thousands of tulips heralding Spring and Cape May's Dutch heritage; September Seafood Festival, memorializing fishermen lost at sea and celebrating Cape May's fishing heritage, with special seafood dishes being served in all the restaurants and hotels, and an outdoor restaurant festival featuring a seafood smorgasbord; Victorian Week, October, featuring tours of the historic district by foot and trolley, fashion shows, slide and film presentations, an antique show, dinner dances, and individual house tours; the Christmas Ball and Community Ceremony, held in December, celebrates the Christmas spirit with tours of specially decorated houses and shops. A Christmas Ball, a tree lighting ceremony, and dancing to the big bands is part of the holiday festivities in Cape May, hailed far and wide as "a top 100 event in North America!"

Many events are sponsored by the **Mid-Atlantic Center for the Arts** (MAC); for information you can call (609) 884-5404 or stop by the MAC office at the Physick Estate, 1048 Washington Street, or visit www.capemaymac.org.

At the foot of Sunset Boulevard, at the very southernmost tip of New Jersey, is **Sunset Beach,** in Cape May Point, with a completely unobscured horizon line, which is unique on the East Coast. The spectacular sunsets here are due to atmospheric conditions created by the meeting of the Delaware Bay and the Atlantic Ocean. In season, a 40-year-old tradition is honored, and "Taps" is played every night as Old Glory is lowered.

When the weary and satisfied traveler is back—safe and snug at home—we authors hope the followers of this Jersey guide will drop us a line and let us know just how their Jersey jaunt went. We sincerely welcome any interesting Jersey stories or travel tidbits (did you have a sighting, or an encounter with the Jersey Devil?). Any valid suggestions, thoughtful recommendations, or legitimate complaints may well wind up in future editions of *O' NEW JER-SEY*. Vacations quickly and fondly become a memory; but today and tomorrow will hopefully find us again winding down that long road or trail.

Writer Gertrude Stein once told a friend that he may as well stay in the same place, not go anywhere. What for? While we are not advising staying in a stasis point, we have suggested all along that there is no need to travel thousands of airplane or railroad miles to have a good time. Looking at a vacation slide (on a home-viewing projection screen) of a group of friends, or the entire family standing in front of "Old Barney" lighthouse on Long Beach Island in New Jersey, may be just as vital as seeing this same group posing in front of the Eiffel Tower, the Pyramids of Egypt, or the Great Wall of China—and think of the money saved! Driving slowly in a leisurely manner down the old back roads and enjoying the passing scenery has been our basic credo. What's the hurry, anyway? If you are hungry, tired, or angry don't forget to take time off the road to enjoy a cruller and a cup of coffee—or maybe a malted milk shake at a Jersey diner. Many farmstands on the back road will offer a glass of free cider or a lump of maple sugar as a pick-me-up. If you are lost and you can't tell where you're at on the map—stop and ask for directions. Remember, most Jersey back roads will eventually lead you to a busy thoroughfare, a gas station, or a major highway. You may need to take a break from driving or even a nap if you can. Most major roads will have designated rest stops and encourage the taking of naps or coffee breaks. Watch for signs along the big highways that point to rest areas. Another option (if tired) is to exit the Parkway or Turnpike and check into a roadside motel somewhere.

Often it is desirable to have a specific destination in mind along with a travel plan; but there are those kind of Sunday drives where it is just fine to amble and wander without a destination in mind. Stop the car and get out and walk? To some this might seem like a radical idea. What, me walk! It is, of course, not a good idea to wander onto private property. What looks like an open field can

License plate attachment, enamel on metal, featuring the famous Mobil Oil Company red Pegasus.

sometimes turn out to be a farmer's bull pen. A number of beaches in the land of Jersey require day badges during the summer season, so there can be costs involved. This also means that to take a walk in certain state parks you must pay a fee. Beaches and parks require maintenance—and money is needed to maintain the ecological balance in these regions, so please don't complain too much about costs that continue to rise and fall. In the case of the Jersey beaches, fees have been reduced in recent years, making them more accessible to the greater populace, so sometimes costs can change for the better. Off-season, from September through the middle of June, the beaches are free.

We also hope that drivers will take care not to hit deer and other animals who cross the highways, sometimes darting in front of a vehicle without warning. The title of one of Stevie Wonder's songs is "Don't Drive Drunk!" On the recording of this song there is the sound of a crash and of shattered glass. While we are not telling drivers not to have a cocktail, beer, or wine with dinner, we are advising them to **DRIVE SOBER!** And **DRIVE SAFELY.** Have fun!

Index

Authors Robert Heide leaning (left) and John Gilman standing (right) with the 1954 Plymouth Belvedere convertible they enjoy driving around New Jersey. Here, they are hanging out in one of their favorite summer places— Ocean Grove.

Write to the authors at: St. Martin's Press
175 Fifth Avenue
New York, NY 10010

Happy trails!

ROBERT HEIDE was born in Irvington, New Jersey. JOHN GILMAN was born in Honolulu, Hawaii. They are both residents of Manhattan who have spent many years on the byways, backroads, and super-highways of New Jersey, enjoying the small towns, industrial areas, seaside resorts, diners, and interesting spots along the way. Both authors have written extensively about the state of New Jersey for such periodicals as *The Village Voice* and the *Daily News*. Gilman is a pop-culture archaeological historian and preservationist. Heide is a published playwright whose plays have been performed in New York in Greenwich Village at the Cherry Lane and Caffe Cino and in the East Village at Cafe LaMama and Theater for the New City. His play *The Bed* was filmed by Andy Warhol; and he wrote the screenplay for Edie Sedgwick for Warhol's *Lupe* based on the life and death of screen star Lupe Velez.